Crucible Vietnam

Crucible Vietnam
Memoir of an Infantry Lieutenant

A. T. LAWRENCE

McFarland & Company, Inc., Publishers
Jefferson, North Carolina, and London

LIBRARY OF CONGRESS CATALOGUING-IN-PUBLICATION DATA

Lawrence, A. T., 1946–
  Crucible Vietnam : memoir of an infantry lieutenant / A. T. Lawrence.
      p.   cm.
  Includes bibliographical references and index.

  ISBN 978-0-7864-4517-2
  softcover : 50# alkaline paper

  1. Lawrence, A.T., 1946– 2. Vietnam War, 1961–1975 —
Personal narratives, American. 3. United States. Army —
Officers — Biography. 4. Veterans — United States — Biography.
5. United States. Army — Military life — History — 20th century.
6. Vietnam War, 1961–1975 — Vietnam — Central Highlands.
7. Central highlands (Vietnam) — History, Military — 20th
Century. 8. Vietnam War, 1961–1975 — Casualties. I. Title.
  DS559.5.L38 2009
  959.704'342092 — dc22
  [B]   2009033817
British Library cataloguing data are available

©2009 Albert T. Lawrence. All rights reserved

No part of this book may be reproduced or transmitted in any form or by any means, electronic or mechanical, including photocopying or recording, or by any information storage and retrieval system, without permission in writing from the publisher.

On the cover, *from the left*: October 1967, age 21 — drinking rice wine with village elders at a Montagnard funeral, central highlands; August 1968 — serving as battalion S-3 Air, after 11 months in the war; June 1968 — the author (left) with an unnamed private atop an armored personnel carrier; *background* ©2009 Shutterstock

Manufactured in the United States of America

McFarland & Company, Inc., Publishers
  Box 611, Jefferson, North Carolina 28640
    www.mcfarlandpub.com

To my father, in loving memory

Acknowledgments

I owe the deepest gratitude to Ronald Chrisman, who took the time to assume the role of editor by painstakingly reading my manuscript and providing me the essential and critical guidance that enabled me to reshape the manuscript so as to enhance its content and readability.

I want to thank all of the soldiers who served with me in the Second of the Eighth; I have changed the names of the men in my platoon, as well as other names in the manuscript, where I deemed it appropriate in order to respect their privacy.

I wish to thank Roger D. Jorstad, Director, Department of Defense Statistical Information Analysis Division, Defense Manpower Data Center, who provided me with the yearly breakdown of Americans killed in action through 1975; these are illusive statistics, for which I was resolved to obtain the official DoD numbers.

I want to thank Dr. Jonathan E. Czarnecki, my professor at the Naval War College, who encouraged me to see the movie *We Were Soldiers*, which was based on the Moore and Galloway book *We Were Soldiers Once ... and Young: Ia Drang: The Battle that Changed the War in Vietnam*, and then provided unfaltering encouragement for a story of infantrymen in the highland jungles of Vietnam.

I also wish to thank my father, who steadfastly believed in me, no matter what dreams I pursued.

Contents

Acknowledgments	vi
Preface	1

PART I: 1965–1967

1. Welcome to the Army!	5
2. A Brief History of Vietnam	15
3. Advanced Infantry Training and Officer Candidate School	30

PART II: 1967–1968

4. Situation (September 1967)	41
5. The School Solution	64
6. Ambushed in a Rice Paddy	87
7. The Battle of Dak To (October–November 1967)	95
8. From the Perspective of Our Under-Strength Platoons	105
9. The Montagnards	116
10. Tet and the Turn of the Tide	123
11. Back to the Boonies (May–July 1968)	140
12. Last Six Weeks (August–September 1968)	162

PART III: 1968–1970

13. Homecoming (September 1968)	171
14. Stateside Army	178
15. Return to Civilian Life	199

PART IV: 1970–Present

16. The Journey (1970–Present)	209

Appendix A: Comparison of Vietnam War Casualties to Other American Wars	217
Appendix B: Army Medals	220
Appendix C: U.S. Hostile (Combat) and Non-Hostile Deaths	223
Chapter Notes	225
Bibliography	233
Index	239

Courtesy Mapping Specialists, Ltd.

Preface

On an overcast day in San Francisco, shortly after the millennium, I went to see the Vietnam War movie *We Were Soldiers*, starring Mel Gibson (based on the Moore and Galloway book *We Were Soldiers Once ... and Young: Ia Drang: The Battle That Changed the War in Vietnam*). I had read the book when it was published ten years earlier, and I still recalled a quote in the book that was borrowed from Ernest Hemingway, "War is a crime. Ask the infantry and ask the dead."

It was as though I had awakened from a dream, or from a long slumber, for the movie rekindled memories of my own experiences as an Army infantry lieutenant in that faraway war that had never truly relinquished me, as though it had firmly entrenched itself within me, for memories of war never really forsake us; their talons have sunk too deep to expunge and, like a hair shirt, they have become both a steady torment as well as a somber comfort.

I was motivated to put pen to paper because there was an aspect of the Vietnam War that I wanted to address, namely the deprivation and stark terror that one experiences in a foxhole. I had four assignments in Vietnam: I served as an infantry platoon leader for three months, then as commanding officer of the division mortar battery for five months during which I commanded about one hundred soldiers, then again as an infantry platoon leader for another three months, then a little more than a month as the S-3 Air for our battalion, a position considered to be nearly as hazardous as that of a platoon leader.

I was a commanding officer as a second lieutenant in wartime (in charge of the division mortar battery), which is exceedingly rare, for though a platoon leader leads a platoon, he is not formally considered a commanding officer. Only the officer that commands the entire company is classified as a commanding officer, and this position is generally filled by a captain.

I kept no journals while I was in Vietnam, and am therefore writing extensively from wartime memories, which have remained quite vivid over the years. I am also committed to writing only about events that I experienced, supported by my readings on the subject, and my studies at the Naval War College during 2002.

I arrived in Vietnam during September 1967 and departed the war during

September 1968. I served with the Fourth Infantry Division up in the Central Highlands of Vietnam before, during, and after the Tet Offensive. Throughout this time the Army employed "search and destroy" tactics, which were in effect from the spring of 1965 into late 1968 — for the first three and a half years after the arrival of American combat units.

Less than five months after Tet, General William C. Westmoreland, the promulgator of "search and destroy" missions, was replaced by General Creighton Abrams who introduced the concept of "clear and hold" that would bring the troops in from the jungles to secure the hamlets, as well as place greater emphasis on training and upgrading the South Vietnamese military. This was a move away from the attrition tactics of "search and destroy" that had been employed with a great deal of bloodletting.

In large part, I was prompted to write this book because my nine other classmates at the Naval War College were all young professional Navy officers, about twelve years out of the Naval Academy, who had chosen to serve their country for at least twenty years. They had never before met anyone who had received a notice from his draft board and then become an officer, and certainly not at the young age of twenty. By the time I was twenty-one, I had experienced more combat than most of these officers would experience throughout their entire military careers. They all envied me.

At the time of my attendance at the Naval War College, I was in my fifties and working as a civilian for the Department of the Navy, yet I was considered an authority in the field of contingency contracting because I had deployed to West Africa, along with the Marines, during the spring of 1996 to assist with the evacuation of nearly 450 Americans and 1,700 foreign nationals from Liberia after the outbreak of civil war in that country. One year later, during the spring of 1997, I was deployed once again to West Africa to assist in the evacuation of 2,530 people from Sierra Leone, which included more than 450 American citizens, when civil war erupted in that country. After these two operations, I was considered an expert in this type of Noncombatant Evacuation Operation (NEO), while the Navy was intent on training up its officers to handle these duties, and so I was extended the privilege of attending the Naval War College (College of Naval Command and Staff).

I have provided a brief historical overview of the French and American involvement in Southeast Asia as well as a timeline of contemporary events that transpired during my time in the Army, which are intended to be of interest to university students of today as well as Vietnam veterans. By their brevity, they do not pretend to be scholarly contributions, and, in this regard, I apologize in advance to scholars who might consider my efforts as generalized to some extent.

The Vietnam War was fought before the days of the all-volunteer professional military of today. In those days the United States *compelled* many of its young men to serve in the armed forces, unless of course they had the means to remain in school, where they were thus deferred from serving. Then, as now, the affluent generally did not serve in the military; they relied on others to fulfill that duty. The citizen soldiers of the Vietnam era served out their two- or three-year commitments, and then they returned to their civilian worlds. For many of these soldiers, their country had called them. They did not volunteer, and therein lies the difference.

I have come to find that the experience of war has followed me long after I returned from the battlefield. I have found this to be a startling revelation.

Part I: 1965–1967

1

Welcome to the Army!

I

During October 1965, one month after I turned nineteen, I received a notice from my draft board directing me to report for my induction (draft) physical within two months. At the time I was sailing the South Pacific, working as an officer in the merchant marine for the Oceanic Steamship Company out of Sydney, Australia. My parents had divorced when I was in my early teens, and, after completing a year of college, I could no longer afford to remain in school or stay at home, and was thus compelled to look for full-time work, which I found in the merchant marine, where opportunities were expanding as a result of the military build-up in Vietnam.

I entered the Army during January 1966 and was sent off to the war in Vietnam during September 1967. If I had remained in school, instead of going out to work for a living, I would have received a college deferment and I would not have had to risk my life by going off to war. It seemed clear to me that the life of a college kid was considered more valuable than the life of some working stiff, or some guy struggling against poverty in an urban ghetto. Well, I knew from early on that life was not fair.

Upon receiving the notice to report for my draft physical, I returned to California from Australia and immediately drove over to my local draft board to the south of San Francisco where I had been raised up through my teenage years. Many draft boards, like mine, tended to draft young men as soon as they turned nineteen; only if they were unable to meet their quotas would they then reach down for the eighteen-year-olds. I explained to the administrators that I had a merchant marine job in Australia and that I needed time to give proper notice to my employer.

The draft board people curtly informed me that I could no longer leave the country because my induction into the Army was imminent, and so I was compelled to abruptly terminate my employment with the Oceanic Steamship Company, and obliged to travel across San Francisco Bay to the Army base in Oakland where I underwent my draft physical, during which the doctors made me drop my pants, turn my head and cough, while they checked to ensure that I didn't have a hernia, then they looked to see if I had flat feet, which, according to "AR 40–501: Standards of Medical Fitness, para. 2–10 (b) (4)," was disqualifying if you wore prescription shoes or complained about pain while walking, as this could result in the government ultimately being required to pay disability compensation down the line. After successfully passing my physical I was classified 1-A (available for unrestricted military service) and informed that I could expect to receive my formal draft notice anytime within the next four months.

I was incensed that the uncompassionate bureaucrats at my local draft board had the gall to tell me that I could not leave the country, and, in my anger, I went to my bank, drew out all of my money and caught a plane bound for Mexico City where I went on a party binge, even though I knew that partying only provided short-term gratification at the expense of long-term happiness. Still, partying does seem to effectively alleviate stress and anger.

I had traveled around much of Mexico for nearly three months when I was seventeen, and I was happy to be back once again less than two years later, though this time I spent all of my time in Mexico City. After about three weeks I flew back to San Francisco, and several days later I went over to the sleazy city bus station at Seventh and Mission and caught the Greyhound bus across the Bay Bridge to the Army Base in Oakland. The base was primarily a processing center for bringing young men into the Army from the San Francisco Bay Area.

Some people, when they heard that I had gone to Mexico after receiving the notice from my draft board, just assumed that I was attempting to escape the draft by fleeing the United States, but nothing was further from the truth. I simply wanted to party, and I was rebelling against those who told me that I was prohibited from leaving the country. I mean, who was really going to stop me?

At the Oakland Army Base, I stood in a row with a mixed bag of young men in the late afternoon, raised my hand and swore allegiance to the U.S. Army, or the United States, I'm not sure which. It was January 14, 1966, and I now belonged to Uncle Sam.

Though the draft had been in continual effect since shortly before World War II, with the passing of the Selective Training and Service Act of 1940, a total of 382,010 young men were drafted during 1966, the largest number of draftees for any year during the Vietnam War.[1] After we had sworn our oaths, men in Army uniforms, who seemed courteous and pleasant enough, rapidly herded us onto buses, which proceeded southward along the Pacific Coast for a little more than a hundred miles to Fort Ord, astride the Pacific Ocean.

My bus was loaded with about thirty guys, mostly teenagers who appeared to have been scooped up off the city's streets. There were some inner-city blacks out of the East Bay, from cities like Richmond and Oakland; there were some Latinos from the Mission District of San Francisco, and there was just a handful of whites that seemed to be from the suburbs and out along the ocean beaches who sported cotton madras shirts. The reason why so few college guys entered the military was that so long as one stayed in school, one was exempt from being drafted. As a consequence, mostly rural and center-city guys, who oftentimes lacked the opportunity to attend college, got drafted.

We arrived at Fort Ord after night had fallen, and then it began. Drill sergeants (as opposed to drill instructors as they are called in the Marine Corps) were waiting for us, screaming at us to get off the bus and into some kind of formation, though it was nighttime and the only illumination provided was from the dim headlights of the bus in the desolate parking lot. They told us that our civilian days were over and that our asses now belonged to Uncle Sam.

We were all promptly marched off to the barber shop where all of our hair was callously shorn off, along with our individual identities, after which we were then shepherded into another room where we were told to strip out of our civilian clothes, down to our underpants, if we were wearing any, and then we were steered through a line along which we were issued heavy cotton olive-green fatigue pants and long-sleeved shirts, t-shirts and cotton boxer shorts, several pairs of socks, one pair of heavy black leather boots (which required time to break in), a belt, a brass belt buckle, and a cap. It was akin to entering prison where all of our personal effects were collected and placed in a marked bag that purportedly would be returned to us upon our release.

We were taught how to say, "Yes, drill sergeant" and "No, drill sergeant." And then we were marched off to a barracks building where we were shown how to stow our armload of new military clothes in our footlockers. Afterwards we were instructed how to make our bunk beds, including the bouncing quarter (requiring the corners of the wool blanket to be tucked under in such a manner that a quarter would bounce when dropped on the taut blanket from a foot above). Next, we were lined up in the barracks and given another screaming lecture about how we were all a bunch of worthless pukes, and then we were told to hit our racks. Nothing was said about dinner. Welcome to the Army!

In the morning we were awoken before sunrise by screaming drill sergeants, telling us that we had less than thirty minutes to take care of our bathroom needs, get into our fatigues and form up outside the barracks. We were then marched to the chow hall where we received our first Army meal—chipped beef on toast (consisting of re-hydrated slivers of dried beef in a creamy evaporated milk sauce, ladled over a piece of soggy toast), more commonly called "shit on a shingle" or simply "SOS."

After breakfast we were required to line up for countless inoculations, even though I had received all of the same shots seven months previously when I had joined the merchant marine, but the Army didn't care, so I got a double dosage of just about everything. We then proceeded to undergo the rather grueling physical training that was intended to build us into soldiers. We learned how to fieldstrip and clean our weapons, even in the dead of night with no light, as this might be a real eventuality on the battlefield. And even though the M16 had been in production for about two years, they were virtually all being shipped overseas to the troops fighting in the war, so we were compelled to train on the heavier M14 rifle that would soon be phased out (except for its use by the Third U.S. Infantry Regiment (The Old Guard) that watches over the Tomb of the Unknowns in Arlington, and whose Army Drill Team continues to perform with the M14).

We were required to memorize and regurgitate, upon demand, the six articles of the Army Code of Conduct:

I

I am an American, fighting in the forces which guard my country and our way of life. I am prepared to give my life in their defense.

II

I will never surrender of my own free will. If in command, I will never surrender the members of my command while they still have the means to resist.

III

If I am captured I will continue to resist by all means available. I will make every effort to escape and to aid others to escape. I will accept neither parole nor special favors from the enemy.

IV

If I become a prisoner of war, I will keep faith with my fellow prisoners. I will give no information or take part in any action which might be harmful to my comrades. If I am senior, I will take command. If not, I will obey the lawful orders of those appointed over me and will back them up in every way.

V

When questioned, should I become a prisoner of war, I am required to give name, rank, service number, and date of birth. I will evade answering further questions to the utmost of my ability. I will make no oral or written statements disloyal to my country and its allies or harmful to their cause.

VI

I will never forget that I am an American, fighting for freedom, responsible for my actions, and dedicated to the principles which made my country free. I will trust in my God and in the United States of America.

The drill sergeants would approach us at any moment, stick their intimidating faces just inches away from ours, and scream, "Soldier, what's the third article of the Code of Conduct?" If we stuttered, or got one word out of place, we would be dropped for pushups and compelled to continue until exhausted. So we made the greatest effort to recite the articles as intricately precise as any Japanese haiku, yet as effortlessly as English devotees would dissect the iambic pentameter of Shakespeare's sonnets.

Although the drill sergeants were big and menacing, and motivated us by fear, we were absolutely struck with terror whenever an officer appeared, for then we were expected to holler "Attention!" If indoors, we had to brace ourselves against the closest wall; if we were outdoors, then we were required to snap to attention and acknowledge all officers with a crisp salute. We did not present one of those medieval open palm salutes that the British favor in order to confirm that nothing is concealed in their hand, going back to knights in shining armor days. No, ours was one of those salutes where only the flank of the hand was pointed toward the other person. We were told that our salutes were different from European salutes because we had never lost a war, and so we were certainly not inclined to give one of those namby pamby open-palm British salutes.

This rigid behavior toward officers was perplexing, for it appeared that even second lieutenants, the youngest junior officers, garnered more respect than the oldest senior sergeants; it was as though officers seemed to merit some mystical and exalted reverence, for even the veteran sergeants who had been in the Army for more than twenty years would snap to ramrod attention and honor all officers with a snappy and respectful salute. Of course, officers were on a different track than enlisted soldiers. An enlisted soldier started out as a lowly private (E-1) and progressed up through the ranks to the highest enlisted rank of sergeant major (E-9). Some sergeant majors are designated command sergeant majors with even greater responsibilities for which only the sergeant major of the Army is imbued with greater honor.

Officers, on the other hand, start out as second lieutenants (O-1), after which they become first lieutenants (O-2), then captains (O-3)—these three ranks are also referred to as junior officers or line officers. Then there are the field-grade officers: majors (O-4), lieutenant colonels (O-5), and colonels (O-6). After which officers ascend to become general officers, first becoming a brigadier (one-star) general (O-7).

II

Everyone who enters the Army undergoes eight weeks of Basic Combat Training (BCT) during which time they receive fundamental rifle training. We also did mile runs and lots of pushups, and we learned how to throw a grenade and put on a gas mask. Upon completion of Basic Combat Training, only one in ten of us remained in the infantry and proceeded on to Advanced Infantry Training (AIT), while the other 90 percent were dispersed among various Army specialties such as Transportation (truck drivers), Engineering, Supply (cooks), the Medical Corps, the Signal Corps, or perhaps one of the two other combat arms (Artillery or Armor).

This distribution of manpower within the Army is quite different from the Marine Corps where every Marine is trained as a rifleman and is required to attend additional infantry training after boot camp, even cooks. The fact that the preponderance of Marines are in the infantry is due to the fact that much of their transportation, engineering, medical, and logistical support is provided by Navy personnel.

The infantry is the most heralded, yet most dangerous, branch of the Army. I enjoyed being in the infantry, probably because I had watched too many John Wayne movies as a kid, or I was not quite right in the head, and yet I felt that if I had to go into the Army I might as well go where the action was. Of course, this was pretty much how a nineteen year-old was thinking in those days. I felt that if I had to go, I might as well go all the way; that's how young I was.

Besides, members of my family had served our country during the War of 1812, the Civil War (from the State of Iowa), and World War II (from the State of California), and now it appeared that I would soon represent my family in another of my country's wars, the seventh major American war to be fought during the last hundred and fifty years; well, maybe the Spanish-American War was not so major, with Americans suffering just a little more than 2,000 battlefield casualties.

My family on my father's side was of English origin, and was considered an old American family in so far as our presence in the New World was concerned, for we were related to Captain James Lawrence who had served in the United States Navy during the War of 1812. I suppose that makes me at least a seventh generation American, claiming lineage back to the parents of James who were living in New Jersey during the 1760s, prior to the outbreak of our American War of Independence.

During March 1813, thirty-one-year-old U.S. Navy Captain James Lawrence (born in Burlington, New Jersey on October 1, 1781), in command of the forty-nine-gun frigate *U.S.S. Chesapeake*, sailed out of Boston Harbor to confront the British frigate *H.M.S. Shannon*. During the fierce battle that ensued, Captain Lawrence was mortally wounded. His last order was "Don't give up the ship!" His dying words became the rallying cry of the United States Navy.

Less than halfway through Basic Combat Training (BCT), my entire company of 220 men was marched into a large classroom and compelled to take a series of tests, which resulted in three of us being *invited* to interview for acceptance into Officer Candidate School (OCS), of which I was one of the fortunate few. So now I began to think to myself, at the age of nineteen, that if I was going to be in the infantry, I might as well be the one giving the orders. I felt confident that I could handle the responsibility and the stress, though only two of us would successfully pass the interview.

The interview board was comprised of a colonel and two majors. OCS was primarily established for college graduates who had not attended a ROTC (Reserve Officer Training Corps) program, and these were the men the board was seeking. Yet for some reason, the interviewing officers seemed impressed by the fact that before entering the Army I had served as an officer in the merchant marine. In those days, in order to secure a job in the merchant marine, one had to be in a possession of a Z-Card (Merchant Mariner's Document) issued by the U.S. Coast Guard, and in order to obtain a Z-Card, one had to have a job on a ship. It was a catch-22 situation; you couldn't get a job without a Z-Card, and you couldn't get your Z-Card without a job. In other words, you had to know somebody. I had met an executive for the Matson Navigation Company when I was knocking around the Mayan ruins on the Yucatan Peninsula in Mexico at the age of seventeen who told me that when I returned to San Francisco, if I ever needed a job, to give him a call. I looked him up a year later and he wrote me a "letter of commitment," which, in essence, was a promise of a job that would enable me to get my Z-Card, though he told me that he really didn't know me all that well and that he had no job at Matson to offer me, so I would be on my own in landing a job at sea.

My father had also served in the merchant marine, nearly thirty years before me, working as an able bodied (AB) seaman for two years after high school, before he even began attending college in 1938. He had sailed on ships of the Dollar Steamship Lines (predecessor of American President Lines), working on "around-the-world" voyages out of Los Angeles, with stops in San Francisco, Honolulu, Shanghai, Hong Kong, Singapore, Suez, Alexandria, Naples, Marseilles, then on to New York and Cuba, before returning to California via the Panama Canal. Six months after the Japanese attack on Pearl Harbor, my father went down to the Port of Los Angeles and successfully passed the officer's exam to become a third mate in the merchant marine, after which he shipped out on a convoy from the West Coast to the island of Midway just a couple weeks after the U.S. naval victory in those waters. Upon his return to Los Angeles, he learned that the Navy was looking for officers, and so he traveled up the coast to San Francisco where he was readily offered a commission as an ensign in the United States Navy.

After obtaining my Merchant Mariner's Document from the Coast Guard at Fort Mason in San Francisco, I found work initially on a troop transport to Vietnam, working as an ordinary seaman, chipping paint most of the time. At the end of that voyage, I was offered a job as a staff officer with the Oceanic Steamship Company (a subsidiary of the Matson Navigation Company), due to the helpfulness of the executive I had met in Mexico.

In any event, I suppose the Army board members figured that being a merchant marine officer might conceivably provide me with the ability to lead men into combat. Still, in most cases, during times of war when the Army must rapidly expand, the United States generally looks to its college graduates to fill its officer ranks; however, with so many college men working the angles to avoid being drafted and sent to Vietnam by either joining the National Guard or simply remaining in school (classified 2-S / deferred because of collegiate study), the criteria for entry into OCS had become more flexible, and, in our great meritocracy, the interviewing officers had the discretion to consider other factors besides a college degree that they felt might foster leadership potential.

No doubt working in the merchant marine makes a young man grow up faster than if he were still living at home with his parents and going to school. Of the 220 men in my basic training company, there was not a single college graduate. Of this total, 218 men had gone no further than high school, and only two men had ever attempted any college studies: A trainee named Don O'Brien had completed two years of college, and then there was me, who had completed one year of junior college. My parents had been the first two people in their families to graduate from university. My mother's family had immigrated to the United States from Ireland in the 1800s, and her mother had been a dancer in the Ziegfeld Follies in New York City before coming out to Hollywood during the 1930s to look for opportunities in film. My father and mother had met at UCLA (University of California at Los Angeles), from which they had both graduated during the summer of 1942.

In any case, Don and I were the only two from our training company who successfully passed the interview board and were recommended for acceptance into OCS. There were a number of Army officer schools, such as the Infantry School at Fort Benning, Georgia; the Artillery School at Fort Sill, Oklahoma; the Armor School at Fort Knox, Kentucky; the Engineer School at Fort Belvoir, Virginia and, the Signal School at Fort Gordon in Augusta, Georgia.

We were afforded the opportunity to list our preferences, though without hesitation I chose the infantry, while, surprisingly, Don chose the Engineer School. He confided to me that he had no desire to join the infantry and face the distinct possibility of losing his life, not to mention his mind. He confessed to me that he considered himself too emotionally sensitive to serve on the front lines—facing death, as well as assaults on his sanity—and therefore he elected to go into engineering. Infantrymen are commonly referred to as "Eleven Bravos," denoting their MOS (military occupational specialty), which was 11B, whereas the MOS for a combat engineer was 12B, and 13B for an artilleryman.

There were four ways to become an officer in the Army: one, graduate from the military academy at West Point (which was producing nearly 600 lieutenants each year); two, graduate from a university Reserve Officer Training Corps (ROTC) program (which turned out 16,306 Army lieutenants in 1968, but only 5,367 in 1973); three, graduate from Officer Candidate School; or four, receive a battlefield commission.[2]

The 1966 Report of the Department of the Army Board to Review Army Officer Schools stated that "ROTC has historically been the primary source of new officers, producing approximately 70 percent of the total each year. The OCS program produced a little over 8 percent, and West Point produced 3.5 percent. The remainder received direct appointments or came in through the drafting of doctors and dentists."

ROTC produces officers for all branches of the U.S. Armed Forces within the Department of Defense (DoD).[3] However, due to the controversies generated by this war, enrollment in Army ROTC programs dropped 78 percent between 1968 and 1973, with the result that ROTC was not able to fulfill its quotas toward the end of the war.⁴

Insofar as battlefield commissions were concerned, only the Marine Corps publicly stated that it awarded battlefield commissions during the Vietnam War. The Marine Corps selected sixty-three enlisted Marines, "whose performance under fire while serving in Vietnam merited a commission," and offered them promotion to the rank of second lieutenant; sixty received their commissions, two declined the offered promotions, and the third promotion was made posthumously. The Department of Defense, in an official communication, has stated that "there were no battlefield commissions within the Army during the Vietnam War." Some Army NCOs state that they were awarded direct commissions, without being required to attend Officer Candidate School, and yet to my knowledge this was done stateside, and not in Vietnam — on the battlefield — and thus it appears that the Army did not consider these to be battlefield commissions in the strictest sense.⁵

September 1965, age 19 — The author as a Merchant Marine staff officer before the Army.

No matter from which avenue a person received his commission as a second lieutenant, they were all deemed to be equivalent. When I received my commission, I would be on the same level as a West Point graduate, except, of course, he would have greater connections than I, and he would be placed on the Army's fast track and guided up the Army's career ladder by all of the "ring knockers" who had preceded him. Still, we would all start out together, on the lowest, yet most revealing, rung of the officer ladder, serving as infantry platoon leaders and leading about forty men into combat.

Initially OCS was only open to university graduates who had not taken ROTC, but when the United States needed to send a military force of more than 485,000 to Vietnam during 1967, and more than 536,000 in 1968, the Army found itself in desperate need of more infantry officers, since so many college graduates were lining up to join the National Guard to avoid being sent to Vietnam.⁶ And so, for a short period of time, the Army permitted some men like me to attend Officer Candidate School, men who had not graduated from university, but who had demonstrated a high general aptitude in a battery of tests and then successfully passed an interview board. Next came the grueling physical and academic training, which nearly a third of the aspiring officer candidates failed.

Would Don O'Brien and I both make it through OCS? According to the odds, only one of us was likely to succeed. Don confided to me that he was from a large and poor Catholic family in Altoona, Pennsylvania, and that he had a brother who was already a Green Beret. Don told me that, when he was a kid growing up, his mother used to send him down to the federal food distribution center, to which he was humiliatingly obliged to pull his little red wagon past his neighbors' houses in order to fill it up with the powdered eggs and milk, along with some bread and big blocks of cheddar cheese that he would then bring home to his family. All the clothes he ever wore were hand-me-downs from his older brothers, including the shoes.

At the end of Basic Combat Training we were finally eligible for a weekend pass, and, as I lived only a hundred miles to the north of Fort Ord, I invited Don to accompany me for a visit to my mother's, since his family was back East. We rode the bus from Monterey up along the Pacific Coast to the Greyhound Bus Station at Seventh and Mission in one of shabbiest parts of San Francisco in those days, where we then caught another bus to the nearby town where my mother lived. My sister Penny, two and a half years older than I, was still living at home and finishing up her studies at college. Don seemed to enjoy his time at my mother's house, and he seemed to develop a genuine liking for the San Francisco Bay Area.

2

A Brief History of Vietnam

I

Prior to sailing the South Pacific I had worked aboard the *USNS General LeRoy Eltinge* (T-AP-154), which had served as a troop transport in World War II, but more recently had carried the 1st Brigade of the 101st Airborne Division to Vietnam during the summer of 1965 (the rest of the division arrived in Vietnam more than two years later, during November 1967).

One of my vivid memories of that voyage was of the airborne soldiers eating powdered eggs at stand-up tables in the galley area. I also remembered their mop detail and how they tied their mops onto ropes and tossed them over the fantail of the ship so they could wash them in the ocean, as so many airborne troopers were getting seasick below decks. The ship had no air-conditioning, so we popped salt tablets like daytime snacks as we got closer to the Equator, and we seamen slept on deck in hammocks whenever feasible. During that time there was virtually nothing in Cam Ranh Bay except two dilapidated piers that jutted out into the water, and our skipper brought the ship alongside the pier without the aid of tugs, simply by issuing verbal orders from the bridge. This was highly unusual, but at the time there were no tugs in the harbor, as this was still the beginning.

The very first American troops to arrive in force, the Marines, had only come ashore in Vietnam a little more than four months earlier at Da Nang, about 100 miles to the south of the DMZ (demilitarized zone). Though the 17th Parallel constituted the border between North and South Vietnam, the DMZ followed the course of the Ben Hai River, which flowed from the Laotian border, just south of the 17th Parallel, to the South China Sea. The DMZ extended for five kilometers (3.1 miles) north to south, on each side of the river.

Once ashore in Vietnam, around the port city of Cam Ranh, I caught a ride in an Army jeep one scorching afternoon in which a twenty-seven-year-old airborne captain was comfortably ensconced, and as we headed down the dusty dirt road toward town, the captain asked me how old I was. I told him that I was eighteen, and he had looked at me and said, "It won't be long before you'll be back here in uniform."

I didn't know what to say. I had observed the young American paratroopers onboard ship, most of whom were just a year or two older than I, and they had all volunteered for the Airborne and were proudly fulfilling their military obligations to their country. I too felt a certain sense of duty, thinking to myself that, if I was called to serve, I would strive to fulfill my obligation, believing that if I were to go out of my way to avoid my responsibility, then someone else would be called to take my place. In any case the captain's prediction was acutely accurate, for I found myself back in Vietnam, with a rifle in my hands, just two years and one month from then, when the fighting was at its worst.

After my encounter with the captain, I felt prompted to do some reading about this small country in Southeast Asia. I was aware of the fact that eleven years earlier, back in 1954, French Legionnaires and paratroopers had been fighting in Vietnam, and had been doing so for more than seven tough years, during which time French Union Forces (made up of Frenchmen, French Foreign Legionnaires, and French Colonial troops from Morocco, Algeria, Tunisia, Senegal, Vietnam, Laos, and Cambodia) suffered more than 74,000 deaths, of which 20,685 (more than 27 percent) were Frenchmen, the best soldiers that France could put in the field, and they were beaten soundly.[1]

French missionaries reached Southeast Asia during the early seventeenth century, though it was not until 1858 that the French military arrived in force, and swiftly captured Saigon in 1859; four years later the French made Cambodia into a French Protectorate and therefore a part of a burgeoning French Indochina.[2] However, it took the French more than twenty additional years before they were able to subdue the area around Hanoi, by 1885, but even then, the French were never able to entirely pacify northern Vietnam.[3] It was the French who had diminished the power of the imperial influence of Hué back in 1885 when they broke up the old kingdom into three territories (Tonkin in the north; Annam in the center; and Cochin China in the south). The word *Indochina* is of French origin, adopted by the French when they were carving out their colonial empire in Southeast Asia, an area that had been enshrouded over time by the cultural influences of its colossal neighbors to the west and to the north — India and China. Southeast Asia is comprised of Vietnam, Cambodia, Laos, Burma, Thailand, as well as a maritime portion that includes Indonesia, the Philippines, Singapore, and Malaysia (Peninsular Malaysia and Malaysian Borneo).

After around eighty years of French colonial rule, more or less, the Japanese made their way into Indochina during 1940 on their drive toward Singapore and stayed through the duration of the war with the concurrence of Vichy France (linked with Nazi Germany which was an ally of Japan). World War II ended on the second of September 1945 with the unconditional surrender of Japan to the Allies aboard the battleship *Missouri* in Tokyo Bay. The Japanese thus evacuated Indochina, while the French remained behind.

Initial United States involvement in Vietnam can be traced back to this time and the administration of Harry S. Truman, which, as early as 1945, due to its fear of communist expansionism (reinforced by the ongoing civil war between the Nationalists and communists in China), decided to support the French in Indochina.

Even though the British granted independence to India, its richest colony, in 1947, France, with a small cadre of Vietnamese converts, tenaciously endeavored to hold onto its Southeast Asian conquest beyond the end of the colonial era. The French came under attack by the Vietminh beginning in December 1946, which marked the commencement of the French Indochina War; and, when the Korean War broke out in 1950, France was able to count on vastly increased military and financial support from the United States.[4]

Nevertheless, during the spring of 1954, France's elite paratroopers and Legionnaires were decisively defeated by the Vietminh on May 7 under the inspiring leadership of General Vo Nguyen Giap. The bloody fifty-six-day battle of Dien Bien Phu had ended, into which the French had poured more than 16,000 troops and suffered nearly 1,300 killed and more than 5,000 wounded.[5] The French had fortified that remote outpost in an effort to protect northern Laos from invasion by the Vietminh, as well as to bring the enemy to a set-piece battle. The Vietminh accepted the invitation for battle against the French fortified position, which, unexpectedly for the French, resulted in a crushing defeat.

Thus ended the French Indochina War, which had been waged for just about seven and a half years—from December 1946 to May 1954. At the time of the battle of Dien Bien Phu, the United States was preoccupied with ferreting out communists at home during the reprehensible McCarthy hearings, and Joseph R. McCarthy, Senator from Wisconsin, had just gone on television to attack the U.S. Army. Besides, at the time, Indochina was so very far away that many Americans could not even locate it on a map.

Dwight D. Eisenhower was president during the battle of Dien Bien Phu; he had succeeded Truman as president during January 1953, just as the Korean War was winding down and approaching a stalemate. This was the same year that Josef Stalin, the hard-line autocratic leader of the Soviet Union (since the death of Lenin in 1924) died. Stalin was succeeded by Nikita Khrushchev, who loved his vodka yet appeared as a peasant at world summit meetings, where he took off his shoe and banged it on the table whenever he wanted everybody's attention. We could never imagine our leaders being so uncouth.

However, Khrushchev had survived the five-month horrific battle of Stalingrad, the greatest military bloodbath in all of recorded history, so Khrushchev knew something about playing hardball, even when his back was up against the wall, or the river in this case. Khrushchev kept harping on the evils of capitalism, but everyone I knew was a worker. I didn't even know any capitalists; I guess they were the fat cats that were exploiting the workers, but even in my neighborhood the plumbers owned their own homes and drove relatively new trucks.

The United States had supported France in its fight in Southeast Asia, especially during the time that the U.S. was fighting in Korea in its effort to stem the tide of communist expansionism in eastern Asia, although it should be noted that the illustrious French Battalion fought with distinction alongside the Americans in Korea as part of the Second Infantry Division. American pilots had flown cargo planes in support of the French at Dien Bien Phu, though the U.S. stopped short of providing the requested bombers of which the French were in dire need in order to avert defeat. In the days of the French, there was as yet no North or South Vietnam. The country was only artificially split in half, as a result of the Geneva Conference of May 1954, when the defeated French were striving to extricate themselves from their debacle, while saving what little face remained to them. Each half contained 16 million people, and each half was slightly smaller than the State of Florida. In essence the French were still striving to hold on to some small pseudo-colonial bastion in the south while vacating Hanoi in the north, which had become untenable, primarily because the Vietminh in the north, around Hanoi, were less than a hundred and fifty miles from the Chinese border, and so they could more easily obtain their supplies, as well as seek sanctuary in China, which was supporting their cause.

The French were able to count on American fear of communism to elicit U.S. support for splitting Vietnam in two. Ironically, both the Chinese and the Soviets also supported the resolution to divide Vietnam. So, even though the French had been defeated and the Vietnamese had prevailed against these European invaders, the world's three major powers of China, the Soviet Union and the United States (along with France) ultimately determined that the country of Vietnam should be "provisionally" divided until countrywide elections, as sanctioned by the Geneva Accords of 1954, could be conducted inside of the next two years to determine the political fate of the Vietnamese people. The Accords also prohibited foreign powers from having any military presence in the area.[6] It should be noted that neither President Eisenhower nor Ngo Dinh Diem signed the Accords, and therefore did not consider themselves bound by them.[7] The Vietnamese were reluctantly compelled to acquiesce to this superpower pressure in order to diffuse tensions between the Cold War adversaries who were still licking their wounds from the Korean War that had ended in a stalemate just the year before, though the inconclusive ending to the war in Korea no doubt boosted the confidence of the Vietnamese communists in pursuance of their goals.[8]

The French really did very little to improve the lot of the Vietnamese other than educate a small percentage of the indigenous population to assist them in their exploitation of that little Asian country; well, perhaps not so little, as Vietnam was more than half the size of France. In reality, regardless of what some history books might say, there was very little romanticism and altruism in colonialism. And yet, under the Truman Administration, "the United States 'had no interest' in 'championing schemes of international trusteeship' that would weaken and alienate the European states whose help [was needed] to balance Soviet power in Europe.' U.S. officials thus concluded that even if the Vietnamese were to obtain independence from France, they would be ... vulnerable to *external control*."[9] External, in this case, meant Chinese or Soviet communist influence.

In 1954 the United States, which was already taking over from the French, endorsed Ngo Dinh Diem (who had spent the previous three years at a Catholic seminary in New Jersey) to lead southern Vietnam, initially as prime minister until he won election to the newly created office of president in 1955, after which he hastily proclaimed southern Vietnam the "Republic of Vietnam," and refused to participate in any all-Vietnam elections as prescribed by the Geneva Accords.[10]

Diem received American support primarily because he was an anti-communist, although he was also a Catholic, which stigmatized him as a product of French colonialism in the eyes of most of his countrymen, who were Buddhists. Consequently, Diem was compelled to apply draconian measures against his fellow Vietnamese in the south in order to remain in power.[11]

By 1954, under the presidency of Dwight D. Eisenhower (1953–1961) and his hard-line Secretary of State, John Foster Dulles, American policymakers adopted the view that Ho Chi Minh and the Vietminh were aligned with Moscow and Red China, and thus part of a burgeoning communist expansionism that posed a threat to the Free World. Eisenhower had pledged, during his campaign, to adopt a more aggressive anti-communist policy, and thus move beyond the passive containment policy of the Truman Administration, which many conservatives alleged had resulted in the loss of China to the communists in 1949, which in turn had encouraged the North Korean communists to invade South Korea in 1950. During 1954, Eisenhower's second year in office, the United States commissioned the world's first nuclear-powered submarine (enabling it to remain under the surface indefinitely and cruise limitlessly) in order to confront the Soviet nuclear threat, while also funding nearly 80 percent of France's total military costs in Indochina.[12]

In this light, the United States took the lead in building a coalition of anti–Communist nations in the region that became known as the Southeast Asia Treaty Organization (SEATO), to which the United States pledged to defend South Vietnam against armed attack.[13] SEATO was established in 1954, just one year after the Korean War had ended, at a time when the American people felt threatened by the spread of communism around the world.

During April 1954, while the battle of Dien Bien Phu was still raging, President Eisenhower made use of a powerful metaphor, referred to as the domino theory, to effectively convey his belief that if Vietnam were to fall to the communists, it would set off a domino effect, whereupon the other countries of Southeast Asia would also fall to the communists—like "a row of dominos."[14]

By the time I was reading about these issues during my senior year of high school in 1964, the manic American fear of the Red Menace had been tempered somewhat, such that it appeared to my way of thinking that most all of these "isms," such as colonialism, nationalism, communism, imperialism, fascism, and capitalism, were simply abstract concepts that political leaders used to manipulate the people. Sometimes, in my most cynical moments, I regarded the domino theory as a political contrivance meant to frighten us in order to justify the expansion of imperialism, or to thwart the mounting tide against colonialism. But back in the early 1950s, the threat of the Red Menace was palpable among our leaders, as well as the American people.

After the spilling of so much American blood in Korea, Eisenhower, during 1953 and 1954, came to the conclusion that the United States should avoid the expenditure of American manpower to fight any more land wars in Asia, while alternatively emphasizing the strategic nuclear deterrent. Nevertheless, in 1955 Eisenhower approved the dispatch of U.S. military advisors to Vietnam to assist the South Vietnamese Army in its fight against the communists.

Many history books cite 1959 as the start of the Vietnam War, as this was the year that Ho Chi Minh declared a People's War to unite all of Vietnam, which led to the formation of the National Front for the Liberation of South Vietnam (NLF), of which the Vietcong constituted its (guerilla) army. The year 1959 was also when Army Major Dale Buis was believed to be the first American to die in Vietnam, when he was machine-gunned down by communists near Saigon on July 8. The Department of Defense later acknowledged that the first American soldier to die in Vietnam was Air Force Tech Sergeant Richard B. Fitzgibbon Jr., murdered by a fellow airman on June 8, 1956. His name was not added to the Wall until 1999.[15] Most U.S. government reports now cite November 1, 1955, as the commencement date of the "Vietnam Conflict," for this was the day when the United States Military Assistance Advisory Group (MAAG) in Indochina (deployed to Southeast Asia under President Truman) was reorganized into country-specific units and MAAG Vietnam was established. MAAG was comprised of American military advisors whose mission was to train the local armed forces.[16]

During the French Indochina war, the Vietnamese nationalists who had fought the Japanese during World War II, and then afterwards the French, were referred to as Vietminh, whether they were from the north or the south of Vietnam, and the Vietminh, at that time, included both communists and non-communists, although under ardent communist leadership. And though these Vietminh "nationalists" were generally perceived as heroes in the eyes of their countrymen, as early as 1956, from the perspective of the Diem government, they were strictly viewed as the bad guys.[17] Thus the Vietminh in the south who had fought the French were no longer considered as heroes by their newly selected leaders; in fact, they were now hunted down as traitors.

Ironically, when Eisenhower briefed Kennedy during January 1961, just before leaving office, he was more concerned about communist Pathet Lao expansionism in Laos than anything going on in Vietnam.[18] Laos, which had been granted full independence in 1954 as a result of the Geneva Conference, was in the midst of civil conflict between the Royal Laotian Army and the communist Pathet Lao that had broken out in 1959 and continued into 1962, ending with the formation of a coalition government and the declared neutrality of that country.

Now that there was a U.S. military presence in neighboring South Vietnam, President Kennedy felt obliged to increase military aid to South Vietnam during 1961. For the majority of us baby boomers, we were all enamored by President John F. Kennedy; we would have followed him anywhere. He was young, charismatic, and he had a vision for the future, but make no mistake, he was also a World War II military veteran and a true-blue Cold War warrior who viewed communism as a global threat, against which he was prepared to use military force.

Back in October 1961, when I was a sophomore in high school, President Kennedy authorized all Army Special Forces soldiers to wear a green beret. By the time I was a senior in high school, I saw more and more of these Green Berets, with their bloused boots and their parachute wings, striding purposefully through the San Francisco Airport — gateway to the Orient. They appeared as indomitable Cold War counterinsurgency warriors, standing as intrepid sentinels in the face of the communist onslaught, impervious to defeat, while embarking on a mystical crusade to make the world safe for democracy.

The year 1961 was also when the CIA-sponsored Bay of Pigs Invasion of Cuba turned into a U.S. fiasco, during which time Khrushchev was still in power. And Khrushchev used all of his powers of intimidation, amassed during his bare-knuckles rise through Soviet politics, to intimidate Kennedy, for Khrushchev was a most accomplished master at bullying people.[19]

It was during 1962 that the U.S. military transitioned from an advisory role to a more active combat support role, as U.S. Air Force pilots and U.S. Army helicopter pilots began to covertly provide air support for ARVN (Army of the Republic of (South) Vietnam) ground troops.[20] Whenever anything is done surreptitiously, it generally indicates that one is hiding something, and in this case the Kennedy Administration was aware that they might very well be violating the Geneva Accords of 1954, which prohibited foreign powers from active combat participation within Vietnam, but they felt that desperate times required desperate measures. The United States was also very much aware that if the elections sanctioned by the Geneva Accords were to take place in Vietnam anytime within the near future, Ho Chi Minh would assuredly win the popular vote, for he was idolized by a great number of Vietnamese throughout the south as well as the north, while those Vietnamese in the south who actually supported the Catholic government of Ngo Dinh Diem were a clear minority. Still, the United States was determined to change the hearts and minds of many more South Vietnamese; it was a hopeless undertaking. As U.S. military assistance and personnel to South Vietnam increased, MACV (Military Assistance Command, Vietnam) was created to assist MAAG Vietnam.

In 1962, France's last major colony, Algeria, gained its independence, China went to war against India over border disputes in the vicinity of Tibet, while the Soviet Union and the United States squared off against one another in what became known as the Cuban Missile Crisis, which many construed to be the opening stage of an imminent nuclear war, when the Soviet Union began placing intermediate-range nuclear missiles in Cuba aimed at the United States. Of course we already had nuclear missiles in Turkey pointed at the Soviet Union, and the United States at the time possessed an overwhelming arsenal of 27,297 nuclear weapons, more than eight times as many as the Soviets. Ultimately, President Kennedy, dealing from a position of strength, responded affirmatively to a private letter from Khrushchev, which proposed that the Soviets would remove their nuclear missiles from Cuba, if the U.S. would remove its nuclear missiles from Turkey and promise not to invade Cuba. In the eyes of the world, Khrushchev and the Soviets were seen as being compelled to humiliatingly acquiesce and remove their missiles from Cuba.[21]

Although the North Vietnamese were striving to unify North and South under a single Vietnamese government, the South Vietnamese leaders seemed to prefer the separation. It appeared that the United States preferred the separation as well, for it seemed impossible that we could ever expect to change the thinking of all the brainwashed Vietnamese communists in the north who seemed so sincerely devoted to Ho Chi Minh, not to mention the large number of Vietnamese living in the South who also appeared to idolize Uncle Ho.[22]

Beginning in 1963, the Buddhists, protesting against the repressive Diem government, started setting themselves on fire while wearing their saffron robes. These human conflagrations were even caught on film and shown on American television. The Buddhist monks seemed to die so stoically, as though they had made a profound moral decision and were at peace with themselves, and for the most part they weren't even communists; it was perplexing.[23]

The Vietnamese government of Hanoi was aided by the Soviet Union and China, much like the Vietnamese government of Saigon was aided by the United States. The Soviets and the Chinese both supplied North Vietnam with millions of dollars a year during the 1960s; perhaps not as much as the United States was pumping into the South, but significant assistance nevertheless, for the Vietnam War was simply a part of the larger Cold War that had grown hot in a small corner of Southeast Asia.

The Vietnamese people, both northerners and southerners, suffered immeasurably as a result of the meddling of these superpowers in their affairs, but no side meddled more than the United States, which actually facilitated the overthrow of South Vietnamese President Diem, which occurred on November 2, 1963, just three weeks before President Kennedy was assassinated in Dallas.[24] Although Kennedy knew in advance of the coup, he was shocked by the death of Diem; events seemed to be spinning out of control, and yet with Diem gone, the U.S. military establishment was filled with hope that the subsequent Saigon government would exhibit more resolve in fighting the Vietnamese communists.[25]

Unfortunately, it soon became evident that the change in government made little difference, for the South Vietnamese Army continued to lose ground. Two other military coups took place within a year of Diem's assassination, and yet the U.S. military support for South Vietnam ploughed on, while our policymakers knew darn well that there was virtually no stable or inspiring South Vietnamese government of any substance.

At the time of President Kennedy's assassination on November 22, 1963, when I was a senior in high school, only 16,263 American military personnel were in Vietnam.[26] Vice President Lyndon Baines Johnson (LBJ) stepped into the presidency avowing to pursue current policies. On November 26, Johnson authorized the planning for increased military activity against North Vietnam, with the result that U.S. military support to South Vietnam would unalterably increase.[27]

During 1964 MACV became the unified command for all U.S. military forces in Vietnam and absorbed MAAG Vietnam because the deployment of American combat units had become too large for advisory group control. U.S. troop levels began to steadily increase as the U.S. advisory role gave way to an active military role. General William C. Westmoreland became the commanding general of MACV during June 1964. This was the same year that China became the world's fifth nuclear power. China had joined the United States (as of 1945), the Soviet Union (as of 1949), United Kingdom (1952), and France (1960) in the elite club of nuclear powers. Now China could become more assertive on the world stage, no longer living impotently in fear of a nuclear attack from the United States, or from the Soviet Union with whom it shared a common border of more than 2,700 miles.

The year 1964 was also when Khrushchev was dumped by the Soviet Politburo (highest executive body of the Communist Party and the Soviet State) due to the loss of face that the Soviet Union had suffered as a result of the Cuban Missile Crisis, as well as Khrushchev's disastrous agricultural policies that had compelled the Soviet Union to import grain from the West.

Khrushchev was succeeded by a troika that included Leonid Brezhnev, as general secretary (of the Communist Party of the Soviet Union); Alexey Nikolayevich Kosygin, as Soviet premier; and Anastas Mikoyan as chairman of the Presidium (the permanent executive committee of legislative bodies such as the Supreme Soviet which had the sole power to pass constitutional amendments), although Brezhnev soon ascended above all competitors to become the undisputed leader of the Soviet Union. Brezhnev did not lightly forgive nor forget the humiliation his country was compelled to endure over the Cuban Missile Crisis. When American combat troops began arriving in Vietnam in force,

Brezhnev and the Soviet Union proved to be a steadfast ally, and major supplier of weaponry, to the North Vietnamese. Conflict was also renewed in Laos during 1964, after a right-wing government coup took over control of the central government, which once again induced the Pathet Lao to take up arms in protest.

During June 1964, I graduated from high school. My high school days were typical of my generation, though being born on the first of September invariably made me the youngest student in my class, as that was the cut-off date; those born one day before me, on August 31, constituted the oldest students in the next class. Even so, I was a good student and played junior-varsity basketball and baseball during my sophomore year in high school. As a teenager I hunted quail and rabbits with shotguns, and deer with a rifle. However, after my parents' divorce I was compelled to give up sports and find part-time work after school during my junior and senior years in order to assist my mother with family finances. In those days, athletics were the defining activities among high school boys in California, and fighting down by the creek behind the schoolyard was the way we settled differences. To be a bright student for an athlete in those days was actually a cause of embarrassment, and resulted in merciless teasing by one's peers.

The day after I graduated from high school, I headed out for Mexico, traveling alone on second-class buses, along with the chickens and the pigs, all the way down to Mexico City where I attended the bullfights and the Jai-Lai matches. I had studied Spanish in high school for two years, but of course that was just an introduction to the language; yet, during my twelve- to fourteen-hour bus rides down the Pacific Coast of Mexico, all of the other passengers were eager and willing to assist me in improving my Spanish. I visited Mexico City, Acapulco, and even knocked around the Yucatan peninsula, exploring the ancient Mayan ruins at Chichen Itza and Uxmal. Afterwards, I returned to California to attend junior college classes in the fall. I turned eighteen just prior to beginning my classes, and was therefore required, by law, to go down to my local draft board and register with the Selective Service System in order to ensure that my country would have a pool of potential soldiers available in the event of war.

II

During August 1964, a U.S. destroyer in the Gulf of Tonkin was allegedly attacked by North Vietnamese torpedo boats, after which Congress wasted no time in passing the Tonkin Gulf Resolution, which virtually handed its war-making powers over to the president.[28] President Johnson now had the authority, extended to him by Congress, to use "all necessary measures" to battle communist aggression in Vietnam, which he proceeded to assiduously apply, especially after he won election to his own four-year term of office beginning in January 1965. The focus of American strategic objectives in Southeast Asia had clearly shifted from Laos to Vietnam.

The United States Constitution (Article I, Section 8) states, "The Congress shall have Power to declare war." However, this was never done in the case of Vietnam, as President Johnson had all the power he needed to escalate the "Vietnam Conflict" (the term used in the Congressional Research Service (CRS) Report and other government documents), due to his expanded authority under the Tonkin Gulf Resolution, and thus he had no cause to go back to Congress for a formal declaration of war.

Though foreign powers, under the Geneva Accords, were prohibited from participating in active combat within Vietnam, after the Tonkin Gulf Incident President Johnson felt justified in dispatching large numbers of American combat troops to Vietnam, who began arriving during the spring and summer of 1965. Johnson also endorsed the active bombing of North Vietnam, while the military persistently argued for wider bombing, which they justified as necessary to protect the soldiers on the ground, who they contended were compelled to fight with one hand tied behind their backs.

In the United States the military serves under civilian political leaders, because fighting and war must necessarily serve a political purpose, for war without a political objective would be irrational; it would simply be war for war's sake, and therefore utterly senseless. Once the political goals are achieved there is obviously no longer any rational purpose in continuing with the fighting. It is for the political leaders to determine when the political objectives have been achieved, or when victory is no longer attainable, and it is for these leaders to decide when hostilities are to cease.

During the Vietnam War, our civilian leaders went to great pains to avoid becoming embroiled in another war with China and the Soviet Union, while our military felt they were being restrained in their bombing missions over North Vietnam. Nevertheless, politicians are expected to grasp the larger strategy, while the military is expected to effectively handle the war-fighting responsibilities, and it is certainly not the job of the military to resolve political issues, for that is the job of our elected civilian political leaders, because they are expected to have the larger perspective of the global situation, and though this might not always be the case, for the most part it is true.

There was a young man I knew from my hometown; his name was Jim Shea, and I knew his parents as well, for our families were friends and often congregated at one another's homes. Jim was six years older than I, and he had graduated from the University of Santa Clara, to the south of San Francisco, before being sent off to Vietnam.

Jim became one of the first U.S. Navy aviators to be shot down over North Vietnam, as this was the time when the United States began its retaliatory bombardment of North Vietnam following the Tonkin Gulf incident. Jim was twenty-four years of age when he was killed in action, and his name is etched on panel 1E of the Vietnam Veterans Memorial (construction of which was not completed until November 1982). Jim left a pregnant wife behind and a child whom he never met. His last letter home read as follows:

> ...The USS Hancock has seen more than its share of combat in the past few months. Our commanding officer is a hard-charging leader, for whom I hold highest respect and admiration. Every pilot is a top-notch man. Our Squadron is both close-knit and spirited, with an outstanding attitude towards life and the nation.... The picture in Southeast Asia is not pretty. There's a multitude of complicated political involvement attached to our every movement and course of action.
>
> It is true that, on the surface, we're engaging North Vietnam, but beneath this lies the turbulent aggression of Red China, with the threatening support of USSR in the background.
>
> We're fighting ideology and tactics so different from our own that I believe the United States hasn't realized yet what the guidelines and policies should be.
>
> To fly over enemy territory, to see anti-aircraft shells explode near you, to drop live ordnance on an actual target — these are the realities of life that seem unreal.
>
> The events have no connection to the real life at home, where the sound of a typewriter in an office replaces the sound of an automatic weapon in a rice paddy, where the sound of a cop's siren means another traffic ticket and not an air raid, where the sound of a steam-driven hammer means a new bridge and not another aircraft launched from a catapult.
>
> To think that in a few months — I'll be back on terra firma ... U.S.A., to rejoin with Susie and our new addition. With these thoughts I'll say God Bless you.
>
> I'll see you soon.
>
> Love,
>
> Jim

Naturally, the bombing incited retaliation by North Vietnam, manifested by the stepped-up infiltration of NVA (North Vietnamese Army, sometimes referred to as the People's Army of Vietnam, or the Vietnam People's Army) soldiers into South Vietnam to engage in face-to-face combat. It should be noted, however, that as early as 1961, U.S. intelligence officers had identified North Vietnamese units in the Central Highlands, which initiated attacks around the town of Dak To, so the North Vietnamese were clearly not playing by the rules.[29] Nevertheless, as a result of the stepped-up NVA infiltration following the Tonkin Gulf Incident, the United States was compelled to bring in larger land-based Air Force bombers to carry out sustained, vice retaliatory, bombing operations over North Vietnam and along the Ho Chi Minh Trail in order to interdict NVA supply lines, and to destroy the will of the North Vietnamese to continue the fight. Land-based aircraft have greater range and can carry larger bomb loads than carrier aircraft, which are compelled to operate from shorter (carrier) runways.

Since the DMZ extended east to west for a little over forty-five miles, it could be sealed off, to a large extent, as an infiltration route, and so the North Vietnamese, in violation of the neutrality of Laos and Cambodia, proceeded to construct the Ho Chi Minh Trail through those two countries, which was actually a network of roads and footpaths, equipped with underground base camps and facilities, extending from North Vietnam, through Laos and Cambodia, to various points in South Vietnam, over which more than a million NVA soldiers made the trek during the war, a journey that took two to three months on foot.

Whenever you have aircraft parked in a war-torn country, you need troops on the ground to protect them, and so, on the eighth of March 1965, 3,500 Marines of the Ninth Marine Expeditionary Brigade, the lead element of the Third Marine Division, stormed ashore near Da Nang, about 100 miles to the south of the DMZ, to become the first U.S. ground combat troops to set foot upon Vietnamese soil (the First Marine Division was dispatched to Vietnam one year later). It was not long before their mission was expanded beyond perimeter defense to include offensive *search and destroy* missions. Da Nang, with a population of 100,000 in 1965, was the fourth largest city in all of Vietnam, behind Saigon (1.7 million), Hanoi (475,000), and Haiphong (220,000).[30]

In the ensuing months, Marine and Army combat ground forces began to arrive throughout South Vietnam in greater and greater numbers. It was during this period that several infantry battalions from the First Cavalry Division confronted main force NVA regulars in the Central Highlands, up along the Cambodian border, as depicted in the Mel Gibson movie (based on the Moore and Galloway book, *We Were Soldiers Once ... and Young: Ia Drang: The Battle That Changed the War in Vietnam*). Prior to this time, during the early years of U.S. military involvement in Vietnam up through 1964, just 261 Americans had been killed in action (KIA).[31]

There are four categories of combat (hostile) deaths: (1) killed in action, (2) died of wounds, (3) missing in action (MIA)/declared dead, and (4) captured/declared dead, of which I consider the KIA figure to be the best determinate for gauging the intensity of the fighting. Additionally there is the category of non-hostile deaths, which includes those missing/presumed dead, and those who die from accidents (by far the largest category, comprising nearly 85 percent of all non-hostile deaths), homicides, suicides, and illnesses.

So, though the first American combat troops to arrive in Vietnam during 1965 were initially tasked with protecting our land-based fighter-bombers, the U.S. aerial bombing of North Vietnam and along the Ho Chi Minh Trail throughout the war would have dubious effect, since North Vietnam was essentially a de-centralized agrarian country for which most of its manufactured goods were obtained from China and the Soviet Union, and the war material coming down the Ho Chi Minh Trail was comprised mostly of replacement infantrymen, rifles, mortars, and ammunition.[32]

Nevertheless, the gloves were off; the war was on. But even with active U.S. support, the South Vietnamese did not seem to be putting up much of a fight. At this time the South Vietnamese military totaled around 350,000, supported by regional and local militias. If they were the good guys, supported by the mightiest military power on Earth, then why didn't they act as though they wanted to win?

The fact of the matter was that the South Vietnamese were dying in greater numbers than Americans; it's just that those damn Vietnamese communists appeared indomitable, and they in turn were supported by our arch-enemies— the Soviet Union and Red China.

During 1965, shortly after China became a nuclear power, Chinese support troops began arriving in North Vietnam to maintain roads, bridges, and rail lines in order to free up more North Vietnamese so they could join the fighting that was escalating in the south. American political leaders had to contend with the possibility of menacing or even killing Chinese troops within North Vietnam, which would thus incite China to send its combat troops into the fray, as had happened during the Korean War. The presence of Chinese troops inside North Vietnam, like the American troop contingents in Berlin (from 1945 until they were withdrawn in 1994) and along the Korean DMZ (1953 to the present), was intended to serve as a deterrent in order to dissuade the opponent from attacking. For even if an adversary did attack the relatively small contingents of foreign troops in these countries, it would inevitably bring down the entire military wrath of the larger powers. Hanoi itself was less than a hundred and fifty miles from China, and the presence of Chinese troops inside North Vietnam did in fact deter the United States from conducting air strikes near the Chinese border.[33]

Vietnam and China had fought one another over territorial disputes along their common border during the past, and most likely there would be more disputes in the future, for the Vietnamese have always had an innate fear of Chinese expansionism into their country, and yet, during the current conflict against the Americans, North Vietnam and China had set aside past differences and become allies.

As a counter-balance to this unlikely alliance, North Vietnam also cultivated the support of the Soviet Union, which clearly considered itself the world's vanguard of communism. The Soviet Union had been a communist country since 1922, following the Russian Revolution that overthrew the tsar in 1917. Then, after its victory over Hitler and the Nazis in early 1945, the Soviet Union rose to prominence as the most powerful communist country in the world. It was the Soviets in particular who supplied the North Vietnamese with much of their weaponry, particularly the AK-47 assault rifle, considered by many to be the best light infantry weapon in the world.

Communist China, on the other hand, was a newcomer to the game, only becoming a communist country in 1949, after winning its civil war over the Nationalists. And although communist China could spawn virtually inexhaustible human waves of infantrymen, it was humbly compelled to rely on the Soviet Union to provide its air force assets.

At this point in time the Soviet Union was the largest country on earth in terms of size, as it spanned eleven time zones and had attained a mass that was more than twice that of the United States (including Alaska). The Soviet Union was in essence the world's last empire, ruled by the Russians out of Moscow, with the third largest population in the world behind only China and India.[34]

During the Vietnam War the Soviet Union was supporting the Vietnamese in the north, who, in essence, were serving as Soviet proxies in its ongoing (Cold War) fight against the United States; although the North Vietnamese did not need much encouragement, and they never thought of themselves as proxies. They considered themselves Vietnamese nationalists, for they were always of an independent bent, as they never allowed themselves to get too close to either the Soviet Union or to China; instead they played these two superpowers off against one another in order to achieve their own ends.[35]

Back in the States, there were no protests to speak of during the early U.S. involvement in Vietnam. In 1963 and 1964 there was a smattering of anti-war protests in America's largest liberal cities like New York, Philadelphia, and San Francisco. However, it wasn't until early 1965, after U.S. ground forces began arriving in Vietnam, that antiwar protests garnered greater media attention, particularly the demonstrations at the University of Michigan in March; a march on Washington, D.C., during April; and draft card burnings at the University of California at Berkeley during May. Yet even these protests occurred early in the war, shortly after the Marines had come ashore at Da Nang, and not many Americans had died — yet. Consequently, the vast majority of the American public at that time was supportive of the direction in which President Johnson was taking the country.

Being from the rather liberal San Francisco Bay Area, I had many acquaintances who opted to take different paths than I, including avoiding the draft altogether and fleeing to Canada. I was never concerned about the decisions that others made, so long as they followed their own convictions. Some people of course had no convictions at all, they were simply accustomed to choosing the easiest path through life, and these people only merited disdain.

By the end of 1965, the first year that U.S. combat ground forces were in Vietnam, the number of U.S. troops stood at 184,000, of which 1,313 Americans had been killed in action; it was just the beginning.[36]

3

Advanced Infantry Training and Officer Candidate School

I

After completing my Basic Combat Training during the spring of 1966, I proceeded on to Advanced Infantry Training (AIT), which was also conducted at Fort Ord, near Monterey. Now that I had unequivocally declared for the infantry, I was marched over to chapel on Sundays where the chaplain struggled to assure me that although the Sixth Commandment stipulates "Thou shalt not kill," to kill for one's country was not a sin.

I had grown up attending church regularly until my parents divorced, and, sitting in my pew, I felt some disquiet in trying to reconcile how war seemed to clearly contravene one of our most sacred Commandments. I would probably need to see a shrink or take some philosophy classes once I got out of the Army, just so I could try to resolve this puzzling paradox, since the chaplain clearly was not reassuring me.

I was one of many soldiers and sailors riding the buses during those days of the Vietnam War, reminiscent of those World War II movies in which everyone seemed to be in uniform. The bus also accommodated young couples and blue-collar workers who could not afford to own a car; yet people seemed pleasant and courteous when they were together, sharing public transportation.

During our Advanced Infantry Training, we became proficient at using machine guns and mortars. And now that we were all destined to serve as infantrymen in the war, we were finally issued M16 assault rifles that were currently being used out in the jungles of Vietnam and were 30 percent lighter than the M14 on which we had trained during our Basic Combat Training.

We also spent hours developing our hand-to-hand combat skills, including *the take down strangle hold*, and *the sidekick to the groin*. We were taught the vulnerable parts of the human body and how to crush our adversary's Adam's apple with one hand. We learned how to apply tourniquets and how to use the cellophane wrappers from cigarette packages to plug a sucking chest wound. We underwent lots of bayonet practice, learning how to parry the thrust of an enemy bayonet, while building up a hatred for our enemies by emitting

3—Advanced Infantry Training and Officer Candidate School

a loud bloodcurdling scream each time we plunged our bayonet into the training dummy, and then we gave a sharp twist to the bayonet, insuring that we had adequately ripped apart our opponent's entrails before emitting another hair-raising scream as we extracted the bayonet from our adversary's body. General George Patton felt that soldiers had to learn to hate the enemy before they could be effective warriors.

After completing my Advanced Infantry Training in California during the summer of 1966, I was sent across the country to attend the Infantry Officer Candidate School at Fort Benning in Columbus, Georgia, commonly referred to within the Army as "The Benning School for Boys." This was the first time that I had been to the South, which appeared quite different from California, for the South had only recently been required, by federal law, to end its oppressive segregation (separation) policies between whites and blacks that had been in place for the last hundred years, ever since the end of the Civil War when black slaves had been set free.

Being from California, I had grown up in the predominately white suburbs to the south of San Francisco, though my environment was not racist. My father in his youth had been on the track team with Jackie Robinson at Pasadena Junior College in 1938, after which they had both transferred to UCLA in 1940. My father had spoken frequently with Jackie, whom he held in the highest regard. God forbid anybody say an unkind word about Jackie Robinson in front of my father.

The Civil Rights Movement actually began around 1954, during the Eisenhower years, at which time the U.S. Supreme Court declared school segregation unconstitutional (even though President Truman had already taken the lead when he ordered the desegregation of the U.S. armed forces in 1948). During 1964, the year I graduated from high school in California at the age of seventeen, President Johnson induced Congress to pass the Civil Rights Act (Public Law 88–352) declaring discrimination based on race illegal.

During August 1966, when I was in Georgia and just getting ready to begin my officer training, the black and white communities were still visibly separated. One day I went into a diner in the southern city of Columbus for breakfast with a fellow soldier who was black. We proceeded to sit on two stools at the counter—and, after waiting for what seemed an inordinate amount of time, even though the diner appeared virtually empty, the hefty white waitress sluggishly came to a halt in front of us. She turned to my friend and asked him what he wanted, then, after she cantankerously took his order, she proceeded to waddle back into the kitchen to place the order with the cook. When she returned from the kitchen and headed back along the other side of the counter in my direction, I caught her attention and asked if I could order? She stopped directly in front of me, leaned forward a bit, and venomously said, "The law says I have to serve him [casting her eyes disdainfully upon my friend], but it don't require me to serve you!"

I was shocked to say the least, but I did not reveal my inner rage to the waitress; rather I continued to sit there, occupying my stool next to my friend, while we proceeded to share the breakfast hour, each of us acting as though nothing unusual had happened.

However, I was truly surprised by the waitress's behavior, not because I was naive about racism, but because of the fact that here in the South, with its one hundred years of enforced separation between the races, this waitress could still feel so self-righteous in defense of such oppressive policies. She probably attended church more often than I, and she may very well have believed that God was on her side, which is what I found really scary. I had a momentary fractional reflection of what it must have been like for the four young college students who sat on counter stools five years ago at a diner in North Carolina, during which time the white waitresses refused to serve them because of the color of their skin.

I attended OCS for nearly six months (twenty-three weeks), from August 1966 into February 1967, so I certainly had more training than the "Ninety-Day Wonders" that the Army had churned out during World War II.

During the officer training I was subjected to the last of the old school approach that was soon considered too severe, but in those days they could wake us at any hour, and the instructors had us out wading through freezing creeks in the dead of night, or going on five-mile runs with full packs. We were always sleep deprived. We did endless PT (physical training); we never walked; rather, we were required to run to all of our classes. Inside our notebooks we carried those table place-mats with a thin layer of sponge on one side and, when we returned to our barracks, we moved off the center aisle toward our bunks by laying down the place-mats, upon which we stepped, and then, while standing on one, we laid out another place-mat in front of us, while picking up the one behind, for we did not want to mar our spit-shined floor; ultimately we leaped up onto our bunks.

However, the TAC (Teach, Assess and Counsel) officers, who constantly monitored our performance, soon came by and intentionally scraped their boot heels through our meticulously spit-shined floor before they departed for the night and, since our floors had to be in pristine, spit-shined perfection prior to inspection the next morning, we had to drag our exhausted bodies out of our racks in the dead of night and surreptitiously get down on our hands and knees, with three of our four extremities resting on sponge place-mats, while using our free hand to spit-shine our floor before going to sleep. By spit-shine, I mean that we applied wax to the floor, then we took little cotton balls that we dipped in water and alcohol, and we worked them over the floor until a beautiful shine developed — this would take hours.

We were constantly harassed while we were eating. We had to enter the mess hall (called a chow hall by the troops), get our trays of food and then sit down at ramrod attention. We had to stare straight ahead while fishing around

3—Advanced Infantry Training and Officer Candidate School

on our plates for the food, hoping to impale something on our forks, because we could not look down, and we were required to bring the fork straight up at a 90-degree angle, and then along a straight line into our mouths. Sometimes the TACs accused us of not looking straight ahead, or of not lifting our forks up from our plates at a precise 90-degree angle, at which time they ordered us to stop eating, get out of the mess hall, and do 100 pushups before returning.

Of course by the time we returned to the mess hall, the mealtime was over. Sneaking food out of the mess hall or buying candy from the vending machines near the barbershop was strictly forbidden, and any attempt to hide food in one's footlocker was grounds for dismissal.

The TACs woke us up around 4:30 each morning by banging garbage can lids together, or simply by hurling a garbage can down the aisle way, which is indisputably more jarring than an alarm clock. We had less than ten seconds, from the sound of the smashing garbage can lids, to be out of our deep, fatigued sleep and be standing *at attention* beside our bunks; nobody slept in the nude, rather we all wore G.I. issue cotton shorts—the baggy kind. The TACs then gave us fifteen minutes to shit, shower and shave—literally, so there we were, about a hundred guys to a bay, with about ten open toilets all in a line, no privacy, everyone trying to take care of all their bathroom business in a quarter-hour before we were required to fall out into morning formation for reveille.

Reveille signals the start of the day, and the time for reveille is designated by the commander, which is followed by the raising of the flag that can only be displayed between sunrise and sunset (though the flag can be displayed after sunset if it is illuminated). Consequently, troops were up and about, and assembling in their reveille formations well before sunrise.

Many people took up the habit of smoking cigarettes in the Army, for smoking was considered "a right, not a privilege," which meant that whatever bad things the military could do to you, they could not take away your right (or your addiction) to smoking. "Smoke 'em if you got 'em" meant a time to rest, so everyone looked forward to a smoke break, even us non-smokers.

At OCS we spent time each day out at the rifle range refining our marksmanship skills to the point where most of us qualified as experts. We were hauled out to the range in the back of uncovered *deuce and a half* (2½-ton) trucks, with benches along the sides and a third bench down the middle for the late-comers who were forced to straddle the bench without a back-rest. I recall sitting on my bench with my back against the braces of the open truck, sleeping in the early morning sunshine, while on my way to the rifle range.

Some days we went out to the grenade range where we would stand behind a three-foot concrete wall, pull the pin to the M61 fragmentation grenade, count out two seconds (one one thousand, two one thousand), then toss the lemon-shaped grenade out in front of us, after which we quickly crouched down behind the cement slab to protect ourselves against any shrapnel blowing back in our direction from a short throw.

There was a deep cement gutter, referred to as a grenade sump, that fronted my standing position in the event I panicked and happened to drop the grenade at my feet, for then I would still have time to kick the grenade into the sump before it exploded, as a grenade has a four- to five-second fuse-delay after the pin has been pulled. Nevertheless, whenever one has pulled the pin and is preparing to throw a grenade, one has the feeling that one is holding onto a live stick of dynamite with a burning fuse, which produces a certain anxiety, mixed with hope, that the grenade will not explode prematurely, and yet the longer one can hold onto the *live* grenade, the less chance the enemy will have to pick it up and throw it back at you.

We developed proficiency in the use of mortars, which I enjoyed because some mathematics are involved in calculating the trajectories of the rounds fired from each of the Army's three sizes of mortars, as well as in the adjustment of the charges on the larger rounds used by our heaviest 4.2" (the diameter of the barrel) mortar. Additionally, we also practiced calling in artillery and air strikes on old dilapidated tanks and bunkers. In essence, all of us infantry officers developed the capability to serve as forward artillery observers, for though an infantry battalion generally had an assigned artillery observer, if we found ourselves operating in smaller units, as companies or platoons, then we infantry officers were required to speak directly to the artillery batteries for fire support.

The TACs continually shouted at us, dropping us for pushups at the slightest excuse, but I was young and strong, and I knew they could not deter me from succeeding, even though most of the aspiring officers, being college graduates, were generally three years older than I. We had to do timed mile runs in full battle gear and combat boots. These runs in combat boots have since been discontinued because of the shin splint injuries they caused, but at the time we were not so concerned; we were young and tough, and I ran the hell out of the course. I never did come in first in the mile run, but I did come in second one time, which seemed to impress the TACs, because it was rumored that the number one finisher had been a college track star.

We conducted jungle training, through the pine forests of Georgia, where the TACs continually reminded us that it was imperative, absolutely imperative, that we continually vary our position in relation to the radiotelegraph operator (RTO) if we wished to have any chance at all of surviving our first fifteen minutes of combat as an infantry lieutenant. They told us that the NVA and VC always looked for the radio antenna, knowing that the platoon leader would be close by, and that is the very person they wanted to kill first; eliminate the leader and the subordinates will become more vulnerable.

Of the 2,648 commissioned Army officers that were killed in action during the Vietnam War, 92 percent were either lieutenants or captains (1,685 lieutenants and 748 captains), also referred to as *junior* officers, and these totals only apply to those officers that were killed in action, and do not include the additional 540 junior Army officers that suffered non-hostile deaths. Amongst the Army's *field-grade* officers, sixty-one lieutenant colonels and eight full-bird colonels were killed in action in Vietnam. Of all the commissioned Army officers killed in action in Vietnam, 9.8 percent (260) were graduates of the United States Military Academy at West Point.[1] Okay, I got the point; after being screamed at countless times, I was sure that when I got to Vietnam, I would keep as far away from my RTO as respectability allowed. After all, it was all about survival — right?

At the very end of our jungle training, we had to go out into the boonies for our map-reading test, which was a critical examination, because if you failed two attempts, you were out of the program and would never be an officer. We were assigned our starting points, issued maps and compasses, and then left to our own devices to follow azimuths through thick woods to find other numbered stakes, but only if we were accurate as to the direction and distance we had traveled. In other words, you have to have some smarts, for if you cannot navigate with a map and a compass, then you're not much good as an infantry officer.

The year 1966 came to an end about two-thirds of the way through my officer training. A total of 4,432 Americans in Vietnam had been killed in action during that year, which averaged out to more than twelve killed each day; things were heating up over there, and most all of us would be heading off to the war sometime within the next eight months, probably during August or September.[2]

Harassment went on unrelentingly throughout the first five months of our officer training, during which time a great number of men dropped out or were kicked out of the program. But then, toward the end of the fifth month of training, around the middle of January, the harassment eased up, and we began to be treated a bit more respectfully since we were soon to become officers.

During the last couple weeks of the nearly six-month training program, we were even permitted to go to the officers' club on the base where we could order drinks at the bar, even though I had not yet attained the legal drinking age of twenty-one. I thought this was pretty special, even though I had frequented bars ever since I began working in the merchant marine at the age of eighteen. Still, I didn't really know a lot about drinking. I remember that many of the officer candidates ordered Singapore Slings because they tasted like an exotic tropical fruit punch, yet contained sufficient alcohol to give one a buzz. I thought it was made with gin, but I wasn't sure. Of course all *real* American men develop a taste for Jack Daniel's sour mash corn liquor that comes from Tennessee. Sour mash simply means that the residue of the previous distillation is used in subsequent fermentations.

It was around this time, during the second week of February, less than two weeks before graduation, that one of my classmates, a young man from New

Jersey named Robert Turnbull, got caught with a candy bar in his foot locker, which was strictly forbidden. So Robert was offered the choice of getting booted out of OCS, or dropping back to the trailing class and repeating the last six weeks of the course.

Robert so much wanted to be an officer in the service of his country that he chose to repeat the last six weeks of the course. Upon his departure from our class, he and I vowed to track each other down after the war. We had lost some of our youthful levity by this point, for the reality was settling in that we would soon be officers and most likely sent off to the war within six months after graduation, where we would soon be responsible for leading about forty men into combat. I had been in the Army for a little more than a year training for this eventuality of going off to war, but it was starting to feel a bit scary, for we all knew that infantry officers in Vietnam had a very short life expectancy.

During the third week of February 1967 I graduated from the officer program and was commissioned an infantry lieutenant in the United States Army with a salary of $303 a month. Officers were obligated to serve in the Army for at least two years from the day they received their commissions, so I was required to serve until sometime into February 1969.

To be commissioned means to be appointed by the president to serve as an officer in the Army of the United States. Though all commissioned officers serve at the pleasure of the president, it is the Secretary of the Army who actually signs the commission. Unlike enlisted soldiers, a commissioned officer cannot be reduced in rank, and a commissioned officer found guilty of bad conduct or dishonorable behavior is subject to dismissal rather than a dishonorable discharge, which is just as bad. When soldiers receive their commissions, a ceremony is held, much like graduating from university, except that we were additionally required to swear an oath:

> I, Albert Thomas Lawrence, having been appointed a second lieutenant in the United States Army, do accept such appointment and do solemnly swear that I will support and defend the Constitution of the United States against all enemies, foreign and domestic, that I will bear true faith and allegiance to the same; that I take this obligation freely, without any mental reservation or purpose of evasion; and that I will well and faithfully discharge the duties of the office on which I am about to enter, so help me God.

I had made a sacred affirmation to God to defend the United States Constitution, which embodies our fundamental principles of government and constitutes the law of the land. I truly considered an oath to be a sacred promise that I would never break.

Usually family members attended the commissioning ceremony, and invariably someone's father or brother stood to the side of the stage and pinned the gold lieutenant bars on the shoulders of the young officer's uniform. I suppose I really didn't go in for too much of that kind of sentimentality, though

I'm sure that my father would have been proud to come out to Fort Benning for the ceremony, but he had recently experienced some business setbacks and really did not have the means to travel out to Georgia, so I just took my gold bars in hand and pinned them on myself. For this occasion we wore our class A service uniforms, which consisted of a shirt and tie worn under an Army green polyester/wool coat with trousers. Officer uniforms had a black stripe around the cuffs of their coats and a black strip running down the outside seams of their trousers.

I was now an officer in the United States Army at twenty years of age. As I walked out of the hall and across the grounds of Fort Benning, all the privates, corporals, and sergeants whom I passed snapped to rigid attention and issued me a crisp salute.

While I was at Officer Candidate School, my sister Penny was offered the opportunity to travel to West Africa and visit with my Uncle Larry, who had married my father's older sister and worked for the Agency for International Development (AID) in Monrovia, Liberia. Soon after her arrival in Africa she secured a clerical job with the U.S. Embassy in Monrovia. I was happy for my sister, as she now had the opportunity to leave home and work overseas. My sister and I had been pretty close when we were growing up, for even though she was two years ahead of me in school (during the Elvis Presley years), she always helped me by showing me how to dress or teaching me how to dance during those most difficult adolescent years. However, when our parents divorced seven years ago, we were starkly aware of the fact that we needed to leave the nest to relieve the financial burden on our mother. In Africa my sister met her future husband John, a Marine Corps guard at the Embassy.

II

After completing OCS, I was authorized a couple weeks of leave before I was required to report to my new duty assignment at Fort Gordon, in Augusta, Georgia, so I decided to travel out to California to visit family and friends. Now that I was an Army officer, I was eligible to fly "*space available*" on military aircraft, so I traveled up to Maxwell Air Force Base near Montgomery, Alabama, in the hope of catching a military hop out West. I traveled to the base in my Army (class A service) uniform and, being as how I was on active duty, I was eligible to fly on all military aircraft.

As I was checking in at the military air terminal, I was informed that an aircraft was in the process of taxiing out to the runway, destined for Colorado Springs, and if I wanted to catch a ride that I should head out to the tarmac posthaste.

I went running out onto the tarmac, and there on the runway apron was a sleek F-111 tactical strike fighter jet that had been especially modified to carry two passengers (Congressmen). The jet had two pilots and a crew chief, as well as room for two passengers. Everyone was cordial as I climbed aboard and off we went.

This was essentially a fighter-bomber jet that could reach a maximum speed of 1,400 miles per hour and fly over 59,000 feet above the earth. During the flight, I noticed that we were flying at a very high altitude, higher than I had ever flown in a commercial airplane, for it seemed as though I could see the fringes of outer space above the blue limit of the sky. As we approached Colorado Springs, the pilot did a barrel roll just for me, where the ground below me started to rotate, and then it appeared over my head, before readjusting itself below me once again as we plunged toward earth.

While I was on leave in California, I saw some of my high school buddies, though we were all still too young to legally enter a bar for a drink. I purchased a two-year-old VW Beetle in Los Angeles to drive back across country to my new assignment in Augusta, Georgia, knowing that I would receive my orders for Vietnam within the next six months.

Upon arriving at Fort Gordon in Augusta, Georgia, I began my first officer assignment, serving as the commanding officer (CO) of a Basic Training company. I was pleased to be assigned a commanding officer role as a second lieutenant, even though this was a peacetime assignment, which didn't mean squat, compared to being a commanding officer in a combat environment.

However, now I was the guy who, simply by my presence, caused fear and trembling among the new recruits, even though I was only twenty years of age. I sympathetically observed the young soldiers, fearfully and frenetically bracing themselves against the walls whenever I walked by in much the same manner as I had done, not too long ago, though half of them were most likely older than I. Nevertheless, it quickly became apparent to me that the Army was run by the old sergeants.

I reported up through the chain of command to some colonel in regards the performance of the troops, and I oversaw the inspections, but the sergeants took care of all the admin stuff, and they seemed to take care of me as well. They all had about twenty years in the Army, while I had a little more than a year, so I was somewhat perplexed as to what precisely was to be my role as an officer. Ultimately I found out: War is fought by young men, especially wars fought in hot humid jungles that suck so much out of a soldier that only the young can endure. The old sergeants did not accompany me to Vietnam; well, at least not all the way out into the boonies with an infantry unit.

When I received my commission in the United States Army during February 1967, I knew that I would most probably be sent to Vietnam within six or seven months, and I knew that a soldier could die there, especially an infantry platoon leader, and so I, like all the other newly minted lieutenants, truly began to live each moment as though it was my last, as though it was forever. It seemed that our Friday night parties were more intense, for we knew that we would soon be going off to war, and we found that when we shared this realization

3—Advanced Infantry Training and Officer Candidate School

with women they were even more willing to give of themselves in order to calm our beating hearts. We had become reckless as well; we were aware that we would be under fire soon enough, and we wanted to squeeze as much juice from the tree of life within the short time remaining to us.

When I received my orders for Vietnam in early August informing me that I was down to my last thirty days before I was to be in the war, I decided to spend my remaining time in Europe since I had never been there, and I had this unconquerable urge to see some more of the world before heading off to a war from which I might not return.

However, my superiors in Georgia considered my desire to leave the country upon receipt of my orders for Vietnam highly unusual, and so I was required to jump through numerous hoops in order to obtain written permission from some general that authorized my travel to Europe while explicitly forbidding me to visit any communist country.

I caught a military hop from the East Coast to West Germany, which required that I be in uniform, and then, upon arriving in Europe, I changed into civilian clothes and stuffed my uniform into my duffle bag, which was my only piece of luggage, and then I headed off to Paris where I spent a couple nights hanging out in various cafés around the Latin Quarter. After France, I traveled on to Amsterdam, just long enough to drink some Heinekens, where no one carded me to discern if I was of the legal drinking age as they frequently did in the States. I was going off to war; I was acting recklessly.

Ultimately, toward the end of my time in Europe, I made my way to Spain where I caught another military flight back to the States. I landed at the Dover Air Force Base in Delaware, after which I rushed down to Georgia to pick up my car, which I proceeded to drive at breakneck speed across the country to my home State of California — my departure point for the war.

I had spent virtually all of my leave in Europe, so now I had just a couple days to spare before my scheduled airplane flight to Vietnam. I had very little time to spend with family. My father was in Southern California at the time, so I did not see him before I departed, though I'm sure we must have spoken on the phone.

So, it was just one of those times, when I simply headed off to do my duty and fight in a war with little family fanfare. I'm sure I told my family not to worry, and that they told me to keep my head down and not to be a hero, and then off I went. I made my way over to the Seventh and Mission Greyhound bus station in San Francisco in my officer's uniform, with my duffle bag slung over my shoulder, and caught the bus to the Oakland Army Base, across the Bay, where I dutifully joined the queue of soldiers that were boarding military buses for the hour and a half ride up to Travis Air Force Base, near Sacramento, for our flight across the Pacific Ocean to Vietnam.

The unique aspect of going to war is that one submitted — to fate, like getting onboard an airplane, or more appropriately a space ship, where, after one is belted in, one is committed and relinquishes control over one's situation. I submitted; I suited up, went through the training, boarded the airplane, fastened my seatbelt, and took off for the war. I had made my decision.

> This above all: to thine own self be true,
> And it must follow, as the night the day,
> Thou canst not then be false to any man.[3]

PART II: 1967–1968

4

Situation (September 1967)

I

We landed in the sizzling heat of the tropics at the Bien Hoa Air Base, about fifteen miles outside of Saigon, and less than 800 miles from the equator. We were herded onto buses for the short ride over to the 90th Replacement Battalion at Long Binh, the largest Army base in all of Vietnam with more than 50,000 military personnel, as well as the location of the notorious Long Binh Stockade (commonly called the Long Binh Jail or simply LBJ), which was the Army prison in Vietnam, while the Navy and Marine Corps maintained their military prison (called a brig) at Da Nang.

Within a couple days of my arrival, during the first week of September 1967, I was apprised that I was to serve as a platoon leader in Company B, of the Second Battalion (of the Eighth Infantry Regiment), within the Second Brigade of the Fourth Infantry (Ivy) Division, up in the mountains of the Central Highlands.

The Fourth Infantry Division soldiers wear a white diamond shoulder patch that is comprised of four green ivy leaves, intended to symbolize tenacity and fidelity, while the word "Ivy" is also a play on words of the Roman numeral IV (the number four). Many of the battle-hardened infantrymen referred to themselves and their division as "Poison Ivy."

The Fourth Infantry Division was one of the three American divisions to assault the beaches of Normandy during the D-Day Invasion. And the history of its most heralded battalion, the Second Battalion of the Eighth Infantry Regiment, where I was headed, had a more ancient history than that of the Ivy Division, stretching back in time to before the Civil War.

During World War II the Second of the Eighth, comprised of 620 soldiers, was the very first amphibious battalion to set foot on the beaches of Normandy at 0630 hours on D-Day, the sixth of June 1944, whereas its sister battalion, the First of the Eighth followed in the second wave an hour later, while the Third of the Eighth and the other two regiments (Twelfth and Twenty-Second) of the Fourth Infantry Division came ashore in the third and fourth waves during the following two hours.

Since the tide at Normandy had a surge of nearly twenty feet as it moved from west to east, Allied forces were required to perform an echelon left movement in their attack along the coast during low tide (so that the landing craft would not risk destruction on the beach obstacles), which meant that the assault troops were compelled to traverse over nearly 500 yards of open beach before they even reached the high tide mark, and since Utah Beach constituted the extreme western flank of the entire Allied Invasion, fifteen miles from Omaha, the next assault beach to the east, Utah was therefore the very first beach on which the assault force touched shore.

Brigadier General Theodore Roosevelt Jr., son of former President Theodore Roosevelt, rode in with the Second of the Eighth and became a World War II legend when he stepped ashore and said, "We're going to start the war from right here."[1]

Twenty-three years later, the illustrious "First at Normandy" battalion (Second of the Eighth), along with two other infantry battalions (First of the Twelfth and First of the Twenty-Second) that made up the Second Brigade of the Fourth Infantry Division, was primarily responsible for screening Vietnam's western border and thereby serving as the first line of defense against those North Vietnamese who were bypassing the DMZ and entering South Vietnam through Laos and Cambodia by way of the Ho Chi Minh Trail.

Our mission was to preempt any offensive assaults by the enemy aimed at the populated cities of the lowlands along the coast, which meant that the North Vietnamese would first have to pass through us—the sentinels of the central highlands.

At the time I did not mind being assigned to these mountainous jungles, for it seemed preferable to serving in the densely populated lowlands along the sea, or the soggy Mekong Delta to the south of Saigon where I would have been compelled to wade through flooded rice paddies, up to my armpits all day.

The U.S. military broke Vietnam down into four quadrants, with I Corps in the far north and IV Corps in the far south, with II and III Corps in between. The Marines were up in the northern half of I Corps that abutted the DMZ (demilitarized zone), a buffer zone of a little over six miles in width that separated South Vietnam from North Vietnam, while the Army was responsible for the rest of the country (the southern half of I Corps, and all of II Corps [the largest corps area in South Vietnam, comprising nearly 50 percent of the total land area], III Corps and IV Corps), although it should be noted that Army troops of the First Air Cavalry Division, in eight months' time, made their way up into the far northern reaches of I Corps (during April 1968), in a joint Operation (Pegasus) with the Marines to relieve the base at Khe Sanh that was under intense NVA artillery fire.

I could have been assigned to any one of three different geographical areas—the lowlands (to the north of Saigon stretching up from III Corps, all the way through II Corps, and up into I Corps), the Mekong Delta (in IV Corps to the south of Saigon), or the central highlands (in the western portion of II

Corps, alongside the Cambodian and Laotian borders)—they were all dangerous places.

The lowlands were the densely populated dry coastal areas to the north of Saigon along the South China Sea, inundated with sand dunes, where the adversaries were primarily South Vietnamese communists—Vietcong, also referred to as VC, Victor Charlie, or simply Charlie by American soldiers. The Victor Charlie descriptor was not intended to praise these southern communists, rather it was simply the manner in which the American military spelled out the alphabet to confirm understanding, such that A was Alpha, B was Bravo, C was Charlie, and V was Victor.

I had ephemeral visions of soldiers in the lowlands sunbathing by the seaside, but fighting in populated areas meant dealing with a lot of booby traps set out along frequently used trails and roads, as well as all of the other sordid unpleasantness of urban warfare.

The Mekong Delta in the deep south was the heavily populated rice-growing alluvial delta formed by the Mekong River as it flowed into the South China Sea to the south of Saigon, and where the enemy soldiers were also predominately VC. In this river delta, American solders were required to wade through interminable expanses of open and exposed rice paddies, for the Mekong River is a major life force in Southeast Asia, and ranks among the top twelve rivers in the world for length, and among the top ten for annual volume (about the same as the Mississippi); it is a mighty river.[2] Its headwaters originate in the Himalayan Mountains of China, within 300 miles of the sources of the Yangtze, the world's third longest river, and the Huang (Yellow), the world's fourth longest river. However, whereas the Yangtze and the Yellow rivers flow to the east through China, the Mekong flows in a southerly direction.

After the Mekong breaks free of Tibet, it forms the border between Laos and Thailand (formerly Siam, until 1939 when the government changed the name to Thailand, meaning *Free Land*, as the country had never been under European colonization, though Thailand was a military dictatorship during most of the Vietnam War). However, when the Mekong reaches Cambodia, it virtually splits that country in half until it reaches the capital city of Phnom Penh, where the mighty Mekong then turns abruptly to the left and rushes southeastward into Vietnam, through which it flows until it reaches the South China Sea just to the south of Saigon where it forms the vast Mekong Delta, which is so immense that it would cover more than a third of Florida.

North Vietnam also has its nurturing river, the Red River, known in China where it originates as the Yuan Chiang (or Jiang), and by the Vietnamese as the Song Hong as it flows by Hanoi nearly a half-mile wide, before it breaks into two branches, one branch heading southeast, and the other branch continuing eastward past Vietnam's third largest city—Haiphong. And although the Red River is less than one-third the length of the Mekong, it nevertheless created the rich agricultural delta of the north, where the conquering French constructed the region's chief port at Haiphong during the 1870s, just upstream from where the river flowed out into the Gulf of Tonkin.

Then there were the Central Highlands in the western part of II Corps, a vast upland plateau astride the Laotian and Cambodian borders that stretched roughly 130 miles south to north, and 40 miles west to east with very few roads to speak of, and where travel was primarily conducted along narrow footpaths. In this area of thick and sparsely populated mountainous jungle, I felt that I, as an infantry officer, would stand a better chance of survival. For even though there were still rice paddies aplenty in the highlands, much of the countryside was inundated with thick, dense jungle foliage where visibility was limited, and therefore the enemy would have trouble picking me out at a distance as the officer. The downside was that we would be predominately fighting North Vietnamese Army (NVA) regulars, the same tough adversaries that the Marines were fighting up along the DMZ, although some small VC cadres operated out of the highland cities as well.

MACV had established a corps-level command (I Field Force) the previous year whose area of responsibility comprised the central highland's twelve provinces. The following units were presently under its control: First Cavalry Division (Airmobile), Fourth Infantry Division, First Brigade of the 101st Airborne Division, and the 173rd Airborne Brigade.

Vietnam had been divided for the last thirteen years, during which time North Vietnam had trained a very well-armed and disciplined national army, many of whom had trained in communist China and were well versed in Soviet tactical doctrine as well. NVA infantry soldiers were formidable adversaries, as they had continually been at war against one foe or another for more than twenty years, and these northern troops were considered to be a more tenacious foe than their communist VC brethren in the South. We would have our hands full.

II

After just a couple of days near Saigon, during which I never saw the outside of the air base and my only thrill was to go shopping at the PX (Post Exchange), I boarded a C-130, one of those typical paratroop airplanes without windows, where everyone is strapped in around the sides of the aircraft, and I flew up into the highlands, to Pleiku, capital city of one of South Vietnam's forty-four provinces with a population of around 30,000, high in the western mountains of central Vietnam, about 250 miles to the north of Saigon and less than forty miles from the tri-border junction where Laos, Cambodia, and Vietnam all touch upon one another.

During the 1950s, Pleiku, in the middle of the upland plateau, had served as the main fortified military encampment for the French in the central highlands. By 1967 it was home to the Fourth Infantry Division, which had constructed sizeable Camp Enari (to the southeast of the city), in the shadow of Artillery Hill, just to the south of Dragon Mountain. The base camp was named in honor of First Lieutenant Mark Enari, who, on December 2, 1966, became the first Fourth Infantry Division soldier to be awarded the Silver Star in Vietnam, for which he lost his life as a result of his efforts. This division base camp was a small city unto itself, comprised of several thousand military personnel, its own heavy mortar battery, its helicopter assault squadrons that included gunship and medevac (medical evacuation) choppers, and its triage facilities to treat the wounded and the dying. It was astonishing to me that my nation could establish such a sizeable war camp smack dab in the middle of another country that lay nearly ten thousand miles from our shores. Nevertheless, over the last two years this had become our party, as we were pretty much taking over. After all, we were the mighty Americans and we would show our South Vietnamese allies how to fight a war.

The Fourth Infantry Division arrived in Vietnam twelve months before my arrival and had quickly moved up into the central highlands to establish its headquarters, although the base also accommodated the 173rd Airborne Brigade and elements of the First Cavalry Division (Airmobile), simply referred to as the First Air Cav; these were the soldiers who wore the distinctive shoulder patch of a black horse's head on a yellow triangular Norman shield, bisected by a black diagonal stripe. This was the same unit depicted in the Mel Gibson movie (based on the Moore and Galloway book, *We Were Soldiers Once ... and Young*) that found themselves in a fight, two years ago in the Ia Drang Valley (named after the river that flows through it), during which they were grossly outnumbered and were badly mauled, even though they inflicted heavy losses on the NVA. It was something to be whispered about. No one who had been there was braggadocio; rather, they were humble survivors.

In the Army structure an infantry division consisted of three brigades, and each brigade was comprised of two or more battalions, and each battalion consisted of two to five companies. Historically, a regiment consisted of just one type of unit, such as infantry, artillery *or* cavalry, while a brigade was comprised of combined arms such as infantry, artillery, *and* cavalry. Now regiments were pretty much absorbed into brigades, and regimental battalions were frequently dispersed among different brigades, although each battalion zealously retained its regimental designate, because that's where the history of the unit resided.

For example, the Fourth Infantry Division was first formed in 1917 during World War I, while the Eighth Infantry Regiment, of which I was a part, was formed back in 1838 and had participated in the Mexican War, the Civil War, the Indian Wars against the Seminoles and the Apaches, the War with Spain, and the Philippine Insurrection, prior to its being assigned to the Eighth Division during World War I, after which it was reassigned to the Fourth Infantry Division.[3]

As a consequence, the pride of the unit resided with the regiment (and its battalions) because regiments (as well as its battalions) could be moved from one brigade to another, or even from one division to another, but the unit always retained its regimental honorific. Although divisions of a sort existed during our Civil War, they did not wear distinctive division shoulder patches. Divisions, as a formal and distinct unit, came into being after regiments, during World War I, when larger masses of troops were required to fight our nation's wars.

At full strength, each of the Fourth Infantry Division's three brigades consisted of around 2,000 frontline infantrymen (excluding headquarters' elements), although the division also included four artillery battalions, three of which employed a total of eighteen 105mm howitzers (usually one battery was assigned to each brigade), while the fourth artillery battalion manned six 155mm howitzers (used where needed). The division additionally included combat engineers (frequently employed to create fire bases for the artillery battalions), medical personnel, an armor battalion (one of only two in country), aviation troops (our medevacs and supply choppers), chaplains, signalmen, military intelligence specialists, Military Police (who seemed primarily concerned about enforcing city curfews when we were in the rear), and other service troops, all of which could result in an infantry division exceeding 15,000 troops.

Though it is difficult to know with any certainty the location of the Fourth Infantry Division's three brigades at any particular time, I was apprised that, three months prior to my arrival, our First Brigade was down in the lowlands along the South China Sea, while the Second Brigade was up in the highlands, and the Third Brigade was wading through rice paddies in the Mekong Delta around Saigon (though just before my arrival the Fourth Infantry Division and the Twenty-Fifth Infantry Division swapped Third Brigades).[4]

One would usually consider it a cardinal sin to split forces in such a manner, with each brigade a hundred miles or so apart from one another, but the rice paddies and thick jungles of Vietnam precluded division-sized operations, or even brigade-sized missions for that matter; most operations were of battalion size or smaller, which tended to increase the initiative and responsibility of the line officers (a commissioned officer below the rank of major), who were frequently compelled to operate quite independently on company-sized operations.

Each of our brigades was comprised of three infantry battalions of around 800 soldiers apiece, and each battalion consisted of a headquarters company and four infantry companies. Each infantry company, at full strength, totaled around 180 soldiers (including six officers), broken down into four platoons, each comprised of forty-three enlisted soldiers and one officer. The numbers do not match linearly because divisions, brigades, battalions and companies each have a headquarters' element that can significantly vary in size. Orders flowed downhill from division, to brigade, to battalion, and ultimately to the companies.

It was the rainy season, so it appeared that all the sandbagged bunkers at division base camp were floating around in a sea of mud. I slogged through the muck and mire from one location to another while subjected to the incessant rain. I saw jeeps and trucks stuck in mud that had risen above their axles. The mud was so deep that when I attempted to move about, it was more like I was wading than walking, as though I was pulling my legs through thick molasses. The base had tents with canvas cots enclosed behind sandbag walls, and tidy little gravel rock paths that ascended out of the mud like tropical islands rising out of the sea. Sand-filled coffee cans were put in place near the tent entrances for cigarette butts, which evinced a garrison aura even in this isolated highland outpost, and I discerned guard towers on top of timber walls, reminiscent of cavalry forts in the days of Custer. There was a Mobile Army Surgical Hospital (MASH) that did triage work to prepare the badly wounded for evacuation to the larger hospitals in Saigon or in Japan. Some American female Army nurses were visible, and even a handful of civilian Donut Dollies, but they were a decided minority in a sea of men. Most of the Donut Dollies were recruited directly out of college by the Red Cross, and they had to be at least twenty-one years of age and single. They were provided just a couple weeks of training before being sent off to Vietnam, where they would make the rounds through the hospitals, passing out books and donuts to the wounded soldiers while telling jokes to make the patients smile.

III

While at the Fourth Infantry Division Second Brigade Headquarters, I found a place to store my duffle bag that contained things I would not need out in the jungle, like my service uniform and dress shirts. I learned that the battalion to which I was being sent, the Second of the Eighth, already had one Medal of Honor recipient, awarded less than six months ago. I was informed that during the last six months the battalion had been relentlessly engaged by the NVA and had lost so many men that its fighting strength had been reduced by nearly a third. As a result, each of the battalion's four infantry companies (A, B, C, and D) hovered closer to 125 men apiece, such that each of the platoons in B Company consisted of just about thirty soldiers, instead of the full-strength complement of forty-four. Company D, to my knowledge, was employed to augment battalion security and to serve as the battalion reserve.

I was aware that each company in my battalion was comprised of four platoons, consisting of three rifle platoons (First, Second, and Third) and one weapons (mortar) platoon (the fourth platoon), which was oftentimes smaller than a rifle platoon because they generally only required seven soldiers for each mortar. The soldiers of the weapons platoon had to lug four M29 81-millimeter (referring to the interior diameter of the barrel, at 3.19 inches) mortars, weighing 107 pounds apiece. Though each mortar could be broken apart into three pieces — the baseplate (48 lbs), the bipod (31 lbs), and the barrel (28 lbs), which we referred to as the tube — along with the sighting mechanism, which weighed four pounds, so some of the mortar platoon guys carried nearly fifty pounds of weaponry in addition to their heavy backpacks.[5]

The Marines and the Special Forces troops seemed to prefer the M2 60mm mortars (just 2.36 inches in diameter) that weighed only forty-two pounds, but these small mortars had a limited range of a little over a mile and fired a round weighing only three pounds.[6]

We felt that our M79 grenade launchers were just as effective as the puny 60mm mortar. The M79, commonly referred to as the "Thumper" or "Blooper," was a single shot, shoulder-fired, break-barrel weapon that resembled an oversized shotgun, of which the shoulder stock was fitted with a rubber pad to absorb some of the recoil. This weapon disgorged a 40mm diameter shell (note: 25.4mm = 1 inch), weighing half a pound, that could cover the distance between the throwing range of a grenade (forty yards) and the closest range at which we could drop our own 81mm mortar rounds (as close in as eighty yards). The M79 had a maximum range of a little over 430 yards, with pretty good accuracy out to 350 yards, and would kill most anything within sixteen feet of the blast — the same effect as a hand grenade. Within three years the M79 was replaced by the M203 grenade launcher, which attached to the M16 rifle and therefore enabled a soldier to fire grenades while still functioning as a rifleman.

In any case, we straight leg (as opposed to airborne or airmobile) infantry types preferred the heavier 81mm mortars when we were out humping the boonies, even though our 81mm mortars weighed more than two and half times that of the 60mm mortar; however, our 81s were capable of firing nine-pound M374 high explosive (HE) rounds nearly three miles, more than twice the distance of the 60mm mortar, and an 81mm mortar round had an effective bursting radius of more than eighteen yards. We also used white phosphorus rounds (WP, also referred to as "Willy Pete"), which upon impact spewed out blazing flakes of phosphorus that would burn through clothing and flesh, right down to the bone.

Mortars were very important to us as they provided our company with its own indirect fire support (meaning they did not need line of sight to the enemy, but rather could fire over hills at grids on a map), like having our own pocket artillery battery, which enabled us to lob explosive shells into high parabolic trajectories that could take out dug-in enemy troops, enemy mortars, and artillery. At OCS I had trained on all weapons utilized by infantry troops, so I was just as capable of leading a mortar platoon as a rifle platoon, but leading one of the three rifle platoons was considered much more glamorous, for we were tasked with carrying the fight to the enemy at close quarters, and thus we would constitute the tip of the sword.

4—Situation (September 1967)

After two nights in Pleiku I boarded a helicopter in the late afternoon for the run out to the west to join my infantry company of a little more than a hundred men, who were dug in, somewhere out there, in the midst of the highland jungle. Infantrymen affectionately refer to themselves as *"grunts,"* a term used both in the Army and the Marine Corps to denote the tired, dirty, sweat-stained foot soldier or Marine who is compelled to hump the boonies all day and then sleep in a foxhole at night. This was it! I was flying over enemy territory, tree-hopping in the chopper to avoid ground fire, then swooping down toward a jungle clearing so the chopper could drop me off within visual sight of the Cambodian border. Sunset was approaching as I debarked from the chopper in the pouring rain. The chopper couldn't wait to get out of there and return to base, so it was up and away before I had even walked away from the wash of its rotors.

I slogged over to report to my company commander while holding onto my rifle and dragging my seventy-pound pack, filled mostly with ammunition and food, with my entrenching tool (collapsible shovel) hanging off the back.

In those days most all of our food was in cans, unlike the lightweight freeze-dried packets that soldiers carry today. I packed several pairs of socks, because I was in the infantry and needed dry feet whenever feasible. I carried battle dressings and some t-shirts, but no underpants, which would have taken up unnecessary room. I carried water, as much as I could reasonably carry, even though water is heavy, but we were in the tropics and were subject to the danger of dehydration, and so some soldiers carried as many as three extra canteens in addition to the one that was hanging off their cotton canvas web belt. We wore a nylon harness (serving as suspenders) that hooked onto our web belts so that our shoulders bore most of the weight, and to which we affixed our grenades (weighing one pound apiece) to our harness, next to our chests, so they could be close at hand.

Of course, during the rainy season we could always obtain water, but there would come days, during the blistering hot dry season that was less than two months away, when we would be compelled to scrounge water out of any festering waterhole.

In addition to our heavy backpacks we wore nearly three pounds of steel upon our heads, for we wore the standard M-1 steel helmets that had been worn by soldiers in World War II and Korea, instead of the light Kevlar helmets worn by today's soldiers. Our steel pots were of a two-piece design; the outer steel shell was stamped from a single sheet of manganese steel, into which was snugly fitted a hard plastic helmet liner with adjustable head straps to keep our steel pots firmly in place. When manganese is alloyed with steel, it dramatically increases the strength of the steel, and virtually all of the manganese used by the Free World in those days came from apartheid South Africa, which made that country a critical trading partner for the United States. We fitted a camouflage cloth cover over our steel pots (first introduced in 1943, during the

Marine and Army assault on Tarawa at the commencement of the Pacific Offensive), and we fixed the cloth cover in place with an elastic helmet band that was designed to hold foliage in order to mask the contours of our helmets, and thus better enable us to blend into the surrounding jungle. We never wore the light cotton boonie hats that the Army was just beginning to issue and which seemed to be favored by Special Forces troops and the Australians.

I was escorted over to my company commander, who was huddled under an olive-green shelter half (groundsheet) in the pouring rain, receiving his next day's orders over the radio from battalion headquarters a couple miles behind us. He was a twenty-seven-year-old captain, while I was the youngest lieutenant he had ever seen in 'Nam, being as how most lieutenants had completed four years of college, whereas I had not.

Most officers, like those out of West Point or ROTC, were generally around the age of twenty-four when they arrived in Vietnam. They had graduated from the Academy at roughly twenty-two years of age, and then they had undergone another year or two of training and command development before they were sent off to the war. Consequently, the other three lieutenants in my company were all twenty-four or twenty-five years of age, and they all sported mustaches which the Army permitted in the war zone, while I had become an officer at the age of twenty, and had just turned twenty-one three days ago, so I was clearly the youngest officer in the company.

No salutes were exchanged in the jungle so as not to advertise to our enemies which of us were the officers. The captain briefly introduced me to the three other platoon leaders who were all drenched to the skin, and then he informed me that I would be taking charge of the second (rifle) platoon. He handed me some maps that were encased in rain-resistant plastic, and a radio codebook that listed the frequencies we were to use on any given day, while apprising me of the radio call signs I was to use in the event my platoon was attacked and I needed to call in artillery or fighter bombers, and then he gave me my orders for the next day: "Lawrence, I want you to have your platoon up before first light, then I want you to lead your men out along this ridge line — here on the map — then continue westward on a compass azimuth of 285°, and search out and destroy any enemy you encounter."

That was it, short and to the point. Three weeks earlier I had been drinking Heineken in Amsterdam; tomorrow I would be leading men through dense, rain-soaked jungle, hunting other human beings. It was incongruous; I felt like one of those patients who is scheduled to undergo surgery and has been contending with the mounting trepidation as the day of the knife inexorably approaches, and then the day arrives, and the patient reluctantly checks into the hospital and is quickly hooked up to the IV and wheeled into the operating room, at which point, one realizes, there is nothing left to do but submit.

My fellow officers kept telling me that I had arrived at just the right time. They told me how fortunate I was to have arrived during the fall of 1967, as we

4—Situation (September 1967)

would surely win the war within the next six months, and I would therefore have just enough time to do some fighting, win some medals, and share in the glory. We would emulate the Israelis who had gone to war against Egypt, Jordan, Syria and Iraq, three months before my arrival in country.

However, Israel had achieved all of its battle victories over its four Arab adversaries in just six days, and thus this third Israeli-Arab war of June 1967 forever after became known as the Six-Day War; in any case, it was a stunning victory for Israel. My fellow officers at the time felt that we were about to do the same thing in Vietnam. However, we were not fighting a war over flat expanses of desert where we could effectively bring in our heavy armor; rather, in Vietnam we were fighting in heavy rain-sodden jungle where small unit infantry tactics were employed and the fight was essentially mano a mano. The Egyptians had lacked discipline and were poorly led, though they had fought tenaciously; the North Vietnamese, on the other hand, had a large, well-disciplined national army, experienced in guerilla jungle warfare as well as main force operations, and they had been actively fighting Europeans and Americans for more than twenty years, ever since the end of World War II; they were battle-hardened, very experienced, and led by first-rate generals. Even the Vietcong guerillas in the south were well armed and reasonably well trained.

In retrospect, the optimism of my fellow soldiers was only wishful thinking, because Americans continued fighting and dying in significant numbers for six more years. Over the next year, during my time in Vietnam, U.S. Forces suffered their highest number of dead and wounded during any twelve-month period of the entire war. The sky was about to fall.

The late afternoon was moving toward dusk, and darkness would soon blanket the jungle. There would be no flashlights, or lights of any kind to illuminate the foreboding darkness, as any light would betray us to the enemy who were prowling out there in the jungle, looking to kill us. The captain also nervously registered the fact that darkness was descending and urgently exhorted me to hustle over and introduce myself to my men, whom I would be leading into combat the next day.

I made my way over to the area of the second platoon through the torrential rain. Dusk was settling in and my men appeared as shadowy forms, yet they all formed up to greet me. My newly issued jungle fatigue shirt and pants were the only clothes visible that were not tattered and filthy, although my shirt and pants were soaked through and through, and my socks and boots were caked with mud. I was self-consciously aware of being the new guy.

The rain continued to fall incessantly, and I was startled by the fact that the legs and arms of my men were covered with jungle rot from the never-ceasing precipitation. The jungle rot looked like some form of ringworm, with purple splotches and peeling skin, somewhat akin to what happens to one's skin if one has been soaking in the bathtub too long, but in this case these men had been soaking in a bathtub for months.

They had all been in combat, and they stood in their filthy worn out jungle fatigues with serious demeanors, sizing me up, trying to discern whether I was a gung ho lieutenant who was going to get them killed, or someone who, if able to survive awhile, just might develop some competency in safeguarding their lives.

My platoon was comprised almost exclusively of blacks and Hispanics; in fact I had three squads of blacks and one squad of Hispanics. Only my radiotelegraph operator (RTO), my platoon sergeant and myself were white. As previously mentioned, a rifle platoon at full strength would be comprised of forty-four soldiers, normally broken down into four ten-man squads made up mostly of privates and corporals with a sergeant in charge of each squad; in my platoon the squad leaders were buck sergeants (E-5s), while the remaining four members of the platoon included a platoon sergeant (E-6), a medic (mine was a conscientious objector and thus did not carry a weapon), a radiotelegraph operator (RTO), and then an officer, referred to as the platoon leader, who was a second lieutenant — me. However, due to combat casualties and soldiers out with malaria, my platoon was down to around thirty soldiers.

The other three platoons in my company were under the command of Southerners and were exclusively white, for there was still a strong military tradition in the South that extended back to the Civil War, and most of the Army infantry forts seemed to be located south of the Mason-Dixon Line, perhaps to benefit from the warmer weather, and it appeared that a good number of infantry officers were Southerners, many of whom had great-grandfathers or even grandfathers who had fought in the Civil War, on the Confederate side of course.

In fact, most of the Army forts in the South were named after Confederate war heroes: Fort Benning and Fort Gordon were both named after Confederate generals who commanded infantry brigades at Gettysburg, while Fort Ord in California, where I had done my initial training, was named after a Civil War general who fought with the Union. The World Almanac doesn't even cite Confederate casualties alongside U.S. casualties; after all, they were disloyal to the Union, and yet their memories continued to be glorified in the South, a stark reminder that just two or three generations ago, Americans fought a very bloody civil war in which more Americans died (as a percentage of the population) than in any other American war. In the South the military was still considered an honorable and noble profession. Being a Californian, I was viewed somewhat as a Northerner, but not quite, for I was a Westerner, and therefore not viewed as a Damn Yankee. Some people are of the view that the United States sent off its black men to fight the Vietnam War, but this is not entirely accurate. "Blacks were found in the same proportion in the Army as they were in the national population, around 10 percent; though blacks seemed to be concentrated, to a large extent, within the combat arms, such that in some infantry units they comprised nearly 25 percent."[7]

4—Situation (September 1967) 53

Each rifle platoon carried two (M60) machine guns, usually carried by the biggest and strongest men in the platoon, as well as eight M79 grenade launchers, one for each fire team. The rest of us carried M16 automatic rifles, affixed with a canvas sling, while the officer, a lieutenant like myself, holstered a 45-caliber semi-automatic pistol in addition to his M16. I presumed that this was so the officer could protect his radio codebook to the death.

Our adversaries were equipped with the AK-47 assault rifle which held a 30-round curved banana magazine that was capable of firing 600 rounds per minute of 7.62-mm (.30-caliber) ammunition, which is about the same size as the .30–06 cartridge that Americans commonly use when hunting elk or bull moose. The AK-47 had been designed in the Soviet Union by Mikhail Kalashnikov back in 1947 as a light machine gun capable of a high rate of fire. The Soviet Army adopted the Automatic Kalashnikov (AK) as its standard infantry assault rifle after World War II; however, by the late 1950s the Soviets began producing updated models such as the AKM (modernized), although production of the AK-47 continued in several Warsaw Pact countries, particularly in Czechoslovakia and Bulgaria, and the Chinese also made a pretty good rendition of the Soviet AK-47, referred to as the Chicom (Chinese communist) Type-56 assault rifle, which also fired 7.62-mm rounds.[8] The AK-47 could be submersed in water, subjected to dust and dirt, and yet still fire reliably, while our puny M16 would frequently jam, unless it was squeaky clean, which was difficult to sustain while wading through rice paddies and the muck of the jungle all day.

Our M16 rifles were manufactured by Colt (out of Hartford, Connecticut), beginning in 1964, and soon replaced the heavier M14 rifle that weighed eleven and a half pounds and fired a standard NATO 7.62-mm cartridge. The M16 on the other hand was a lightweight weapon of less than eight pounds, fashioned out of plastic instead of wood so that it looked more like a toy than a weapon; in fact, it very much resembled the M16 Marauder toy rifle made by Mattel, which also manufactured the Barbie doll. Ironically, the plastic handgrip for the M16 was in fact made by Mattel, of which the early models even retained the Mattel logo.

The aluminum box magazines (a spring-loaded metal clip) for our M16s were designed to hold twenty bullets, though we never loaded more than nineteen rounds because a fully loaded magazine frequently resulted in the weapon becoming jammed. Even though the M16 was capable of firing 700 rounds per minute, we never achieved anything close to that volume of fire due to the limitations of our nineteen-round magazines, though we frequently taped two magazines together, upside down from one another, so that when one magazine became empty, we could simply turn the tapped magazines around and have another nineteen bullets immediately at hand.

We unanimously agreed that the AK-47 was superior to our M16 rifle that only fired a wimpy .223 caliber bullet. We were probably feeling a little bit like

Custer and his men when they dejectedly discovered that some of the Indians possessed Winchester repeating rifles that were superior to their U.S. Cavalry breech-loading carbines. The AK-47 had superior killing power with its larger caliber bullet, while it almost seemed as though the purpose of our dinky M16 was not to kill, but simply to wound and bleed the enemy in order to tie-up other enemy resources such as stretcher-bearers and medical personnel. We even had experts come out to the field from Saigon in a vain attempt to convince us that our M16 was indeed the superior weapon. We clearly saw through their bullshit.

We also carried several coils of rope for crossing rivers, a spare radio that was normally used by the ambush squad, and each platoon carried an axe in the event we needed to finish clearing out a landing zone (LZ) after we had blown down the trees with plastic explosive. Sometimes our company reconfigured itself into four rifle platoons by evenly distributing the mortars amongst the four platoons, although this was pretty rare, and done only when we were caught up under extremely thick triple canopy growth where our mortars could not be effectively employed.

There were no college graduates in my platoon, including me, and every man had seen the elephant (experienced combat), except for me. Probably at this stage, the control that an officer exercises over veterans of war is somewhat tenuous. These men had all faced death and, as a consequence, they had lost much of their fear, especially of authority. Yes, I was the officer in charge, and I would be giving the orders, but I sensed that I had to tread lightly. I wasn't talking to some flaxen-haired Ivy League students raised in the sheltered 'burbs of New Haven; rather I was talking to men from the mean streets of Detroit and the harsh barrios of Los Angeles, each of whom was armed to the teeth, and I was not going to reform them. No, I was going to have to channel their formidable energies toward the killing business, for to try to stand these men up and browbeat or threaten them in any way; well, forget about it!

Since the Fourth Infantry Division had been in country for a year, most of the original soldiers had fulfilled their commitments and returned to the States, one way or another. Consequently, most of the men in my platoon, like me, had also arrived piecemeal. Obviously we had not all trained together as a cohesive unit back in the States and then traveled overseas together, as was the case two years ago when the U.S. military build-up began, or even a year ago when the Fourth Infantry Division first arrived in country. I did not consider this replacement approach to necessarily be a bad thing, for we were not all rookies facing combat together for the first time.

My platoon had a mix of veterans and new guys, which provided us with some degree of continuity. They understood my feelings of being new and alone. Although my fellow officers were older than I, most of the soldiers in my platoon were younger than I. For the most part they were nineteen or twenty years of age, although several were in their mid-twenties. They all seemed too young to die, in my opinion. Being as how I had just turned twenty-one, I was young for an officer, but I was not young among my enlisted troops.

They were cordial; they would give me a chance. Their last lieutenant had been killed shortly after he had taken charge of the platoon, and that was more than three months ago. Those in the know will tell you that the life expectancy of a platoon leader in a full-fledged firefight in Vietnam is about fifteen minutes. In the interim the platoon had been led by Platoon Sergeant Williams, a Silver Star recipient and a hero in everyone's eyes. They had done just fine without an officer, for they had a battle-hardened enlisted sergeant leading them whom they trusted implicitly.

Sergeant Williams was awarded his Silver Star less than six months before, in late February, during which time the entire Company B, with just a little more than a hundred men, was awarded a Presidential Unit Citation when its solders "distinguished themselves by extraordinary heroism" in the central highlands after being attacked by a large enemy force. The soldiers of my company reacted aggressively and "inflicted severe losses on the enemy force, rendering it ineffective for future combat operations," thereby "contributing significantly to the success of Operation Sam Houston (a surveillance operation up along the Cambodian border)."[9] It's highly unusual for such a small unit to receive a Citation from the President. The only other Presidential Unit Citation bestowed upon my unit was awarded not just to my company, but to the entire battalion (Second of the Eighth) during the D-Day Invasion of Normandy, when its four companies were the first troops to storm Utah Beach.

The Presidential Unit Citation was first introduced during World War II and awarded for extraordinary heroism in action against an armed enemy. The unit must display such gallantry, determination, and *esprit de corps* in accomplishing its mission under extremely difficult and hazardous conditions so as to set it apart and above other units participating in the same campaign. The degree of heroism required is the same as that which would warrant award of the Distinguished Service Cross (just below the Medal of Honor) to an individual.[10] The ribbon is ultramarine blue surrounded by a gold frame with laurel leaves. Soldiers of a unit that is awarded a Presidential Unit Citation proudly wear this ribbon on their uniforms above the right breast pocket of their dress uniforms, across from their individual medals, which are worn over their hearts.

Sergeant Williams had been through all that fighting. Nevertheless, infantry platoons are generally led by officers, because a young lieutenant is expected to possess a certain *élan* (essential enthusiasm for combat [military meaning of the term]) that tends to fade even in the most intrepid older veterans. Besides, an officer is also expected to have received some very specialized training, and so my men expected me to be extremely proficient with a map and a compass. They would rely on me to always know where we were, which was no easy feat under triple-canopy jungle where visibility was less than fifty yards and where it was extremely difficult to discern, when gradations were slight, whether one was standing on a hill or in a depression. They would count on me to be competent and efficient at calling in artillery and air support when we were in dire straits. They would rely on me to quickly and effectively call in medevac helicopters to evacuate our wounded and killed. They would watch and observe to see how I would assign the men to take point, which was the extremely dangerous lead position of the platoon as it moved through the jungle, and the men would observe how I would lead them in the attack and in the defense. I was their new leader; they would give me some time, but not much. Within two months of my arrival I would find myself conducting a *search and destroy* mission in the vicinity of Dak To, which would develop into one of the largest battles of the war (along with the Battle of Ia Drang), before the commencement of the Tet Offensive that would follow less than three months later.[11]

I was struck by the fact that the only subject these soldiers ever talked about was war. I had been sipping beer in Amsterdam just three weeks ago, but these men had no interest in talking about Europe, or books, or anything other than telling war stories, and these are not happy stories, rather they are invariably morbid, for they are filled with narratives of losing buddies and of gruesome killing. I found the talk to be troubling and unsettling, so I just sat around like a bump on a log, because I really had nothing to contribute. Tyrone, one of my sergeants from the tough streets of Camden, New Jersey, looked over at me and said, "I'll bet you think that all we ever talk about are war stories."

I replied, "Well, that's what it sounds like to me."

He grinned. "You're right. And after you've been here about six months, that's all you'll be talking about."

They already existed in some mystical place, beyond our prosaic world. They had survived combat, and now they were different. They had faced death and experienced killing, yet it's not as though they were callous—well, perhaps they had become calloused, but they were so young that they still laughed, but in a different way; no longer like young boys, but more like old men.

Would I change and become like them? It was too early to tell, for they had survived their first encounters with deadly combat, as though that gave them a greater entitlement to be irreverent, to be themselves, as though they were one step closer to understanding the meaning of life, and not just the standard sugar-coated façade, but rather the true reality of existence that lay just behind the velvet curtain.

I wanted to have experiences in life, but I did not want to be an old man while I was still young; however, I had run out of options at this point, for I had no more choices to make, except to submit to fate and take my chances. I had nowhere else to go, except forward, where few have ventured—out into the bush, to see the elephant.

IV

I was escorted over to the platoon command and control center, which was a three-man foxhole that I shared with my RTO and my medic. The foxhole was already turning to mud, so we wrapped ourselves in our shelter halves and slept outside of our hole. Nobody possessed an alarm clock, but I had no trouble being up, before first light, at 4:30 in the morning after a fitful sleep.

Some of the surrounding mountain peaks exceeded 6,000 feet in altitude, and though we were in the tropics, one could feel the biting cold that took hold during the late night hours and persisted into the pre-dawn morning; I noticed the frosty breaths of the men around me. I discerned my men moving about in the pelting rain, as night was giving way to the impending dawn and the first glints of light began to gradually transform the darkness into discernable specks of color.

I observed my men taking a small handful of plastic explosive (C-4), which looked like silly putty and was used in our claymore mines or for blowing down trees to create a landing zone in order to medevac out our wounded, and they ever so gently formed the C-4 into a ball in their hands until it was about the size of a large jawbreaker. The explosive material in C-4 is cyclotrimethylenetrinitramine, also known as RDX, which is more powerful than TNT.

They then placed the ball of C-4 on the wet ground and put a flame to it, and it burned intensely, even in the unrelenting rain. They then took an empty C-ration can, with the lid still attached for use as a handle, into which they poured some water, then sprinkled in a packet of powdered coffee or hot cocoa. They then held the can over the blazing explosive while firmly holding onto the attached lid, being extremely careful that the can did not strike the explosive, and this steaming elixir was usually the only hot substance that they ingested during the entire day. The remainder of the day, we ate our food cold. One had to be especially careful around C-4, for if one accidentally dropped a heavy can on it, or stepped on it while it was burning, it would explode.

Fortunately, Sergeant Williams was close at hand to assist me in assembling the men into formation, though each awakening dawn, prior to heading out on our search-and-destroy patrols, it was my responsibility as platoon leader to make the assignments as to which of my men would walk point. The thing about being point for the unit is that not everyone can do it; assignments are not made alphabetically; you need your best soldiers to take the point; in fact, you need two soldiers, one who is in the front and cuts a path through the thick, tangled jungle vegetation with his machete, and the other soldier, just behind the machete man, who handles the compass and keeps the machete man and the trailing soldiers on the assigned azimuth. Both the machete man and the compass man need to be alert to the possibility of enemy activity out to their front, for they, as point, control the movement of the unit, and it is their responsibility to halt the unit if they sense trouble up ahead. Their lives, and the lives of those they are guiding, rest on their skills and alertness. Any daydreaming or loss of focus could cost them their lives, so they must be ever vigilant for danger, lurking out there, just in front of them. Soldiers know this, that it is both an honor and an extreme hazard to walk point.

As we moved out through the tangled jungle I measured distance by assigning two soldiers to each count how many paces we had taken. They were to tie a knot in a length of twine after every hundred paces and apprise me as to the number of knots they had tied, then I attempted to convert the paces into meters, since all distances in the military were computed in meters and kilometers rather than yards and miles. I figured that every pace was a little more than a yard, but still a little less than a meter, and so I calculated that approximately 1,050 paces would equal one kilometer, and then I attempted to transpose that distance, as well as our compass-heading, onto my plastic-covered map with a grease pencil so that I could affirm our location in the event I suddenly needed to call in support from our artillery battery that was located on a fortified hill (referred to as a firebase), about four to five miles behind us. The army utilized the twin rotor Boeing CH-47 Chinook helicopter, capable of carrying 7,000 pounds, to airlift the heavy artillery guns and crews into position.

The scale of our maps was 1:50,000, meaning that everything on the map was one-fifty thousandth its size in the real world. Therefore, one inch on the map represented 50,000 inches on the ground or one centimeter on the map equaled 50,000 centimeters on the ground; thus, 2cm on the map represented 1 kilometer, while 1 inch on the map represented nearly eight-tenths of a mile. The map contained numbered grids running west to east and south to north that formed squares, so that if attacked, I could quickly look at my map and simply call in fire coordinates, such as, "location 76.4 west, 24.2 north," for example, and our supporting artillery battery of six 105 howitzers would then rain down a great deal of lead upon that location with quite good accuracy.

The accuracy of my calculations was critically important, as it was absolutely necessary that I knew where all of my men were when we came into contact with the enemy, because I had to be absolutely certain that none of my men would become casualties of friendly fire (meaning non-hostile fire, in this case referring to possible casualties from our own artillery rounds), before I could even think about getting on the radio and calling for the artillery to unleash its fire and brimstone upon the enemy.

My first day's foray out into the jungle with my undersized platoon of thirty soldiers was uneventful, and we returned to the company perimeter an hour or two before sunset for our second night in the same location, which was the maximum amount of time we ever remained in one place. I think my company commander was simply attempting to ascertain how well I could handle a map and a compass while my platoon was cutting its way through heavy jungle.

V

Most of the time we operated as a company with just a little more than a hundred men. Only just a couple occasions did we ever operate as a battalion with all four companies working together with a combined strength of around five hundred soldiers.

During one of those times, when my company was the lead element of the battalion, my captain ordered my little platoon of around thirty men to serve as point for the entire battalion. We didn't moan or groan at all; in fact, we were quite prideful of the fact that we were given the distinction of serving as point; it affirmed that our battalion commander felt that we were his best company, and that my company commander believed we were his best platoon. Everyone knew that we had been given a silent pat on the back, and we thrived on that unspoken accolade, for we knew that we had earned the honor of leading the five hundred soldiers behind us. In those instances when my platoon was ordered to lead the battalion, then I needed my very best soldiers to take the point, regardless of whether or not they had performed that duty as recently as the preceding day.

Soldiers who are assigned point are subjected to severe stress, which is why the duties of point must be rotated regularly. I learned one important lesson shortly after taking charge of my platoon, when I had assigned a soldier to take point, and he looked at me and said, "But, sir, I was point two days ago; besides it's second squad's turn to provide point." He was correct; I had acted precipitously, so I walked over to the second squad and assigned two men to act as point (machete and compass); they were not thrilled, for this is not an assignment for which people enthusiastically volunteer, and one of the soldiers in the second squad said to me, "Sir, I thought you assigned Malcolm from the first squad to take point, and now you're changing your mind?"

A leader can commit no worse sin than to appear inconsistent in the eyes of his men; I had sinned big time. I realized that I needed to give more thought to my decision-making responsibilities, and that once I made a decision I should not vacillate. The decision, for the most part, should be unequivocal, particularly in a combat environment. Still, assigning men to take point was like playing God, for I was making life-and-death decisions over these men. I decided who was to stand in the greatest danger, for it was the point man who would invariably be the first to die, no matter how much additional time he spent meticulously sticking jungle foliage into his helmet band in order to camouflage himself. Initially, in my youthful innocence, I welcomed the responsibility, but later on I came to find that I did not like playing God; it makes one old before one's time, and I knew that I was not worthy; perhaps none of us are.

Recognizing the hazards of taking point, I found that the most effective approach in making the assignments was to appeal to the soldier's pride. Life is not always fair, and these soldiers were acutely aware of that fact; they simply wanted me to realize that I was not simply giving an order, but that I was also making a request, albeit from a position of authority, for their special skills to guide and safeguard their fellow comrades in arms. They wanted to ensure that I respected them, and that I recognized that the chain of command ironically operates in both directions.

In the military, respect for rank is obligatory, but that does not necessarily mean that one respects the individual. Some people have nothing but their rank with which to compel people to obey their orders, but this should not be confused with leadership. I understand that one does not have to be a nice guy to be a leader, but there must be some personal connection, some degree of empathy and compassion. Humility is appreciated, as it can temper power and authority, which tend to be corrupting; however, humility was not emphasized in any leadership course to which I had ever been exposed, particularly in the military where mission accomplishment is paramount, and where decisions must often be made rapidly while under enemy fire. Leading by example is another time-tested approach that can be quite effective, although ultimately respect must be earned on a personal level; it can never be presumed by rank alone.

On those rare occasions when we did move as a battalion, we had hundreds of men digging in at night, which necessitated that we dig slit trenches that were narrow holes dug in the earth two feet deep, a foot wide, and ten feet in length. Then, when one had to relieve oneself, one straddled the hole and defecated into the trench. This practice concentrated the human waste in a prescribed area of the perimeter, after which soldiers were tasked to cover over the slit trenches by the use of their entrenching tools before we moved out. When we operated as a smaller force, as a company or a platoon, we just found a spot in the jungle and dug our own individual hole with our entrenching tool to relieve ourselves, which we then covered over so that the enemy could not come along and estimate the size of our unit by our spoor.

We never did operate as a brigade with all three of our brigade's battalions (Second of the Eighth, First of the Twelfth, and First of the Twenty-Second) working together, because the dense jungle necessitated that we operate in smaller units. However, on a couple occasions, we did work in conjunction with one of our sister battalions (First of the Twelfth). I even got to know another infantry lieutenant in that battalion, named Eric, who told me that he was also from the San Francisco Bay Area, from Marin County on the other side of the Golden Gate Bridge, and that he had once worked as a waiter in a small German restaurant near the top of Mount Tamalpais.

On subsequent meetings, Eric and I always sought each other out, because it is very comforting to speak with someone from the same region as yourself, as though you inherently understand one another.

VI

The Battle of the Ia Drang was fought up in this remote highland country a little more than two years previous. During October 1965, the Third Brigade of the First Air Cav Division had been intently searching the central highlands for the NVA and Vietcong, who were known to be operating in regimental-size units (around 2,500 soldiers for a full-strength NVA regiment, generally comprised of a headquarters element and three battalions).

On October 19, the Thirty-Third NVA regiment attacked the Special Forces camp at Plei Me (approximately forty miles south of Pleiku and only thirteen and a half miles to the east of where the major Ia Drang Battle took place four weeks later). The Plei Me camp consisted of a CIDG (Civilian Irregular Defense Group) force comprised of twelve Green Berets and 350 Montagnard mercenaries of the Jarai tribe. Fighting raged for six days before the NVA broke off contact on the twenty-fifth of October, without achieving their objective of overrunning Plei Me.[12]

Soldiers of the First Brigade of the First Cav Division were brought into the area from An Khe (thirty-one miles to the east of Pleiku) to pursue the enemy, and on the first of November the First Cav engaged elements of the NVA Thirty-Third Regiment, killing ninety-nine of the enemy.

Less than two weeks later, the Third Brigade commander received intelligence indicating that the enemy, in force, had moved to the west of the Plei Me Special Forces camp into the Ia Drang Valley, and he decided to quickly send one of his battalions (First of the Seventh) into the valley to conduct a reconnaissance in force in hopes of pinning down the elusive NVA Thirty-Third Regiment, so he could then bring in his other two battalions to destroy the enemy.

The First Battalion (of the Seventh Cavalry Regiment), commanded by Lieutenant Colonel Harold (Hal) Moore, consisted of three rifle companies (averaging 117 soldiers each), and one weapons company of eighty soldiers, totaling 431 soldiers altogether.[13]

These cavalry troops rode helicopters instead of horses, and they had all trained together back in the States and arrived in Vietnam as a cohesive unit. They were elite infantry soldiers and brimming with self-confidence and proud of their unit, probably much like George Armstrong Custer felt when he led this same Seventh Cavalry Regiment into the valley of the Little Big Horn eighty-nine years earlier, back in 1876.

It was rumored that the last song that Custer heard as his regiment rode into battle was the old Irish drinking song, "Garry Owen," sung by his Irish troops.

> Our hearts so stout have got no fame
> For soon 'tis known from whence we came

> Where'er we go they fear the name
> Of Garryowen in glory.

Off they rode, the men of the First Battalion of the Seventh Cavalry, into the valley of the Ia Drang on November 14, 1965. Three NVA battalions (drawn from the Thirty-Second and Sixty-Sixth NVA Regiments) were there to greet them, along with a VC battalion, totaling altogether around 2,200 soldiers, outnumbering the Americans by more than five to one.[14] The Americans were engaged by the enemy before all of their companies had arrived at the landing zone X-Ray, though by the end of the day all four of the First Battalion companies were on the ground together, and an additional rifle company from the Second Battalion (of the Seventh Cavalry) had also arrived to strengthen nighttime defenses.

During the morning of the second day (November 15), a second rifle company from the Second Battalion arrived on the battlefield, during which time the Americans found themselves engaged in fierce fighting. Also, the same morning, another battalion (Second of the Fifth Cavalry) was dropped at an LZ a little more than two miles away and proceeded to make their way on foot to link up with the six companies of the beleaguered Seventh Cavalry. Fighting broke off during the afternoon, but erupted again after midnight and continued throughout the hours of darkness.

As the third day dawned (November 16), the Americans had three battalions in the field (First of the Seventh, Second of the Seventh, and Second of the Fifth) — the equivalent of one brigade. Sporadic fighting continued throughout the afternoon, such that, by the end of the day, after three days of fighting, the Americans, initially outnumbered by more than five to one, had suffered seventy-nine killed and 121 wounded.[15] However, the enemy appeared to be severely crippled by infantry, artillery, and air strikes, as they broke off contact on the fourth day (November 17) and appeared to be on the run, retreating westward, back into Cambodia, only three miles away.

The First of the Seventh was airlifted out of the Ia Drang Valley, while the Second of the Fifth and the Second of the Seventh (with one rifle company from the First of the Fifth) moved out of the area, on foot, in separate directions toward new landing zones further north and northeast, in order to put some distance between themselves and a scheduled B-52 strike that was intended to obliterate suspected NVA positions on the Chu Pong Massif near the Cambodian border to the southwest of LZ X-Ray. The B-52s were based out of Guam, which lies 13° north of the equator, the same latitude as Pleiku, and they would make the uninterrupted 5,200-mile round-trip flight to Vietnam by refueling in-flight, though some of the newer long-range B-52s could make the entire round trip on a single load of fuel. The B-52s could fly at an altitude of 50,000 feet, such that the enemy could not hear them coming, and the first sound they heard was the thunderous explosion of the huge bombs, which could create a crater in the midst of the jungle the size of an Olympic swimming pool.

Some of the troops of the Second of the Seventh felt that they were embarking on "a walk in the sun," and away from the carnage they had inflicted upon the Thirty-Second and Sixty-Sixth NVA Regiments, which appeared to be in full retreat. They began their march early in the morning, and by midday they were feeling the increasing weight of their backpacks under the blazing hot sun. Around 1:00 in the afternoon, just as they were reaching their new LZ (Albany), the 400 soldiers of the battalion were ambushed by the Eighth Battalion of the Sixty-Sixth NVA Regiment, which had not yet seen any fighting and was fresh and at full strength (550 soldiers), along with remnants of the elusive Thirty-Third NVA Regiment (that was still recovering from the losses it had suffered in its attacks against Plei Me and its fighting against the Air Cav's First Brigade a little more than two weeks earlier). Fierce fighting erupted, which continued for sixteen hours and resulted in the virtual annihilation of three American infantry companies and the deaths of 155 of their comrades, the highest number of Americans killed in a single day during the entire war.[16] Lieutenant Colonel Moore in his recent book (written when he was a retired lieutenant general) stated that although the Army talked up the American victory at LZ X-Ray, its commanders in the field intentionally downplayed the massacre at LZ Albany, which led to a failure in the Army to learn critical lessons from its disasters.[17]

No one serving in the highlands ever forgot the battles of the Ia Drang, contemplations of which kindled persistent anxieties about the possibility that, one day, our battalion could conceivably find itself in a similar situation, outnumbered by five to one, and fighting for its life. Tales of the ferocious battles of the Ia Drang induced mythical, yet foreboding, reflections in our minds, evoking uncomfortable recollections of Custer—confronting inconceivable disaster.

5

The School Solution

I

Though I found the movie *We Were Soldiers* about the Ia Drang battle interesting, it was evident that the combat scenes were filmed amongst scrub oak trees in California, and therefore the movie failed to capture the primeval and forbidding darkness of the tropical jungle. Though it is not just the play of light and shadow that characterizes the steamy jungle, it is also the smell, which invades the nostrils with a damp, musky stench of undying decomposition, of decaying, sodden leaves being transformed into a malodorous ooze.

Shortly after the Battle of the Ia Drang, Army combat troops ceased wearing any metal on their fatigues that could reflect sunlight, such as my lieutenant's bars, nor would we wear any insignia, designating rank that could enable the enemy to identify the officers and senior sergeants. I wouldn't even wear the fabric insignia that officers wore in base camp and at battalion headquarters. Rather, at the company level, we all dressed in the same filthy non-descript jungle fatigues, encrusted with grime and sweat (the more roomy cotton jungle fatigues, the pants of which had six pockets, came into being shortly after the Battle of the Ia Drang). In the rear, enlisted men wore their corporal's stripes or their sergeant's stripes on the sleeves of their fatigue shirts, while officers wore their insignia on their collar lapels. For example, a lieutenant wore his lieutenant's bar (gold for a second lieutenant and silver for a first lieutenant) on his right lapel, and his branch insignia (crossed rifles for the infantry) on his left lapel.

In the hot damp jungle, if one had a choice, one would go around in a t-shirt, but long sleeve fatigue shirts were de rigueur in order to protect our arms against malarial mosquito bites, as the Army suffered more than 40,000 cases of malaria between 1965 and 1970 alone.[1] We were required to take two different types of anti-malarial pills: A large orange pill (containing 300mg of chloroquine and 45mg of Primaquine), and a small white pill, administered only to soldiers in the central highlands, to my knowledge, containing 25mg of Dapsone (diamino-diphenyl-sulfone), which is primarily used in the treatment of leprosy.[2] These pills were intended to protect us against *Plasmodium vivax malaria* as well as *Plasmodium falciparum*, the malignant malaria that can kill, both of which are transmitted by the female Anopheles mosquito. Malignant malaria can involve a number of complications, such as low blood pressure, kidney failure, hemorrhaging, liver damage, shock, and coma that may prove fatal.

Malaria is not a virus, but rather a disease caused by protozoan parasites (single-cell microscopic organisms of the genus *Plasmodium* that can only survive by infecting a host). The female Anopheles mosquito itself serves as a host to these parasites, as do those to whom she passes them on when blood-feeding. We would take the large pill once a week, and the small pill every day. It was a command responsibility to ensure that the men took their pills, for it was thought that some soldiers might shirk their duty by not taking their pills, preferring to contract malaria so as to escape combat.

While out humping the boonies we never bunched up; we always kept a distance of about five meters between one another; for in that way, a grenade could take out only three of us at most. At OCS we had been taught to continually vary our position in relation to the RTO so that the enemy could not easily identify who was the officer leading the unit, for the enemy would always be looking for the radio antenna sticking up, so they could target the officer nearby for their primary kill. It's based on the guillotine theory, whereby the quickest way to kill the body is to cut off the head. This is why people openly say that an infantry lieutenant has a short life expectancy in combat. There's a reason why one of every ten of the 58,220 Americans who died in Vietnam was a commissioned officer (5,930 [10.2 percent]).[3] And if one included the 1,239 (non-commissioned) warrant officers that died, most of whom were helicopter pilots, then the ratio of officers to enlisted men who died in Vietnam rises to more than one in eight.[4] Yet from the very beginning, my RTO, a sinewy white boy from North Carolina named Wade Kershaw, was right on my ass; everywhere I went, he was sure to follow. I would speed up, he would speed up. I would zig, he would zig. I was getting edgy. Finally, I turned around and said, "Kershaw, do you always have to hug my ass? I thought you and me were supposed to vary our positions?"

My RTO boldly stared me down and said, "Sir, in heavy jungle, in the event of an ambush, we don't have time to run around trying to butt fuck each other; we need to be close together all the time."

He knew better than I about survival, while I was still concerned about propriety. Like most veterans of combat, Wade didn't talk a whole lot; he was a matter-of-fact kind of soldier, who performed his job exceedingly well. And so I came to realize that there is the school solution, and then there is the real world solution, which, for some inexplicable reason, cannot be taught in school. There is no greater teacher than personal experience.

When I moved with my platoon, I was usually positioned about one-third of the way back from the front. At OCS I was taught that if I led from the front of the platoon, then I would be ineffectual in leading the men behind me, and it would be the same if I attempted to lead from the rear. The optimal position was about one-third of the way back from the front whenever we moved in a column formation and snaked our way through the dense foliage. In Civil War days, officers led from the very front, but then, for the most part, they were all up front — in a line, so as to concentrate their musket fire. The war in Vietnam required soldiers to take more initiative than in Civil War days, operating as small as a five-man team, formed out of a squad, because rifles now had much greater range and accuracy, so that fire and maneuver, along with concealment, were the keys to victory, and survival.

When moving in column, the men formed into two parallel lines, each with a head and a tail, each averaging about fifteen men (it would have been slightly more than twenty men if we were at full strength), moving parallel to one another; at the two heads were the points, each led by a soldier with a machete who cut a path through the jungle, step by step, followed closely by a compass man who kept the platoon on course. This was generally the formation we assumed when moving through the jungle, though on some occasions, during night moves or crossing expansive rice paddies, we moved in single file. Whichever the formation, I was still positioned about a third of the way back, though I was ultimately responsible for ensuring that my men were on the proper compass heading, and so I was also using a compass and sending orders up to the points if I felt they were diverging from the prescribed azimuth, since it was harder for them, because they were breathing and sweating more profusely than I, and the thick jungle or tall grass up at the very front of the column could easily cause them to become disoriented.

One day, as we were cutting our way through exceedingly thick jungle, some dark malevolent force seemed to rise up from the earth and viciously slap me across my face. It slapped me so hard that it blurred my vision. At first I didn't know what to do, but the pain was so excruciating that, I must confess, it caused me to let go of my rifle as I went scrambling blindly down a steep ridge toward a small stream that I had glimpsed in the distance.

I ran through thickets and dense foliage until I reached the stream, in which I doused my face in its cool mountain water, but the inexorable pain persisted, and I found myself howling from the torment. My men and my medic came rushing down the slope after me, carrying my rifle, and they tried to soothe me, but I was in tremendous pain.

It turned out that the soldier in front of me in the column had accidentally knocked a hornet's nest from a tree branch, and then he had inadvertently kicked it off to the side of the path, with the result that I had been stung in the face by more than twenty of the large angry wasps. Many people died from so many stings; I did not, but I was not in much shape to lead my platoon, until my medic shot me up, no doubt with some painkiller, and in my drugged state I was able to continue the march, since one had to keep up, for no one was ever left behind.

Usually, when we were in pain or required some suturing (from accidental machete cuts), our medic supplied us with Darvon (Propoxyphene) tablets. Darvon is a narcotic analgesic that works in the brain to decrease pain, of which one of its advisories stipulates that it should not be used by people who are suicidal or easily addicted to alcohol or other substances. On this occasion I needed more than just some lightweight Darvon.

My platoon was habitually shorthanded and always desperately in need of replacements. It struck me as strange that the Army never seemed to run short of truck drivers, supply clerks, or cooks in the rear; in fact, there was always a plethora of those specialists, but we always seemed to be running short of frontline infantry troops, which were the guys needed to do the fighting. Stranger still was that everyone who enters the Army undergoes Basic Combat Training, during which every soldier learns the rudiments of the infantry, so why did we always have a shortage? If virtually everyone in the Army had initially been trained in the infantry, then why were we continually operating understrength? I could only surmise that our division headquarters was having a hard time getting soldiers to come out into the jungle to get shot at, but then again, who is really in a hurry to die?

At times I led a platoon of only twenty-five soldiers. Though just like Custer, we felt that we could easily fend off five times our number. After all, we were Americans; we were winners, and so we were not unduly concerned about the incredible resolve of our adversaries, or the fact that they had been fighting for more than twenty continuous years.

The men in my platoon spent virtually all of their time in the jungle; they might come back to the division base camp once every three months or so for a brief period of less than a week; just long enough to take some hot showers, eat some hot food that did not come out of cans, drink a cold beer or two, pick up some more ammo, and then they headed out once again into the jungle, where they lived like animals, conducting search and destroy missions, hunting other human beings to kill.

Exotic vegetation proliferates in the tropical jungle, where thick clusters of bamboo provided an innate sense of security, as thick stands of bamboo could even deflect 50-caliber bullets, and a 50-caliber is a hell of a large bullet, for caliber refers to the diameter of the bullet, and a 50-caliber bullet is five-tenths of an inch in diameter. But even so, a 50-caliber bullet had a hard time with bamboo, as several stalks grew from a single root, and often these stalks formed an impenetrable screen through which we could not effectively cut our way, even with our machetes. It was while we were entangled in these bamboo stalks that we occasionally ran into bamboo (green tree) vipers, entwined in the leafy stalks or on tree branches, and though these poisonous snakes were generally nocturnal, they would aggressively attack if disturbed, regardless of the time of day. And though their bites were seldom fatal, they could be very hazardous as these snakes tended to bite soldiers on the neck and shoulders because they remained up in the foliage, and rarely descended to the ground.

There was a profusion of plant life in these highland jungles: Bamboo seemed to grow everywhere it was wet, which was most everywhere. Palm trees thrived here, growing to towering heights of more than 100 feet. There were the prized hardwoods of ebony and teak. There were banyan trees whose aerial prop roots enabled them to spread laterally, as though they were sprouting additional trunks, and there were cardamom trees with yellow flowers that tended to grow in clusters, the fruit of which is used to produce a spice used in curries and teas. I spotted huge centipedes on these trees, about eight inches long, that were purple with extended yellow legs which were capable of giving a vicious bite, the venom of which caused extreme pain. Cinnamon trees grew in the forest, in the shade of taller trees, and there were cinnamon ferns nearly three feet high, as well as agarwood trees whose massive trunks were covered with bumps, the oil of which was used in incense and in French perfumes, and there was a profusion of wild orchids and exotic forms of cypresses, all of which added to the phantasmagoria of the rain forests of the highland jungle.

Vestiges of the French colonial presence could still be observed by the sizeable tea plantations that were continuing to be cultivated in large swaths of cleared out jungle, and there were also some rubber tree plantations, and rubber trees, at one time, had existed only in the Amazon rainforest before being transplanted to Vietnam by the French during the colonial era.

Toward the end of each day we sought out some suitable high ground from which to prepare our nighttime defensive perimeter. We started digging our foxholes, usually two-man or three-man foxholes, as twilight was approaching. It took a full hour, sometimes two, to dig a hole in the ground that was four feet deep and sufficiently wide to accommodate two to three men. We used our entrenching tools, which were small collapsible shovels with wooden handles, painted Army green, which, when extended, were just a little over two feet in length (27½ inches, to be exact), so much of the digging was done while we were on our knees. It was obviously easier to dig during the wet season than during the dry season when the ground became as hard as granite.

Later, in the black of night, when it was time to try to get some sleep, though still raining, we wrapped ourselves in the shelter halves that served as an insulation blanket, much like a wetsuit insulates a surfer, though we still felt wet and miserable throughout the night. In this fashion we slept out on the soggy ground in the driving rain, but our shelter halves provided us with some warmth, even though we were soaked through and through.

We did not carry sleeping bags because they would have taken up too much space and weight on our backs, and they never would have dried out in the tropical jungle. And even though the torrential monsoon rains cascaded from the skies for more than half the year, we didn't even bother to carry the waterproof ponchos that the soldiers wore in base camp, because they were too bulky and heavy to carry through the jungle; rather, we carried just our shelter halves that were made of cotton, and though these shelter halves were not waterproof, they could retard water to some extent.

A second shelter half was carried by every other soldier, and whenever feasible we tied the ends of the additional shelter half to some bamboo or tree branches above our heads in order to break the fall of the rain somewhat, even though the rain still seeped through the shelter half, and then we strove to get some sleep in the pitch-black jungle.

When used as a tarp, the shelter half also served as a means of catching drinking water from the rain-laden skies if we were not close to a stream or a river. In an effort to avoid becoming totally immersed throughout the night, we dug shallow trenches around our sleeping spots with our entrenching tools so that the water forming on the ground coalesced into rivulets and flowed around our bodies.

Nevertheless, wrapped only in our shelter halves, we were subjected to the drenching rain and persistently violated by the soaking wetness, while continually exposed to bites from malarial mosquitoes, bamboo vipers, stinging ants, and other creepy crawlers, not to mention attacks by the enemy, all of which caused us to continually jerk into wakefulness at the slightest sound or the merest sense of nighttime movement in the jungle, which inevitably resulted in a tortured sleep.

There was obviously no electricity in the jungle, and under triple canopy rain forest the sun rarely pierced — it got dark early. Shortly after sunset the jungle became as black as tar, and our sense of hearing came to predominate over our sense of sight, which is why a whisper seems to carry so far at night.

Each night three squads dug foxholes, while one squad forewent digging; instead they were sent out into the darkness to set up an ambush. I kept in contact with the ambush squad via whispered communications over the radio, as it was my job to call for artillery if the ambush squad got into trouble, and, as previously mentioned, it seemed that even a whisper could travel an inordinate distance through the inexhaustible darkness. We used PRC-25 portable radios, referred to as a prick-25, which was a backpacked FM receiver-transmitter that weighed a little less than twenty pounds and had a maximum range of seven miles, depending on the weather. The radio was powered by a dry cell battery, which weighted more than four pounds and had an average life span of about twenty hours, so we were required to carry at least four spare batteries, between re-supply deliveries.

Occasionally, I accompanied one of my squads out on ambush (while leaving my platoon sergeant in charge of the platoon perimeter), during which I observed that the men on ambush duty did not sleep at all, as they felt too frightened and vulnerable. We all simply squatted and waited in the incessant rain, hoping to catch the enemy moving at night, for this was the time that the North Vietnamese felt most secure. My superiors highly frowned upon a platoon leader accompanying a rifle squad out on ambush, because if the enemy were to mount a full-scale attack, then the officer should obviously be with his largest group, so I rarely informed my superiors that I was going out with the ambush squad, though I considered it necessary in order to understand what my men were going through, and to gain their respect. In Vietnam I came to understand that rules, regulations, and procedures, unlike laws, are not etched in stone; they can be subject to flexible interpretation at times.

The squad assigned to ambush duty waited until darkness, then quietly slipped out of the defensive perimeter, strictly adhering to absolute silence as they moved out a couple hundred yards away from the rest of the platoon. Stealth was paramount, as any clanking metal, coughs, or lit cigarettes could spell doom, and it did seem that sound traveled faster and more clearly through the denser cold night air than through the heat of the day.

The under-strength squad of about eight men would settle into a position along a footpath or a trail junction in the thick dark jungle, without a moon to illuminate the shadows. They would surreptitiously set some claymore mines out in front of their position, then hunker down in the wet leafy undergrowth and wait for the enemy to walk into the kill zone. Our claymore mines weighed about three pounds and were comprised of a plastic casing, packed with a pound and a half of C-4 plastic explosive, which, when detonated, blasted out 700 steel balls that would scythe through anything within fifty meters (about fifty-four yards) out to its front. And because the claymore mine was somewhat fan-shaped, it blew out the balls in a 60° arc that engulfed an area fifty meters wide at its optimal killing distance.

The ambush squad crouched down in the nocturnal gloom, enduring the interminable rain without digging any foxholes, finding whatever leafy cover was available, simply letting the wet settle in, under a moonless night. They did not talk or light cigarettes; they waited patiently and ever so silently for the enemy to walk into the trap. On occasion we reaped rich harvests of death during these ambushes, mostly human, though I recall one night when a Bengal tiger accidentally tripped one of our claymore mines and was killed, which saddened all of us. Still, the discovery of the tiger motivated all of us not to fall asleep when on watch at night. Tigers are indigenous to Asia; they are the largest of all cats, weighing up to 500 pounds (while a lion maxes out at a little over 400 pounds), though they had to be pretty desperate to sink to eating human flesh, which is not the best meat available.[5]

Ambush duty was not an assignment for which soldiers volunteered; rather, it was the result of an order from an officer that resulted in the assigned squad getting virtually no sleep for the night while placing themselves at considerable risk. For those of us who were back in the nighttime perimeter, we would be settling into our foxholes, which were not exactly executive suites; however, they did provide us with greater protection against incoming mortar rounds. At least in our foxholes we had the opportunity for some tortured sleep.

If it was a two-man foxhole, then one soldier was on guard for a three-hour stretch, while the other soldier slept, and then the roles reversed, and since night fell early in the jungle, the nights lasted nearly twelve hours, so soldiers in the company perimeter could get close to six hours of broken sleep. The three-hour sleeping interval was not designed to provide the soldier with a deep, sound sleep, but rather was designed around the fact that three hours was about the limit for a soldier to be alert on guard duty during the night. However, even then, with the threat of being eaten by mosquitoes, bitten by bamboo vipers, dragged away by a tiger, or having your throat slit by the enemy, a decent night's sleep was an elusive desire.

Even amongst the soldiers remaining within our platoon perimeter, a couple of two-man teams were required to depart the perimeter and serve as "listening" posts, about twenty yards in front of our platoon during the night. These two-man listening posts, like the people on ambush duty, did not dig a foxhole; rather, their duty was to set out claymores in front of themselves and then to crouch down and "listen" for any noise that might indicate that the enemy was sneaking up on our position. If they detected the enemy creeping up toward us, then they were to detonate their claymores and throw their grenades, but not fire their rifles which would give away their positions, thus making them easy targets, and then they were to hightail it back to the platoon perimeter.

The NVA were very adept at creeping up on our positions and turning our claymore mines around so that they faced our own men — the sneaky bastards. This is how they played at war; they took incredible risks. Amazingly, the face of our claymores was stamped in big, bold, raised capital letters: FRONT — TOWARD ENEMY. I often thought that we were ironically making it very easy, even for a blind man, to determine the lethal direction in which the claymore should be pointed.

We sometimes rigged our claymores to trip wires (before inserting the blasting cap into the top of the mine) if we were setting them out in front of our nighttime perimeter, but if we were out on ambush, then we ran a wire from our claymore to a handheld electrical detonator (clacker) that was small enough to be held in one hand, and in this manner we could control the detonation.

One could generally throw a grenade out about thirty or forty yards, though a good athlete could throw it as far as fifty yards. The grenade had a four- to five-second fuse delay once the pin was pulled, and the grenade could efficiently kill anyone within a radius of sixteen feet of the blast. We sowed a fair amount of death upon the enemy by the use of grenades, particularly during nighttime ambushes, though we had to be careful that the grenade did not get hung up in the overhead growth and fall back on our own position.

At night, I felt safer with the moon, for then my nighttime visibility was extended. In the infantry, the lieutenant took charge of the platoon during the daylight hours and during all movements; however, at night, after the unit had halted and dug in, the platoon sergeant took over from the lieutenant, and set up the listening posts and designated the positions for the machine guns, ensuring that they had interlocking fields of fire, so that if the enemy was brazen enough to attack us, they would be caught in the crossfire of our automatic weapons. Although it took some pretty crazy fools to assault dug-in troops in the dead of night, in this way the NVA believed, by closing with us, they could nullify our artillery howitzers, by making us hesitant about firing for fear of injuring friendly troops, leaving us with just our own mortars to provide indirect fire support.

The NVA seemed impervious to fear, unless they were captured, and then they started quaking in their "Ho Chi Minh sandals," though sometimes they wore low-cut canvas shoes with rubber soles. We were scared as well, because in the pitch-black darkness we could not see a damn thing, and every moving shadow appeared threatening, so it was best not to move around too much, or one might become a casualty of friendly fire, because in the darkness, every movement, even from behind, appeared threatening.

Before arriving in Vietnam I was not really aware of the protocol of having the platoon sergeant take charge of the platoon at night. Maybe I had been asleep during that class at Fort Benning, though I doubt it, because as soon as the TAC officers saw a candidate's head begin to dip, they cracked us over our plastic infantry-blue helmet liners with the short sticks that some of them carried, which brought us back to rigid attention. Still, this issue of the platoon sergeant taking charge at night seemed pretty important when I discovered the rationale, for this was the time when the platoon leaders made their way over to the company commander to discuss the day's accomplishments as well as any lessons learned, while receiving our ops orders for the next day's hunt (search-and-destroy mission).

Orders flowed downhill from the colonels at brigade, who were comfortably ensconced in their reinforced bunkers with wooden floors, somewhere in the rear, and they seemed to move us around like chess pieces on a huge green board, the strategy of which was only understood by themselves. These were the senior colonels in starched fatigues who kept us forever on the move, through miles of thick and virtually impenetrable jungle toward one objective after another. Sometimes the bush would be so thick for a mile or more out to our front, without the slightest footpath, that we were required to chop our way, foot by foot, through the dense foliage in the raging heat. Sometimes the foliage towered above us, like being in a dense fog where one couldn't see more than three feet to either side, and then we no longer cared about the noise, because noise we made, for we were simply struggling to reach our assigned destination for the night.

We were proximally closer to battalion than brigade, and the battalion leaders congregated in a hastily erected tent over dirt, protected by the head-

5—The School Solution

quarters company, though occasionally augmented by one of our infantry companies. Those of us out on our search-and-destroy missions received advice from our battalion S-3 Air, flying overhead in a chopper who was some unfortunate Army captain who had probably been coerced into this extremely hazardous assignment, not too far above us, and he apprised us of streams in our vicinity, or hills out to our front that would make for an ideal nighttime encampment. We were grateful for his help, though even we in the infantry felt sorry for the poor guy, whose life expectancy was not much greater than ours if we got into a good-sized firefight.

Battalion headquarters was comprised of various staff elements: S-1 handled personnel issues such as bagging and tagging the dead as well as requesting replacements; S-2 handled military intelligence, which many outside the specialty derided as the ultimate oxymoron (though they were mistaken, for death by friendly fire clearly deserves that distinction); S-3 handled operations and training; S-4 handled logistics; and the S-5 was responsible for Civil Affairs, which pertained to any dealings or interaction we might have with the Vietnamese.

S-3 was the most heralded staff element because this was the staff officer who issued the daily search-and-destroy assignments, coordinated artillery support, and ensured medevac choppers were standing by, while his assistant, the S-3 Air, generally did double-duty as the deputy S-3, when he wasn't hovering above the battlefield. Nobody envied the S-3 Air, even if he was a staff officer who had the luxury of sleeping in a tent back at battalion headquarters at the end of the day.

If we found ourselves in a daytime ambush, then the unfortunate S-3 Air would have to linger over the firefight, dodging bullets while assisting us with the plotting of artillery fire by relaying fire coordinates to our artillery Liaison Officer (LNO) back at battalion, who was responsible for directing artillery fire and close air support (entailing communication with an Air Force Liaison Officer back at brigade). Units closer to the coast would also be able to call for carrier air support through Navy or Marine Air Liaison Officers. The artillery LNO relayed the fire coordinates we provided him to our supporting artillery batteries. Sometimes artillery officers were parceled out to infantry companies to serve as forward artillery observers, but they were in such short supply that our company never had the luxury of their presence.

Meanwhile, further back of battalion HQ, at brigade headquarters, the full-bird colonels in starched fatigues were drinking iced tea in a relatively comfortable bunker with wooden flooring, cooled by fans or even portable air-conditioners. They busied themselves by looking at a flat map tacked to a piece of plywood, while those of us out in the bush were looking at a terrain of mountains and streams that was anything but flat, yet which needed to be traversed in order for us to reach our next objective.

The perennial questions invaded our minds: If you're not out walking the walk, then how in the hell do you know what your men are up against? There seemed to be no consideration to ensure that speed of movement was at a pace that would enable us to put out flankers, and so most of the time we were ordered to hasten the pace at the expense of posting normal security on our flanks, which obviously contributed to the higher casualty figures we were compelled to absorb, but these peripheral exchanges of small-arms fire on our flanks did not seem to unduly concern our senior officers in the rear, for they were intent on getting us into a regimental-size engagement where we could blast the hell out of the enemy with our artillery and fighter aircraft.

This outlook, from the lofty and secure height of brigade, no doubt affected the way in which we on the front lines thought about headquarters, for the full-birds appeared to be thinking less about us, their killer angels, than of their own glorious careers. At least battalion headquarters was out forward in the vicinity of our infantry companies, and so they were proximally closer to us, they did not wear starched fatigues, and they sent out the poor S-3 Air to assist us in our daytime movements when the skies were relatively clear, which was not very often during the incessant rainy days of the monsoon season.

On only one occasion was my company required to augment the security for our battalion headquarters, which generally employed the headquarters company for that purpose. A headquarters company is smaller than a line company (derived from Line Infantry, meaning those soldiers that made up the bulk of the fighting force and who traditionally fought in tight disciplined formations, though generally applied nowadays to all combatant troops, including armor and artillery). Generally, a battalion headquarters company, at full strength, consisted of about a hundred soldiers, and they were not assigned frontline search-and-destroy missions; rather, they exclusively provided security for the headquarters staff.

It was unbearably boring duty as our battalion commander and his staff usually employed most of my men to fill sandbags and construct burlap and dirt walls around their Operations tent and their sleeping tents because these senior officers had absolutely no intention of rolling up their sleeves and digging their own foxholes or filling their own sandbags. If given a choice, we would rather be far away, out in the boonies, hunting the enemy instead of filling sandbags for these staff officers. A bunker constructed out of sandbags (serving essentially the same purpose as bricks) was impervious to most small-arms fire.

It is during the early pre-dawn hours of the morning that one is most vulnerable to attack, just before first light when people are transitioning into wakefulness; so generally we were all up and awake by 4:30 AM, and since we had soldiers alternating at sleeping and standing guard in their foxholes throughout the night, no one got a full night's sleep, so we were habitually sleep-deprived, and thus we always seemed to be fatigued.

War is not a nine-to-five job; in fact, the most successful hunters are those who are able to outsmart their prey and thus gain the element of surprise. This is accomplished by anticipating the prey's movements and habits, and this sometimes entailed moving at night, which the enemy would not expect of Americans. The added danger of war is that the prey is just as smart an animal as the hunter, if not smarter. Perhaps in war, where both the prey and the hunter have weapons, there is no prey at all, only hunters.

Survival depends on the intensity of the survival instinct within the animal; if an individual has become too soft, to the point where he fails to sleep with one eye open, then he has given the advantage to his prey — the other hunter. It's not the most natural behavior for an American, who inherently tends to become spoiled in his affluent society, to adopt the ever-vigilant instinctual alertness of the hunted animal. Still, humans are very adaptable, and the survival instinct exists within us all. It was as though we civilized men were compelled to suppress our civilized selves, while allowing our primordial instincts to predominate and thereby convey us back into the primeval morass of eons ago, into the kill-or-be-killed mentality of the jungle. Of course there were those, like the indigenous Montagnards, who were literally born in the jungle and learned its ways of how best to hunt and survive in this fetid environment, but we Americans could learn, and learn we did.

I slept at night in a three-man foxhole because I was with my radiotelegraph operator (RTO) and my medic, while the rest of my men shared two-man foxholes. My medic, a short and slight-of-build Latino named Diego Suarez, was a conscientious objector (classified 1-A-O / available for noncombatant military service only), which meant that he did not believe in killing, yet here he was, in the midst of the battlefield, except that he did not carry a weapon. He never spoke about his convictions; he was a healer, not a warrior, yet he was a capable medic who humbly accepted our respectful sobriquet of "Doc."

One evening, as sunset was waning, and our color-vision was transitioning to smoky grays, we captured an enemy soldier. One of my men had encountered the North Vietnamese soldier along a trail. Both soldiers were carrying their weapons and approached within twenty paces of one another before they were able to distinguish, in the looming darkness, that they were from different sides; the NVA wore dark green cotton shirts that appeared similar to ours from a distance. My man aimed his weapon at the enemy soldier and pulled the trigger, but his M16 automatic rifle jammed, and so he hollered, "Didi mau" (scram) at the enemy soldier, who took off running, right in front of me and my RTO.

My RTO fired a burst, and the North Vietnamese soldier crumbled to the ground. I figured he was dead, but as I approached his prone body I observed no blood, and incredulously realized that he had simply fainted — in the midst of a dead run! The bullets had passed so close to his head that he had fainted from stark terror.

My RTO tied him up, and I directed that the three of us would each take a turn at guarding the prisoner during the night. My medic Suarez, who was small in stature as well as being a conscientious objector, reminded me that he did not use a weapon. I told him not to worry, that if he observed the prisoner trying to escape, all he had to do was wake me.

It must have been around three in the morning, while turning over in my sleep, that I was jarred by a primordial sense of foreboding, which prompted me to tear myself awake, and out of my half-closed eyes I saw, there in front of me, Suarez and the prisoner wrestling for a rifle, in what appeared to be a menacing embrace. The prisoner had somehow untied his hands, and had made a grab for one of the rifles. My medic and the North Vietnamese soldier were fighting for their very lives over the weapon. The enemy soldier was fighting to survive, and, if he were to gain control of the rifle, he would have killed us all.

I felt myself rising and moving, as though in slow motion, as if I was mired in quicksand, as if in a somnolent dream, while surging toward the enemy soldier, whom I pummeled to the soggy ground with my fists. Suarez and I then subdued the struggling, clawing man, and then I tied him up again, really tight this time, by applying a clove hitch, reinforced with a half hitch, known as a "jam" knot, which I had used in the merchant marine, for this knot becomes tighter the more one struggles against it. I suppose I could have just as easily finished him off with my bayonet and put an end to our concerns about any future escape attempts, but the thought never entered my mind.

Nobody went back to sleep, and I sat there, in the faint glow of the approaching dawn, reflecting in some existential fashion, as though I was observing myself from a distance, in space and time, thinking to myself how close I had just come to dying, while in my sleep. Some say that this is the best way to go, but it gave me the shudders. I want to look death in the face when it comes for me.

We walked our NVA prisoner with us throughout most of the following day, with his hands bound behind his back and his mouth gagged with a t-shirt, except for brief moments when he was offered food and water. Ultimately a passing re-supply chopper was diverted to our location to pick him up and take him back to division base camp for interrogation.

II

One thing about the war in Vietnam was that no matter how hellish it might become, it would be over for me in one year, as that was the extent of my combat obligation. Unlike my North Vietnamese adversaries, some of whom had been fighting their entire adult lives, I was not required to serve for the duration of the war. If I could just survive for twelve months, then Uncle Sam would send me home. However, with an average of more than thirty-five Americans being killed in action each day over those next twelve months, 365 days seemed like an interminably long time. Years later, armchair military quarterbacks opined that one of our most egregious tactical errors was that we limited the combat tour of our soldiers to one year, while pointing out that during World War II some soldiers had fought for the duration, though at least during that war there were frontlines and the rear, and units could be rotated in and out of combat, such that very few soldiers from that era were exposed to sustained combat for more than 300 days a year. For all American wars after Vietnam, our military leaders attempted to rotate combat units about every six months, for even they realized that a soldier exposed to continuous combat for an entire year was an inordinate amount of time.

Lieutenant General W. R. Peers, Commanding General of the Fourth Infantry Division wrote in his Senior Officer Debriefing Report (AD502432) for the Period 1967–1968, "The one-year tour of duty in SVN has proved highly advantageous for American and other Allied forces. It is one of the main reasons why the morale of Allied forces in SVN has remained consistently high. It provides the individual a goal to which he can look forward."

The monsoon in Vietnam runs from May through October in the highlands (though there is still a fair amount of rain in April and November as well), during which time it rains nearly twenty-four hours a day, with just a couple sporadic breaks of intense scorching sunshine. I arrived in Vietnam toward the end of the monsoon season, during which time I was carrying the last book of J. R. R. Tolkien's *Lord of the Rings* trilogy in the hip pocket of my fatigue pants. It was a thrilling story of a battle between good and evil that presaged the end of the world, and the book enabled me to escape from my day-to-day wartime reality into a fantasy escapist world. But was it fantasy, and was it really escapist? After all, the author himself had served as a twenty-five-year-old second lieutenant in the British trenches during World War I at the battle of the Somme. The tale itself was about war, yet I was captivated by the fantasy struggle from which I hoped that goodness would prevail, though the odds appeared poor, but then, in the world's darkest hour, an army of elves came to fight alongside men and dwarfs against the unrelenting forces of evil, and it was only by the greatest coalition of free spirits that there could be any hope at all of prevailing over the ubiquitous forces of darkness.

I took Tolkien's paperback book out of my fatigue pants pocket from time to time, whenever I had a moment to read, which was not very often, and only during daylight hours, such as a break for chow. Consequently, the book had become a soaking, coagulated glob of mulch, which required me to carefully peel off each waterlogged page, one by one, and then I held each page delicately by the fingers of both hands, and I read each side. By the time I had read the page, it was already beginning to crumble in my hands, so I just balled up the page in my fingers and broke it into little paper globules, which would soon break down in the mud and muck of the jungle, so that nothing would be left behind for the enemy to find, not even Tokien's masterful tale, which provided the only respite I was able to find from the daily macabre humors of war.

Nighttime in the jungle during war is a dangerous time. We were attuned to listen for the slightest noise coming to our ears from out of the eerie blackness, squinting to discern any movement or variance in the shades of black out to our front. This was not camping; rather, this was surviving. It was an animal's existence. In these threatening surroundings, as exhausted as we were, after spending ten to twelve hours during the day cutting our way through the searing, steamy jungle in search of the enemy, we did not sleep soundly. We were constantly fatigued, and yet we were compelled to be persistently alert, even while sleeping, with our rifles close at hand. For no matter how prepared one is, in the darkness, if attacked, confusion reigns, and a rifle just out of reach can sometimes be impossible to find.

On one occasion my platoon was probed at night by the enemy and one of my men was unable to locate his rifle in the darkness, though it could not have been more than three feet out of his reach when the first enemy mortar rounds struck, and so I called for him to come over and get down behind me, but now we were one less rifle, and the inattentive soldier had let us down, and he knew it. This was a very expensive lesson to learn; fortunately for him it was not fatal, but almost. The enemy, at night, only came in complete darkness; I never knew the NVA to attack when any light was cast by the moon.

The NVA utilized Russian-made 82mm mortars that were just a tad larger than our 81mm mortars, which enabled the NVA to drop our smaller captured rounds down their tubes, while we were unable to drop their slightly larger rounds down our tubes. I considered this to be a brilliant stratagem on the part of the enemy, whether by design or dumb luck, except for the fact that we were the mighty United States Army and rarely had to economize on ammunition. Our only problem was if the weather prohibited re-supply, since we only carried enough ammunition to sustain us through three days of combat. Let's face it: ammunition is made out of steel and is heavy.

The NVA also used rocket-propelled grenade launchers (RPGs), which were, in essence, 40mm rocket launchers. We, on the other hand, had trained on M40 recoilless rifles back in the States, which had a rifled barrel that fired a 106mm round, and had replaced the smooth bore bazooka of World War II days. Though in Vietnam, most of the time, if we needed to take out enemy bunkers, we simply used the M72 LAW (Light Anti-Tank Weapon), a portable one-shot disposable weapon that fired a 66mm round.

At night, in order to see in the dark, we launched illumination parachute flares out in front of our positions from our mortars. The flares rose nearly two thousand feet up into the night sky, then ignited, and began their leisurely descent toward earth, while their blazing brilliant-white 500,000-candlepower lit-up an area 1,200 yards in diameter for seventy-five seconds, until the lofty illumination flares ultimately came down to earth.

Ever afterwards, whenever I watched a fourth of July fireworks celebration that glorified an old wartime battle, the nighttime illuminations involuntarily rekindled stark memories of Vietnam within me. While everyone else was sighing "ooh" and "aah," I was back in time, observing how the exploding fireworks turned the night into day, and thus facilitated the killing business.

In the pre-dawn morning, those of us not already up on guard duty awoke in the pouring rain and struggled to untie our mud-encrusted boots in order to replace our soaking wet socks with the pair that we had dried against our chests during the night. This practice thus lessened the degree of jungle rot that we were all trying to mitigate. It was also part of my responsibility, as platoon leader, to regularly inspect the feet of the men in my platoon, as jungle rot on the feet could decimate an infantry platoon more thoroughly than malaria.

Upon arriving in Vietnam we had all been excited to be issued jungle boots that had olive-green nylon-mesh uppers that breathed better than the all-leather black boots we had worn stateside, and they even had drain holes that allowed the water to escape. They also had a steel plate inserted mid-sole to help protect against pungi stakes, which abounded in the fetid paddies, and they were impossible to discern in the murky water, and though they were only heat-tempered bamboo pointed stakes with baked-on shit at the tips, they were still sharp enough, and sufficiently hard enough, to pierce right through the sole of one's combat boot and penetrate several inches into one's foot. Nevertheless, these boots were a definite improvement in the jungle, because whenever the rain stopped and the sun broke out, our jungle boots stood a better chance of drying out than was the case with the all-leather boots.

At night one had to be very cautious about lighting a cigarette, as the flame from the lighter, or the glowing tip of the lit cigarette, could give away one's position to the enemy. It was during my first month in Vietnam that I smoked my first cigarette; I felt nauseated at first by the taste, but smoking seemed to calm my nerves and suppress my thoughts about food and fatigue.

The very first thing that many American infantry troops did, upon surviving the first wave assault on the beaches at Normandy during the D-Day invasion, was to take a piss, and after that they grabbed a quick smoke. Most every soldier in the Army carried a Zippo lighter, even if he did not smoke, for it worked even in heavy rains when ordinary matches would not suffice. The Zippo has been manufactured in Bradford, Pennsylvania, since 1932; it is a windproof cigarette lighter, sheathed within a rectangular brass or steel case that keeps the innards dry even when immersed in water, though soldiers in 'Nam preferred Zippos with a chrome finish. The lid is attached to the body with a welded hinge, and the wick is encased in a wind hood that enables a person to light a cigarette in strong breezes. Most everyone had their Zippo lighter engraved, of which the most popular engraving was derived from Psalm 23 and read, "Yea, though I walk through the valley of the shadow of death, I will fear no evil for I am the evilest son of a bitch in the valley."

It was a continual struggle to keep our cigarettes dry; we wrapped them in plastic if we could, and then, when we extracted one from the pack, we cupped it with our hands to try to keep the rain off of it so that it would light, and also so that the enemy would not see the burning tip, especially at night in a slimy smelly foxhole where any visible illumination could cost you your life. Still, unavoidably, the pack of cigarettes often became a soggy mess, and even then we went to great lengths to dry them out, and then smoke them in their dank tobacco-stained brown wrappers.

From time to time we were resupplied by choppers coming out to the field, as we could only carry about three or four days' supply of food and ammunition, and these re-supply visits required us to determine what we could reasonably carry away with us in the heavy packs on our backs. Those who had survived their first combat experience never scrimped on ammunition. I wore two olive-green ammunition cotton bandoliers slung diagonally over my shoulder and across my chest, each of which held seven magazines and allowed for faster reloading than pulling magazines from the ammo pouches on our web belts. I also carried a reserve of at least ten additional magazines in my backpack and in the pockets of my fatigue pants. Whenever possible we carried even more ammo—extra grenades, perhaps a claymore mine, some 100-round belts of ammo for the machine gunner that weighed six and a half pounds apiece, and a nine-pound mortar round for the weapons platoon, as we were well aware that any of this ordnance could save our lives in a moment of crisis. A veteran would even get rid of the heaviest C-ration cans, like ham and eggs, and ham and lima beans, while retaining just the cans of bread, pound cake, crackers, and fruit cocktail, as well as the packets of powdered coffee and hot chocolate, cigarettes, and toilet paper that came in the accessory packs. Each C-ration meal also included a small can that contained either jam, peanut butter or cheddar cheese; the cheese came in four different flavors, one of which contained caraway seeds, and to this day I cannot tolerate the taste of caraway seeds, as I had eaten them in 'Nam to the point where just the smell could turn my stomach.

Due to the fact that we were not supplemented with any fresh fruits or vegetables in the bush, where we were compelled to eat our food exclusively out of cans that were notoriously deficient in vitamins if they had been stored for excessive periods of time or exposed to high temperatures, I observed vestiges of scurvy among some of my soldiers, revealed by their bleeding gums. At least the French in Vietnam had issued raw onions to their troops out in the boonies to ensure that their soldiers did not suffer from lack of vitamin C.

We assisted the new replacements, who were struggling under the weight of their heavy backpacks, and who were foolishly inclined to divest themselves of ammo so they could carry more food. My sergeants and I approached them and started tossing out the heaviest cans to lighten their load. The resupply choppers also brought out cartons and cartons of free cigarettes to the soldiers in the field, and each C-ration meal came with a packet of four cigarettes and a book of matches. The cigarettes were primarily Chesterfields and Lucky Strikes, and, since the production of C-rations ended in 1957, before the wide use of filter cigarettes, all of the C-ration cigarettes were non-filters. Surplus C-rations were consumed in Vietnam until they were eventually depleted and replaced by MCIs (Meal, Combat, Individual) that came in the same metal containers as C-rations, but offered more menu choices.

Essentially we were provided with free cigarettes to console us while we were fighting and dying. This was before the days when the United States began to strive to become a smoke-free society, though the stress of war from time immemorial tends to induce soldiers to smoke in order to alleviate fatigue, hunger, and fear. Most of the soldiers would forgo the cartons of non-filtered Camels, considering them too strong; so I would take them, for I was their leader, and therefore I selected last.

We constantly struggled against the debilitating fatigue of moving through the hot, humid jungle, which nevertheless incessantly sapped our strength. We were always sleep-deprived, such that, toward the end of a long, grueling day of humping the boonies, it oftentimes took all of our effort simply to focus on the legs of the man in front just to keep moving with the unit, especially for the soldiers who had been on ambush duty the night before, as they would go more than thirty-six hours without sleep. More often than not, it was while we were in this fatigued state that we frequently came into contact with the enemy, though, even in those instances, our heart-pumping adrenalin would generally override our lassitude.

When we were cutting our way step by step with machetes through the thick jungle foliage in the sweltering heat, we were lucky if we were able to cover seven miles over a ten-hour period. Additionally, in extremely thick jungle it was sometimes impracticable to put out flankers, even though their absence increased the vulnerability of our column to surprise attack against our flanks.

Whenever feasible we put out flankers, as per our classroom training, but then this reduced our speed of movement in heavy jungle, and, much of the time, speed of movement was paramount, and so, regrettably, we simply did not have the luxury of taking all necessary precautions, such as protecting our flanks. Frequently our unit, be it of platoon, company or battalion size, had orders to cover a certain distance in a specified period of time in order to flush out the enemy, or to take up a blocking position in anticipation of intercepting the enemy. In those instances we simply had no choice but to step up the pace, which meant more noise and more sweat. This is the bane of the infantryman — to march, march, and then march some more, like Sisyphus, King of

Corinth, who was condemned in purgatory to ceaselessly push a huge bolder up a hill, without making any discernable progress.

Day after day we were out humping the boonies while struggling under the weight of our seventy-pound packs, for we were all mules in the infantry; nobody received special treatment, whether officer or enlisted, everyone had to carry his own weight, though some carried more, particularly the machine gunners with their heavy guns. The M60 weighed more than twenty-three pounds and was fed by metallic 100-round split-link belts with a tracer every fifth round so that the gunner could observe the trajectories of the bullets and make adjustments accordingly to increase his accuracy. I, on the other hand, got tired just carrying my lightweight M16 that weighed less than eight pounds. However, nobody had it tougher than the mortar guys who had to heft their heavy mortar tubes, bipods, and forty-eight-pound baseplates. We were all in the shit together, and this shared deprivation formed the deepest of bonds.

Of course everyone wore their dog tags (2" long and 1⅛" wide, with rounded corners) on a steel ball chain around their necks. In the combat zone we wrapped our stainless steel dog tags with green tape so that they would not reflect light or make a clanking sound when they knocked together. The dog tags listed our names, our service numbers, religious affiliations, and blood types, so if one was wounded and needed a transfusion or a limb amputated, or something equally grotesque, then the surgeons would be able to ascertain our blood type from our dog tags, even if we were unconscious, which was a comforting thought.

Each of us wore two dog tags, because, in the event we were killed, one of the dog tags would be sent back with the body, while the other would be retained by an officer. As an officer I was instructed to tie one of the tags onto the dead man's bootlaces, but if his legs were blown off by a land mine, some people mentioned that I was to wedge the dog tag between the dead man's teeth; the dog tags even had a notch at one end that many assumed was for this very purpose, but in fact the notch was inadvertently caused by the stamp machine that held the dog tags during their production.

The other dog tag, retained by the officer in the field, would be used to corroborate the death, and thus confirm who was present and accounted for, and who was lost. Even if you had been blown away beyond recognition, your dog tags might enable the remnants of your body to be identified so that you could be delivered to your family back home; this was a macabre though eerily consoling thought, for there seems to exist within all peoples the strongest impetus to return home — whether dead or alive. We never left a fellow soldier behind; we always brought him back with us.

During 1985, a young genetic professor in England discovered DNA fingerprinting, leading to the first trial in the U.S. two years later to absolve a criminal by DNA identification. As a consequence, DNA testing has made it extremely unlikely that any more tombs to unknown soldiers will ever be erected, because identification can now be made from even the tiniest fragment of bone. The Tomb of the Unknowns (more commonly referred to as the Tomb of the Unknown Soldier) in Arlington National Cemetery contains the remains of an unknown soldier from World War I, as well as the crypts of unknowns from World War II and Korea. Additionally, there was also a crypt to contain an unknown from the Vietnam War, but then in 1988, those remains were identified through DNA testing, and thus removed and returned home to his family.

We also wore our P-38s on our dog tag chains, which were the tiny steel can openers that came with our C-rats, which barely qualified as chow, since more often than not we had to eat our food cold. The P-38 was a small-hinged piece of metal, only 1½ inches in length, with a blade portion that one jabbed into the can, and then one worked the can opener with the thumb and forefinger. The directions specifically warned that one should "sterilize before re-use," but nobody paid any attention to that advisory, as food poisoning was the least of our worries.

One day, during my third week in the jungle, our company commander received orders from battalion to conduct a night movement with the mission of cordoning off a nearby Vietnamese village that was suspected of giving aid to the enemy. Night movements are disconcerting, because this is not man's natural element. Why is it that most children seem to have an inherent fear of the dark? On this occasion my company commander ordered me and my small platoon to lead our company of just over a hundred men. The night, though alien, was protective. I could not see far into the jungle, but neither could anyone else, and we weren't sweating through the blistering heat of the day. It almost seemed innocuous, like a Boy Scout outing, and yet silence was the key to survival at night. I suppose that silence was always a critical element of survival, but the night instinctively compelled people to speak in whispers.

We were moving cautiously, approaching the suspected enemy village, and we were moving solely with what little illumination was provided by the opalescent moon in its waning crescent stage. I was moving stealthily along a jungle trail over which I observed that many feet had passed. I could discern that the path was heavily traveled, and quite recently, because the grass had been trampled flat and had not yet risen back up; my heart was in my throat.

I stopped to ascertain our position on my map, while my RTO shielded me with his shelter half; I quickly turned on my flashlight, equipped with a red filter to lessen the range of its illumination, for I needed to verify our position from time to time in order to ensure that I was on the proper azimuth to the village, and also that I would instantly know the exact map coordinates of our location, so that if all hell broke loose I could immediately and effectively call in artillery, but I had to hurry, because I was responsible for the entire company, and the captain was back there, somewhere, waiting impatiently.

I moved back down the trail, with moist leaves slapping me in my face, past my crouching men to Sergeant Williams, in order to discuss my findings and to seek his advice. Perhaps I was a little uneasy in the dark. We were both crouching down on one knee, talking in whispers, though I must have appeared a bit agitated, for Sergeant Williams gave me a quizzical look, and then he reached into his backpack and pulled out a bottle of Jack Daniel's whiskey and offered me a swig. I gratefully obliged; I could feel the warmth and the dauntless courage of the corn liquor fortifying my body.

This was the only bottle of liquor I ever saw in the field during my entire time in Vietnam, as alcohol was strictly forbidden out in the boonies. Sergeant Williams was a war hero in the eyes of everyone in the platoon, including me. He was pretty much the last of the old breed; he was older than most platoon sergeants, being around twenty-eight years of age. He was not one of those "shake-and-bake" sergeants who had been sent to the NCO (non-commissioned officer) school for accelerated promotion to the rank of sergeant in just six months, whereas in the peacetime military it would normally entail six years or so before an enlisted soldier moved up to the rank of staff (E-6) sergeant. Sergeant Williams was already on his second tour in 'Nam and had been a staff sergeant before he arrived in country on his first tour. He had been running the platoon without an officer for some time, and obviously he could competently do it all.

In any case, while I was becoming adjusted to the methods of fighting in the jungle, as opposed to what I had been taught in the States, I found myself deferring to Sergeant Williams for tactical advice. Why not? He had the combat experience, and I was the rookie. Still, he was a strong personality and, as such, might diminish my development. He pretty much ran the platoon.

As we neared the village, we began to spread out in a wide arc in order to cover the approaches to the village, and then we waited patiently for the first early morning glimmer of light before moving on into the village. When we moved into the village at first light we discovered some Chicom Type-56 assault rifles underneath a rice stash, indicating that the villagers were indeed providing support to the enemy, and so we gathered all of the villagers together. We had the village men squat down and put their hands behind their heads, and we told them not to talk, yet one inscrutable old man kept blathering away, and I saw Sergeant Williams yelling at the old man to "shut the fuck up!" But the old man, who appeared to be past sixty, kept right on jabbering, since he obviously did not understand a word of English, and to be yelled out by some mean-looking giant with a rifle in his hand must have been terrifying, and then I observed Sergeant Williams stride over to the old man and viciously kick him in the side of his face. And the old man went down like a sack of potatoes, with a broken jaw, and now he could only emit silent gurgles.

Sergeant Williams was a "bad ass," and for the life of me I could not understand why some people could be so brutal toward a defenseless person. The prisoners were squatting with their hands on top of their heads for Christ's sake, and rifles were pointed at them, and they were scared shitless—literally. Maybe the old man was telling the other prisoners to rise up against us and make a grab for our rifles, but I didn't think so. I felt that the old man was simply so terrified that he simply could not stop blabbering. But I was the novice, and Sergeant Williams had seen so much more combat than I.

III

Sergeant Williams, Silver Star and all, had become brutalized by the war. I had not yet crossed that Rubicon; I still saw these terrified souls as people. However, I also know that those who have not been to war are unable to fully comprehend what it feels like to be ambushed and to lose your buddies, then to go into the nearest village, find enemy weapons, and want to take out your anger on those people closest to hand, whom you believed had supported the very enemy that had just killed your comrades. Still, you are always you, whether you are wearing a military uniform, a policeman's uniform, or the coat and tie of a businessman, or whether you are sitting around the table with your wife, or walking your child to school. You are always you, cloaked in the humanistic and religious values in which you were raised. I understand the harsh training required to mold a soldier, as well as the dehumanization that results from killing, but through it all, you are still you, and you are always accountable for your actions. Article VI of the Army Code of Conduct states, in part, "I will never forget that I am an American, fighting for freedom, *responsible for my actions*, and dedicated to the principles which made my country free." There are no excuses when it comes to ethics.

To kill a man is against my values; however, my country tells me that to kill in this instance is okay, because my country has sanctioned this killing, but they do not tell me that it is the moral thing to do. I know innately that kicking a defenseless man in the head is against my values. If I am pointing a weapon at close range at an unarmed man, then he is clearly under my power and he is morbidly frightened, yet still he is a man, though he dare not run, so he faces the barrel of the rifle and submits, and he fervently hopes to live to see another day, while the soldier with the rifle hovering over him holds the power over life and death. Many a young soldier who had never before had such power, now found that people would fearfully submit to his supremacy, begging him not to take away their lives, and the young soldier now stood in the combat zone with the power of God. If you want to play God, proceed at your own risk.

Not everyone is enlightened, for some people, their dominating trait is anger. Had the young soldier read Aristotle's Nicomachean ethics? Had his parents raised him lovingly, or was he beaten and unloved as a child?

Now here was our young soldier in the combat zone, face to face with the enemy, whom, in his eyes, he considered responsible for the deaths of his buddies. What was he trained to do? This was the issue. As soldiers, we were taught little about compassion; rather we had been taught to kill, but that was still no excuse. There are some things the Army cannot teach, for some things can only be learned intuitively. We know, without anyone telling us, the difference between right and wrong, and for this reason alone we are unavoidably responsible for our own actions.

One week later Sergeant Williams had a relapse from a severe case of malaria and had to be evacuated from the combat zone. He did not return, and I was left in charge. If Sergeant Williams had not been medevac'd, I probably never would have truly taken over the leadership of the platoon, but now, in his absence, the soldiers of the platoon clearly looked to me as their leader.

I certainly owe Sergeant Williams a debt of gratitude for enabling me to survive my first four weeks in the combat zone. I felt that I had been groomed by the best, and that I could henceforth lead my platoon with confidence. We can learn from anyone, whether they be above us or below us in the chain of command. I have seen officers whose egos or vanity have convinced them that they must possess all of the answers, for they are in charge, but this is a demented manifestation of leadership, because I have yet to meet anyone who has all the answers. No matter how high one rises, it is necessary to still keep one's feet on the ground, because the laws of physics preclude us from flying.

6

Ambushed in a Rice Paddy

I

Sometimes, while on patrol, we broke out of the jungle, into a man-made clearing that had been hacked out of the dense foliage to create a sparsely populated highland village, comprised of some thatch huts and surrounding rice paddies. In country like this, where the rain fell relentlessly, not much could be harvested, except for rice, which thrives in water.

A rain forest is defined as a forest that receives more than sixty inches of rainfall a year, and yet the rainfall in the central highlands exceeds eighty-five inches each year, which is even more amazing when one considers that the rainy season in Vietnam only lasts for about six months. The central highlands receive the most rain in all of Vietnam, over eighteen inches during the month of August alone, and 40 percent more rain each year, on average, than does Saigon or the Mekong Delta. The city of Seattle, in America's Pacific Northwest, is infamous for its incessant rain, which falls every month, slacking only in July, and yet less than forty inches of rain fall on Seattle throughout any given year.[1]

The villagers in the central highlands constructed earthen dikes to enclose the water-filled rice paddies, each of which was generally about twenty yards across, and then the villagers interlocked the paddies so that there might be three to five paddies stretching out for fifty to a hundred yards or so. The villagers planted the rice shoots at the end of the dry season, and then they allowed the paddies to flood with rain and river water, after which the rice would begin to grow in this soup. When the paddies were flooded, the water could rise as high as one's armpits.

Traversing a rice paddy was always fraught with potential danger, because they are so open that we were clearly exposed and therefore extremely vulnerable, yet sometimes the jungle foliage encircling the rice paddies was so thick that we had no choice but to file straight across the paddies. We waded down into the flooded malodorous bog, climbed up over a dike, then descended once again into another paddy. The water in these pestilential miasmas was stagnant, muddy and fetid, with all kinds of flotsam, including mosquito larvae and water buffalo feces applied as fertilizer, for a buffalo, different from a bison, has few sweat glands in its skin, so it cannot cool off by sweating; rather, it cools off by slogging around in streams or paddies. I also observed leeches swimming all around us, looking like little tadpoles with wiggling tails, in search of warm blood, and we were the most attractive host. The leeches could sense our body heat and our nutritious blood, and thus they swam around our ankles, attacking our bodies between our boots and our pants, or, if the water rose up to our armpits, then they would also invade down our pants at our waists.

When we reached the other side of the rice paddies, I posted half of my men out forward for security, while the rest of my men dropped their pants and burned the already engorged leeches off their ankles and penises with lit cigarettes; even the non-smokers carried cigarettes for this purpose. It was amazing to me how quickly these leeches could engorge themselves with so much blood, and they possessed a natural anesthetic in their saliva so you couldn't even feel them sucking your blood. They also had an anticoagulant in their saliva, so that when they did let go, there would still be a fair amount of bleeding. Once the first group of soldiers took care of their leeches, they then posted security while the rest of us took care of our leeches.

II

One hot, muggy afternoon, during my second month in Vietnam, my company was traversing a series of rice paddies in single file in order to limit our exposure to pungi stakes, and my little band of thirty was the trailing platoon. As a consequence, we were just getting ready to enter the first paddy as the lead element of the company was exiting the paddies on the far side. The rain had ceased and a scorching hot sun had broken out, and I noticed that there was not a breath of air to ease the stifling heat, and when I gazed up at the sky, over the open expanse of the rice paddies, it appeared that even the clouds were standing still. I could see more than fifty yards out to my front, and I observed the movement of the men up ahead, all dressed in olive-green with camouflage canvas wraps on their helmets that effectively blended into the green and brown of the jungle paddies.

In the sweltering heat our steel pots were weighing down heavily on our heads, making us dizzy, and we had difficulty just trying to keep our weapons and our hefty packs above the muddy paddy water that was reaching for our armpits. The filthy putrid water was soaking our butts and warming our balls, tempting most men to piss in the water while they were wading across, even though our battalion S-3 had warned us about pissing in the paddies, inferring that something malevolent might sense our warm urine and swim right up our penises and horribly infect us, or, at the very least, our dicks would become a magnet for leeches (which I believed to be true). And though the paddy water was tepid, it imparted a sensation of refreshing coolness to our baking bodies, which were inescapably exposed to the blazing midday sun.

6—Ambushed in a Rice Paddy

We were keeping silent, because we knew we were very much exposed and vulnerable, particularly for those of us who had entered the water last, for now nearly fifteen minutes had passed since the first soldier had entered the paddies, which was sufficient time for the enemy to consolidate their forces, if they happened to be in the neighborhood.

Soon after I entered the first paddy there was the unmistakable staccato sound of automatic weapons fire, and so we all ducked our heads, but we were in water up to our chests, so that's about all we could do, duck our heads a little. And then we came to realize that one of our own men, a new officer, on the far side, had decided to test-fire his M16, while my platoon was just beginning to traverse the paddies, so he could ensure the paddy water hadn't jammed his weapon. All veterans knew this to be sheer idiocy; no veteran would ever test-fire his weapon in the combat zone, unless the entire unit did it together, and certainly not while standing up to our armpits in a rice paddy. The new officer was smiling, but the rest of us were not, for one never knew how close the enemy might be.

By the time my platoon was emerging from the rice paddies, our captain and the lead platoon had passed out of sight of us onto the other side of a small ridge. Some of the troops from the platoon in front of mine had reached the gentle grassy slope beyond the paddies and were indulging in a break — sitting down and sipping from their canteens, when all of a sudden, all hell broke loose, as a barrage of AK-47 automatic fire assailed us from the side of the paddies from which we had recently departed.

The volume of enemy fire kept increasing, and the rapid clipped cadence of the fire began to sound like a buzz-saw, and bullets were hitting people, and I saw one soldier go down with a bullet through his leg that started to bleed profusely, and he was hollering for a medic, and other soldiers were hit and lay bleeding and dying. We hunkered down and returned fire amid the acrid smell of gunpowder that hung heavy in the air, while bullets were striking all around us, and people were continuing to get shot.

I scampered further up the bank onto a small knoll, and quickly released my pack in order to lighten my load and to present a lower silhouette to the enemy. As I dropped to the ground, I rolled away from my pack, as all veterans had instinctively learned to do, though oddly this was never taught in school. I wondered why? Maybe the instructors wanted to circumvent the subject of death, since they knew that the odds of an infantryman dying in combat were pretty high, being as how 70 percent of all Army hostile deaths in Vietnam were borne by infantrymen, and this is particularly astonishing when one considers that only 10 percent of the Army troops in Vietnam were in the infantry.[2] Unfortunately, this was a practice that new guys took some time to learn, for it was not instinctive, to move away from one's reserve ammunition, and then come back to it.

During the ambush, virtually all of my men were down on their stomachs, including myself. Very few of my men were returning fire, as they did not want to reveal their positions to the enemy and thus draw fire upon themselves. I must confess that I also wanted to hide in any depression I could find and not draw attention to myself; yet I was the leader, and this realization at least prompted me to look around, and I saw Kershaw, my RTO, up on one knee, just five feet behind me — waiting, for me, to issue some orders, any orders. However, I felt as though I was in a hornets' nest, and the buzzing of bullets was making it difficult for me to even think, as though the fog of battle had discernibly stunned me, but then I was afflicted with a moment of clarity, when I acknowledged to myself that I, as the officer, was expected to set the example, and if my RTO could be up on one knee communicating with our company commander, then so could I, and therefore, with a conscious force of will, I rose up on one knee in the face of whistling bullets crackling all around me.

So now we were two guys up on one knee, congregating around a radio antenna, which seemed to advertise to the world that here was the command and control team. It seemed to me that we had become two sitting ducks. Frankly, I could never understand why any enlisted soldier would ever volunteer to be an RTO. Was this moment eating into my life expectancy of fifteen minutes for an infantry lieutenant under enemy fire? How was Kershaw able to expose himself to such risk? My unencumbered knee was shaking, but at least I hadn't pissed my pants. I felt terribly vulnerable, and I fearfully hoped that I would not be shot in the face or in the groin; I even shifted slightly to shield my groin; that's about all I could do, as the bullets were whizzing about, simply grit my teeth and strive to do my duty, or, more simply, try not to appear as a coward in front of the men whom I was expected to lead.

You cannot see the bullets; you cannot dodge the bullets, for an AK-47 bullet travels at 2,400 feet per second, which is more than twice the speed of sound, so you just submit to fate, meaning that you have absolutely no control over the situation. I recall reading a Civil War history that described the behavior of a young federal infantry lieutenant under fire at Gettysburg, who was flinching and ducking his head in the face of the firing, and his captain strode right up to him and told him to stop flinching and to stand like a man.

If you can stand like a man in a hailstorm of lethal bullets, then you have been initiated, my friend, and you have tasted of a triumph that no one can ever take away from you, for you have looked at death and prevailed. You did your duty, you honored your country as intrepidly as all of those who had gone before you, of whom quite a few had paid with their lives, and you proudly, though no doubt fearfully, followed their shining examples, and that was no small feat.

Perhaps this was my moment of truth, when pride predominated over fear. I would rather take a bullet than appear as a coward in front of my men. Sometimes I reflect on what I might have done if my RTO, who had been through more combat than I, had not set the example, or if Sergeant Williams had not been evacuated. Who knows? Perhaps I would have been squeezing myself into my steel helmet instead of rising up to one knee and exposing myself. Life is like that, filled with "what if's?"

As the ambush continued to unfold, I was compelled to grab the radio handset from my RTO and change the radio frequency so that I could talk directly to our artillery LNO at battalion who was in direct communication with our supporting artillery battery about five miles to our rear, since my captain was on the other side of the ridge and did not have line of sight to the enemy. I requested that they bring down a shower of burning hot metal upon the enemy positions, and then I walked in the exploding rounds until they were bursting only about fifty yards away, and some of the shards of shrapnel from a couple erratic rounds were ripping right through our own positions, splintering the trees around us, yet we were still drawing automatic weapons fire because the enemy was willing to take their chances with the exploding artillery rounds, so long as they could get off some nice clean shots at us from across the rice paddies. They were intent on shooting us to pieces.

I could hear bullets whistle by me as they passed to my right and to my left, but a bullet that passed directly over my head made a very distinctive sound, like that of a cracking whip. I have heard this cracking whip sound numerous times. People say that you never hear the bullet that has your name on it; well, of course you wouldn't hear that bullet, because it's traveling faster than the speed of sound, and it will hit you in dead silence, for you can only hear the bullets that have already passed you, either to the side or over your head.

In the midst of the ambush I expected to see my entire life of twenty-one years flash before me; however, that did not happen. I had no cosmic insights; instead, I had the most mundane thoughts. I was thinking of how tired I was, and I was so thirsty that I found myself longing for the taste of an ice-cold beer. I realized that combat was not at all like the movies where everyone was standing up and courageously firing back at the enemy. The true reality is that people tend to crawl into themselves, and they are reluctant to return fire. Yet it is only when you are able to return fire at a higher rate than your adversary that your opponent will begin to lower his head and reduce his volume of fire. If you do not return fire, then your adversary just keeps blasting away.

One job of the officer is to kick ass—to get people to return fire. So I had to overcome my intense fear, stand up, and proceed physically down the line, slapping men on their steel helmets while ordering them to return fire. Now I was conspicuously the only soldier up on both feet, entirely vulnerable, walking the line along a grassy knoll, nakedly exposed, though at least I was a moving target, and yet I was compelled to move at a measured pace so as to calm my men, and, surprisingly, I discovered that once I had utterly submitted to fate in this instance, my heartbeat slowed perceptively, and I was able to think more lucidly. And though I could hear bullets hissing all around, I moved up and down the line unscathed. Perhaps it was a miracle, or, more likely, our adversaries were just piss-poor shots.

It is an obvious fact that one cannot dodge a bullet and that is why there are so many head wounds, because one has to raise one's head to fire one's weapon. Our steel pots would deflect a small arms round, but even our steel helmets would not stop a round that came at us directly—from in front or from the side. To my right I saw one of my crouching men hit by a bullet and fall inert along the grassy slope.

Even during these terrifying moments I never thought I would die, though I did encounter soldiers who had premonitions of death, from which a torpid listlessness seemed to creep into their demeanor, such that it did seem that death would find them, as though these soldiers had relinquished their will to survive. Yes, I believe that a perceptible sense of languor had set in amongst these men, as though the fight had been taken out of them and they were drained, perhaps because of what they had done or what they had seen, such that it almost seemed as though they had already surrendered to the peaceful darkness that seemed to linger all around us. However, I was too young and far too full of life to be overly concerned about death.

As our reactive response to the ambush proceeded and we had finally generated a steady volume of return fire, we were ordered by our brigade commander, hovering high above us in his helicopter, to assault back across the rice paddies and attack the enemy on the other side.

I must say that I never saw a brigade commander in Vietnam walk the ground while their men were fighting. Those that I observed preferred to be way up high, out of range of the bullets, while seeing the battle as their golden opportunity to be written up for a Distinguished Flying Cross (awarded for heroism beyond the call of duty while participating in aerial flight). I'm talking about the full-bird colonels at brigade, for there are two ranks of colonel: A lieutenant colonel wears a silver oak leaf insignia and usually commands a battalion, while a full colonel wears a silver eagle insignia and usually commands a brigade (consisting of two or more battalions). I'm sure there must have been some full-bird colonels who walked the ground, but I never met one. Most of the time these full-birds flew high above the killing zone, issuing orders out of a helicopter, and they were certainly not riding in the low-flying chopper of the battalion S-3 Air Operations Officer, the unfortunate son of a bitch who was ordered to fly right on top of the ground action and serve as our forward artillery observer. The S-3 Air had serious survivability concerns; he was probably sitting on his steel pot in order to protect his balls, while chain-smoking Camels and trying to keep his hands from shaking, while the colonel flew higher, with steady hands. And it was this full-bird colonel who would lean on our company commander, who in turn was compelled to obey orders, and thus we were ordered to counter-attack back across the rice paddies, exposed, and up to our armpits in a sea of floating water buffalo turds.

Most of my men were screaming four-letter epithets, or giving the bird to the full-bird flying high above us, though I do not think the colonel heard any of us, or noticed the obscene hand gestures, and some of my men, I do not doubt, pointed their weapons up toward the sky in umbrage against what they considered to be such insane orders. We wanted to believe that our brigade commander had our best interests at heart, and that perhaps he would call for air strikes in addition to the artillery, but when men are ordered to conduct a slogging assault across exposed rice paddies against an entrenched enemy, then we unequivocally knew that this full-bird truly hungered for that Distinguished Flying Cross.

At times in Vietnam there seemed to be confusion as to who was the enemy, for if you expect soldiers to die as a result of your orders, then you must at least be willing to put yourself in harm's way as well; this is the role of the infantry officer, and nothing less can engender respect. Once an officer rises above the level of a line company, he is no longer in the front lines; he is now issuing orders from a safer place. Success for the brigade commander was measured by the number of confirmed enemy kills that we could produce for him. So, from the brigade commander's perspective, repelling an ambush meant little; we had to counterattack, then remain in the contact zone and police the area to confirm how many of the enemy we had killed.

It's one thing to be wading across expansive rice paddies in file or in column when you feel relatively confident that the enemy has not yet discovered your presence. It's another thing altogether to assault, in line, shoulder to shoulder, while wading chest-deep across rice paddies in the face of a known enemy.

We were afforded the ludicrous consolation of having our own machine guns fire over our heads to provide covering fire; yet those were our orders, and so we formed up together and proceeded to wade back down into the reeking bog.

Slogging across the rice paddies, shoulder to shoulder, recalled to my mind the futile and pathetically sad charge of the British Light Brigade cavalry of a hundred years ago: "Their's not to make reply, Their's not to reason why, Their's but to do and die."

We traversed more than fifty yards of muddy open water, knowing that if the enemy were at the far end of the rice paddies in force, we would be in dire straits. The machine guns on our side kept up a steady fire over our heads as we re-crossed the paddies; I could hear lots of cracking whips; they sounded the same, whether they were coming from behind or in front.

As we slogged back across the paddies, we received some sporadic sniper fire, indicating that the enemy was apparently pulling out. Still we maintained a steady volume of fire as we proceeded across, and then we rushed up onto the far bank as though we were hitting the beaches at Iwo Jima.

We began searching through the thick, tangled jungle for enemy bodies. This was somewhat akin to conducting an Easter egg hunt, as we would spot splashes of blood on some leaves, then check the ground to see if a body was visible, then look for any turned-up dirt, indicating that a body may have been dragged away. It was not easy to find enemy bodies because the North Vietnamese were as dedicated as any American in retrieving their dead. They carried leather straps that looked somewhat like belts, to which they attached a plug of wood. They would then hook the wood piece to their comrade's pants, and then drag their buddy away, oftentimes under intense fire. They were some very tough dudes, and we all admired the respect they held for their dead.

Meanwhile, we continued to search for blood trails, anything that might indicate a confirmed kill. One of my men rushed up to me with a tattered jacket and a pair of pants, saying, "Wadda ya think, lieutenant? You think maybe we can claim two kills from these?"

We had no confirmed enemy kills that day, and this task of scouring the bush in search of enemy bodies was detested by the soldiers out in the boonies, for it simply put them at additional risk, and they knew it.

The officer who had brought on the ambush by test-firing his weapon had put himself at grave risk, for, even though he most likely would not be put on report, thoughtless behavior of this sort prompted soldiers to ask themselves, "Is my officer going to get me killed, or is he going to look out for me?" If the troops felt the officer was going to get them killed, then the officer was considered a liability. Perhaps this is the case in all armies; I mean, there is some reasonableness to this view of expendability, if one truly believes that their leader is irrational and going to get them killed. However, this is generally not an issue to be decided by the rank and file, for this would be an impractical way to run an army.

One historian has written that the Army finally admitted, three years after my departure from Vietnam, "that fragging (pulling the pin of a grenade, then rolling the live grenade toward someone) had resulted in ... murders, 80 percent of them officers."[3] I had heard stories within my own battalion of officers who had become the victims of their own men, and I certainly believe that acts of this nature did in fact take place. It should be noted that the Department of Defense has officially stated that 236 homicides were committed in Vietnam, compared to 9,107 accidental deaths.[4]

7

The Battle of Dak To (October–November 1967)

I

Toward the end of my fifth week in the jungle, during the second week of October 1967, my battalion was assigned to conduct *search and destroy* operations in a place unfamiliar to us all at the time — a place called Dak To, which was situated in the northern extremity of the central highlands plateau.

Dak To was just a small garrison town of less than 2,000 that supported a Civilian Irregular Defense Group (CIDG). It was really more of a military camp than an actual town, only a couple miles off of Highway 14 (the main asphalted north/south artery through the highlands) alongside a dirt road that was actually labeled on our maps as Highway 512. This narrow rough road extended for only twelve miles in length, running due west until it dead-ended at the Laotian border. In fact, the last three miles of Hwy 512 were shown on our maps as simply a trail, not even a road any more, before it simply disappeared off our maps once it reached Laos.

This slender artery had served as a major NVA infiltration route into South Vietnam (off the Ho Chi Minh Trail) for many years. Dak To also served as a major forward operations base for SOG (Studies and Observations Group), highly classified reconnaissance teams, made up primarily of indigenous Montagnards that were dispatched across the border to monitor enemy movements along the Ho Chi Minh Trail.

Thirteen years previously, back in February 1954, elite French troops had been outnumbered and virtually wiped out at this northern linchpin of the central highlands. As early as 1961, the very first NVA units to infiltrate into South Vietnam did so through the central highlands along this very same route and initiated attacks against the town of Dak To. More recently, just four months ago, the 173rd Airborne Brigade had tangled with the Twenty-Fourth NVA Regiment around Dak To, losing nearly a hundred soldiers killed in action, but this time there would be an entire NVA division to confront.

The small town of Dak To was about twenty miles north of Kontum, the capital city of the province with a population of 14,000, though we had now moved north of Cambodia, and when we gazed westward, we were now looking across the ridgelines into Laos. The country of Laos shared a common border with North Vietnam, and then formed about a third of South Vietnam's western border in the north, while Cambodia leaned up against the remaining two-thirds of South Vietnam's western border to the south. The French had incorporated the country of Laos into French Indochina during the 1890s, which is the only landlocked country in Southeast Asia, bordering China in the north, Burma and Thailand to the west, Cambodia to the south, and Vietnam to the east.

Laos seemed more menacing than Cambodia because it shared a long common border with North Vietnam of roughly 500 miles, and the NVA had enjoyed free run of eastern Laos for a long time. Laotian communist guerillas, referred to as the Pathet Lao, had been active along the Laotian contiguous border with North Vietnam for the last twenty years. The closer we approached to Laos, the edgier we became. This was Indian country; it was scary here, because the North Vietnamese could engage us where and when they chose, and then they would quickly disperse back across the border into their sanctuaries where we were prohibited from following.

We relieved the Second Battalion of the 503rd Infantry Regiment of the 173rd Airborne Brigade on October 12, and for the ensuing two weeks we were the only battalion in the area of Dak To. It almost reminded me of the Yosemite Valley in California, for it was a narrow valley wreathed by towering mountains, except that everything was dense tropical jungle green, including the jagged mountain peaks. From a distance, Dak To almost appeared as the emerald city of Oz. Our mission was to assist ARVN and Special Forces in the area, as well as securing the Dak To airfield and providing security for engineer road and bridge construction parties that were upgrading four miles of Route 512 that lay between Dak To and the proposed Ben Het Special Forces camp (completed early in 1968) that was located even closer to Laos.

Though unknown to us at the time, the NVA had already dug extensive bunkers throughout the slopes that ascended up out of the valley, and they were waiting for us. One early morning, we moved out on patrol westward through the valley, and then we began to climb up through the thick vegetation on one of the steep slopes that enclosed the valley from three sides. After a short time we found ourselves walking right through an NVA bivouac area of battalion size. It was empty, but cooking fires were still visibly smoldering. The enemy had been cooking their rice and tea less than an hour before. They knew we were here, and so they had faded back into the undergrowth, but they had not run away. They were out there, just beyond the clearing, and they were waiting for us to come to them.

It was spooky, eerie to know that the enemy, in force, was so very close. I noticed that the palms of my hands were sweaty, prescient that we might soon find ourselves in contact with the enemy. Yet even when we were this close to them, we still did not chamber a round. We had bullets in our clips, and the clips in our weapons, but we did not draw a bullet from the clip into the chamber of our weapons until we could see the enemy, or had drawn enemy fire, for we knew that the chances of someone inadvertently failing to ensure that their safety was on, and accidentally firing a round and hitting one of our own men was too high to risk. Back in the States I had observed deer hunters who chambered a round in the midst of their fellow hunters, so that they could improve their chances of getting off a shot at a deer before the animal could spring away, and yet this scenario would only occur in the unlikely event that they might happen to walk up on a deer unobserved. They were idiots, and I don't mean the deer.

Very real comparisons can be drawn between the Battle of the Ia Drang Valley and the Battle of Dak To that was soon to erupt. Both battles were fought in the autumn, at the very end of the monsoon rainy season, though the Battle of the Ia Drang was fought in 1965, whereas the Battle of Dak To was fought in 1967. Both battles were fought up in the western highlands, about ninety miles apart. The Ia Drang battle occurred about forty miles to the southwest of Pleiku, while the Dak To battle was fought in the Annamite mountains of Kontum Province, about fifty miles to the northwest of Pleiku. They were the two largest American battles of the Vietnam War prior to the Tet Offensive that erupted three months later on the thirtieth of January 1968.

We were all aware of the ambush of a battalion of the Seventh Cavalry Regiment in the Ia Drang Valley two years earlier. That was the fear, to step into a situation where you were grossly outnumbered, and then overwhelmed. It was the George Armstrong Custer syndrome, when Custer led this same cavalry regiment into the grassy valley of the Little Big Horn River in present-day Montana, after which he made the unforgivable mistake of splitting his force before continuing on along an open ridge with just one battalion of a little more than two hundred men. They probably felt invincible, for, after all, they were professionals. They no doubt felt that they could take on two or three times their number as they proceeded to head out along the barren grassy ridgeline, where they soon reached a point that afforded them a wide vista of the sprawling Indian encampments below them off to their left, and then the hair on the backs of their necks must have stood up, when they saw countless tepees stretching out into the far distance.

They ruefully observed the Indian warriors gathering on their horses down below them, and then the Indians began to sweep in their direction, like an onrushing stampede. Custer and his men would have counted more than two thousand vengeful Sioux and Cheyenne galloping toward them, and the Indians possessed rifles as well; some even possessed .44 (caliber) Winchester repeating rifles that could fire more rapidly than the .45 Springfield breech-loading carbines of Custer's men.[1] Perhaps, at first, Custer and his men believed that if they could gather together, they might drive the Indians away; but very quickly they realized that the Indians would not be deterred, and so Custer and his men were all stripped of their lives, while suffering gruesome deaths. I doubt that many of them willingly or stoically embraced their immortality.

Although my battalion was the first unit to conduct search-and-destroy missions into the hills to the south of Dak To, where we stumbled upon some of the enemy bunker complexes, the NVA were not yet ready to engage in battle, as they were still in the process of bringing in more regiments, and so they simply permitted us to walk back down the steep jungle slope, unmolested, back to the village of Dak To.

I can only surmise that the NVA were intent upon assembling a division-size force of five full regiments, and that most likely only their lead regiment had arrived on the scene, while their strategic plan called for an entire division to be in place so they could tie up two or three American brigades, rather than just our small undersized battalion.

Since the Fourth Infantry Division was responsible for this area of operations (AOR), it quickly brought up the three battalions of its First Brigade (First of the Eighth, Third of the Eighth, and Third of the Twelfth) from the west of Pleiku to augment our Second Brigade, as well as three battalions from the 173rd Airborne Brigade (the First of the 503rd, Second of the 503rd — the very battalion that we had relieved less than three weeks earlier — and the Fourth of the 503rd). The Fourth Infantry Division also called in two battalions from the First Brigade of the First Cavalry Division.

Ultimately, around 4,500 American troops were involved in the ensuing battle, as well as six ARVN battalions and several CIDG companies led by Green Berets, supported by fifteen batteries of artillery, while the NVA fielded its entire First Division, comprised of four infantry regiments (Twenty-Fourth, Thirty-Second, Sixty-Sixth, and 174th), three of which had their full compliment of 2,500 soldiers, along with one artillery regiment (the Fortieth), as well as one VC battalion (304th), totaling 11,196, although some of these troops were employed for diversionary attacks against the city of Kontum to the south.[2]

As early as the fifteenth of October, intelligence reports had indicated "the build-up of enemy forces in preparation for the Battle of Dak To." October 25 is cited in the After Action Report as the first day of the Battle of Dak To, which states that on this day the "2nd Battalion 8th Infantry conducted operations in Dak To and vicinity." However, after our search-and-destroy missions, our battalion was pulled out of Dak To and deployed westward to take over First Brigade's mission of screening the border area, while fresher units were brought in to Dak To and given the formidable task of storming the NVA bunkers.

When people think about the Battle of Dak To, they tend to focus on the five-day assault up Hill 875 by the Second Battalion of the 503rd Infantry Regiment (of the 173rd Airborne Brigade), during which 113 American soldiers were killed, including around twenty soldiers who died instantly as a result of a direct hit from an errant bomb, dropped by an American plane.[3] Another 170

American soldiers, in addition to those of the Second of the 503rd, were also killed in the battle, which actually consisted of a number of separate engagements that stretched over a period of roughly thirty days. The area of operations around Dak To was the command responsibility of the Fourth Infantry Division, and fatalities of the battle were also sustained by the First and Second Brigades of the Fourth Infantry Division, the First and Fourth Battalions of the 503rd Infantry Regiment of the 173rd Airborne Brigade, and two battalions (one each from the Eighth and Twelfth Cavalry Regiments) of the First Brigade of the First Cavalry Division (Airmobile).[4]

On the third of November the Third of the Twelfth (Fourth Infantry Division), which had just relieved our battalion, found themselves in the first major engagement of the battle, as they clashed with elements of the Thirty-Second NVA Regiment along the ridgelines south of Dak To. The next day, the Third of the Eighth (Fourth Infantry Division) fought off two battalions of the Thirty-Second NVA Regiment, while, further west, the Fourth of the 503rd Airborne (173rd Airborne Brigade) traded fire with elements of the Sixty-Sixth NVA Regiment. During this phase of the fighting, combat was continuous for the next ten days, at the end of which time the Thirty-Second and Sixty-Sixth NVA Regiments began to withdraw to the southwest, while the Twenty-Fourth and 174th NVA Regiments stepped forward and entered into the battle.

On the fifteenth and seventeenth of November, the 304th VC Battalion initiated mortar attacks against the city of Kontum to the south in order to relieve pressure on the NVA regiments fighting around Dak To. On the eighteenth of November the Twenty-Fourth NVA Regiment battled ARVN forces to the northeast of Dak To, which continued on and off for twelve days. Also on the eighteenth of November, the Second Battalion of the 503rd Infantry Regiment (of the 173rd Airborne Brigade) engaged in the battle's largest action, the five-day fight for control of Hill 875, which was stoutly defended by the 174th NVA Regiment. After two days of stubborn fighting to take the hill, the Second Battalion of the 503rd was reinforced by the Fourth Battalion of the 503rd, and they were joined on November 22 by the First Battalion of the Twelfth Infantry Regiment (of the Second Brigade of the Fourth Infantry Division); the hill was finally taken on the twenty-third of November — Thanksgiving Day.

The battle for Hill 875 was a perfect allegory of this war of attrition. It had cost the lives of more than a hundred American soldiers to take the hill, yet once they gained the summit, after the NVA had withdrawn, they promptly vacated the hill, which swiftly turned back into jungle and the domain once again of the NVA.

At the end of the fighting, the Second of the 503rd (173rd Airborne) had suffered 113 KIA, the Third of the Eighth (Fourth Infantry Division) forty-six KIA, the Fourth of the 503rd (173rd Airborne) forty-five KIA, while the First of the 503rd (173rd Airborne) had twenty-four KIAs. The Third of the Twelfth

(Fourth Infantry Division) also had twenty-four KIA, and this was the unit that relieved us just a couple days before the heavy combat began, and they were the first unit to be involved in a major engagement around Dak To. This battalion also suffered 155 wounded, in addition to their comrades that were killed in action, meaning that more than a third of their infantrymen had been either killed or wounded. If they hadn't replaced our battalion just before the fighting erupted, then we would have been in their place. Twelve other American units also suffered KIAs, though in lesser numbers.[5]

Few major battles per se took place during the Vietnam War, because the thick jungle dictated that it be a war fought amongst small-size infantry units, and yet, during its time in Vietnam, the Fourth Infantry Division suffered 17,760 battlefield casualties (either killed or wounded), which was only 4,900 fewer than the Division suffered during its entire involvement in World War II, which included the Division's D-Day assault on the beaches of Normandy, its liberation of Paris, the Battle of the Bulge, and its attack across the Rhine River where they became the first American soldiers to set foot on German soil. And it should be noted that of the ninety-one U.S. Army divisions deployed in all theaters during World War II, the Fourth Infantry Division is ranked third on the list for highest number of battlefield casualties, behind only the Third and Ninth Infantry Divisions, both of which had entered the war in North Africa during November 1942, more than a year and a half before the Fourth Infantry Division stormed ashore on the beaches of Normandy. The battlefield casualties (killed and wounded) sustained by the Fourth Infantry Division in Vietnam would have placed it among the top ten of the ninety-one U.S. Army divisions that fought in World War II.[6] Perhaps with so few major battles in Vietnam, there was less glory than in World War II, where masses of soldiers in division-strength were pitched into battle against the enemy, and cities were liberated with grateful people waving flags, but that did not mean there wasn't a considerable amount of bleeding taking place in Vietnam.

At the end of the bitter fighting around Dak To, the Americans had suffered 283 killed and 1,188 wounded. Our ARVN and CIDG allies suffered sixty-one killed and 253 wounded. The enemy had lost 1,644 killed (verified body count, not estimated) before they were finally forced to withdraw. Much of the success for the enemy's defeat was attributed to "the fact that he was caught while" still "moving toward selected and, in some areas, previously prepared positions" in preparation "for an attack that he calculated would demonstrate his ability to take and hold an area and give him the victory he so desperately needs." After the battle the First of the Eighth uncovered an extensive underground tunnel and cavern complex in the vicinity "with hospital areas along with eating and sleeping facilities."

Major General W. R. Peers, commanding, additionally stated in his *After Action Report—Battle for Dak To* (completed on 3 January 1968) that the "length and violence of the engagement and the overall significance of the battle have made the events that occurred in the vicinity of Dak To, from 2 October [when Fourth Infantry Division "units were having scattered and light contact with reconnaissance and trail watcher parties" as the "NVA were moving large forces into southwest Kontum Province"] to 1 December, the most important that have occurred in the Central highlands since the 1954 Geneva Convention." The After Action Report further surmised that more than 2,000 of the enemy were estimated to have been killed in action, with the Thirty-Second NVA Regiment suffering the greatest number of enemy deaths (600); however, "the difficult terrain and dense vegetation in the area greatly assisted the enemy in his evacuation of casualties," for which the enemy was willing "to risk fresh casualties to police his dead and wounded."[7]

Although the ferocious battle around the small village of Dak To was considered a tactical disaster by the NVA commanders in the field, it was viewed as a strategic success by the NVA High Command, as their primary objective was to draw U.S. troops away from the populated areas in preparation for the Tet Offensive that was scheduled to commence two months later on the thirtieth of January 1968 — the first day of the Vietnamese (and Chinese) lunar New Year, ushering in the year of the Monkey; in this respect the NVA were quite successful.[8]

II

Ultimately the North Vietnamese disengaged from the battle of Dak To by simply slipping back over the border into Laos and Cambodia, where we were forbidden to pursue. I could not physically discern the borders between these countries; they did not appear to be separated by a clearly marked river or highway, but rather by thick mountainous jungle that seemed to stretch out to the west as far as I could see. I suppose the higher ridgeline delineated the border, for the area shown on my map abruptly ended, just out in front of me, reminiscent of the voyages of Columbus, during a time when many people believed that a point would be reached out to the west where one would simply fall off of the edge of the earth, into a deep dark void.

I am certain that the American soldiers who fought in the battles of the Ia Drang and Dak To did not think of these clashes as victories, even though they had inflicted considerable casualties upon the enemy. The American veterans of those engagements acquired a deep respect for the NVA and knew that they were in for one hell of a war. The North Vietnamese had been in a constant state of war for the last twenty-two years, during which time they had fought against the Japanese, then against the colonial French, and now the Americans. They were adept at jungle fighting, for after all this was their environment, and they were undisputedly the best in the world in the art of camouflage.

It was right around this time that Defense Secretary Robert S. McNamara began to have doubts about the ability of the United States to win the war, and he was becoming troubled by the continual escalation of the conflict. He sent a written memo to President Johnson expressing his misgivings about the war, and was fired shortly thereafter.[9] Years later McNamara claimed that President Kennedy himself had begun to have doubts about U.S. involvement in Vietnam and was determined to pull the military advisors out just as soon as he was elected for his second term, which would have commenced nearly three years earlier—during January 1965.[10]

Unfortunately we will never know about this potential turn of history, because Kennedy was assassinated during his first term, after less than three years in office. In one sense, we were not truly at war until after Kennedy was gone, and Johnson had been elected in his own right and began sending combat troops, in large numbers, to Vietnam during the spring and summer of 1965, such that by the end of the year there were 184,000 American military personnel in Vietnam, and this number doubled within just one year, by the end of 1966.

If one considers that South Vietnam was slightly smaller than the State of Florida, and if one realizes that only 22 percent of all the Army soldiers in Vietnam were in combat roles, with the remaining 78 percent providing support, then this meant that during 1965 less than 40,000 soldiers were actually out in the jungle trying to kill the enemy.

Some contend that only 15 percent (versus 22 percent) of the soldiers serving in Vietnam were actually in combat arms (10 percent serving in the infantry, and 5 percent serving in the artillery and armor). However this 15 percent figure does not take into account medics, helicopter pilots, and combat engineers, which many contend should also be added to the mix, so I have elected to stay with 22 percent as being a realistic, albeit conservative, percentage of those soldiers in Vietnam at any given time that were considered to have served in combat roles.[11] I have heard of people using higher ratios than 4 to 1 in referring to support troops, some have used ratios as high as 9 to 1, but I assume they must be focusing on the 10 percent infantry figure, whereas I consider the 4-to-1 ratio as being more realistic, based on the 22 percent figure of soldiers serving in combat roles. In addition to the three combat branches (Infantry, Armor, and Artillery), the Army has thirteen other branches (Air Defense Artillery, Adjutant General Corps [admin], Aviation, Chemical Corps, Corps of Engineers, Finance Corps, Medical Service Corp [of which its medics served in the field with the infantry], Military Intelligence, Military Police Corps, Ordnance, Quartermaster Corps [supply], Signal Corps, and Transportation) as well as some additional specialties, such as chaplains and lawyers (Judge Advocate General's Corps).

If only 22 percent of the Army troops who served in Vietnam were in combat roles, then, for every soldier out in the jungle seeking to engage the enemy, there were four REMFs (rear-echelon motherfuckers) in the rear providing support by driving trucks or working as clerks or supply guys, and those guys might pull some guard duty around the division base camp perimeter, but the fact of the matter is that of all the Army soldiers who actually went to Vietnam, only about one in five was out in the field hunting the enemy, and if you take away the medics, helicopter pilots, and engineers from this mix, then only about one in seven soldiers in Vietnam was actually in the combat arms.

Now, during November 1967, approximately 107,000 combat troops were out in the jungle (again this is probably a high number), which was increased by an additional 10 percent during 1968, and another 1 percent during the spring of 1969, after which the numbers began to decline, but even 107,000 or 118,000 combat troops was still an insufficient number to win a war in a jungle country that stretched more than 600 miles in length from north to south, and averaged more than 100 miles in width from east to west. In any case, the war in Vietnam became a war of attrition in which each side was simply trying to wear down the other side by bleeding them dry; it was death by a thousand cuts (Ling Chi), the old Chinese torture method, employed by the Song Dynasty of a thousand years ago, whereby small bits of flesh were cut out of the victim over a period of days, during which the torturers went to great lengths to prolong the victim's agony prior to death.

I have seen bodies that had lain out in the tropical sun for just a day or two and the skin had turned a purple-black color, as though they had been burned, and they were bloated to nearly twice their size, looking like plump sausages, as though, at any moment they might burst open and their entrails would spew forth. Only their uniforms, encasing these human sausages, appeared to keep the skins from bursting. Of course you could smell these putrefied bodies before you saw them, perhaps a quarter of a mile away, or more if a breeze was blowing. I have seen dead bodies on stretchers, stacked up eight high in a 2½-ton truck. I have seen things I wish I had never seen.

Death could assume many forms, from terrorized rictus to placid repose. One day we received enemy fire against our unprotected left flank, which compelled us to hit the ground and respond with a fusillade of automatic weapons fire as well as grenades. Afterwards, as we combed the jungle out to our front following the engagement, we came across an enemy dead who appeared to be serenely sleeping on his side. He was wearing shorts, an opened green cotton shirt and sandals, and I could discern no visible blood. He had been down just a moment, so he still had some color, though he was beginning to turn pasty. I felt that if I just bent down and assisted in helping him up, that he would just spring to his feet, but he remained in peaceful repose, and then I observed a tiny puncture wound, just below his ribcage, but I could find no exit hole, so the bullet must have hit a rib bone or two, and then ricocheted around his insides, slicing up his internal organs, and I could see, as we turned him onto his back, that his intestines were starting to spill out from the puncture wound, and that it was evident that he had given up the ghost and departed the world of the living. His animated spirit was no longer evident in the body; it had departed, somewhere, leaving behind just an inanimate hunk of flesh. It could very well have been my bullet that did the damage, for we were all exchanging fire.

It's strange that some people can suffer the most devastating shocks, including traumatic amputations, with their legs being ripped from their bodies by a land mine, yet still survive, while others receive what appears to be a pinprick, and yet it sucks the life right out of them. Who can understand what keeps the animate spirit living within the body? With what tenacity does the spirit hold on to life? Does the spirit feel pain and suffering? From what I have seen, I'm inclined to say yes.

8

From the Perspective of Our Under-Strength Platoons

I

During the Vietnam War the military was enamored by statistics, with the result that the enemy body count became the most critical determinate of the Defense Department for evaluating the progress of the war. This emphasis on statistics was attributed to Robert S. McNamara who had been appointed Secretary of Defense by President John F. Kennedy back in January 1961, a position McNamara held for more than seven years, until February 1968.

McNamara had been born in San Francisco and obtained his undergraduate degree in economics from the University of California at Berkeley in 1937 before proceeding on to the Harvard Business School where he obtained his MBA (Master's in Business Administration).

After university, McNamara served as an officer during World War II, mostly doing statistical studies in support of the air war in Japan, after which he joined the Ford Motor Company where he worked for fourteen years, rising to become president of the company, a position he held for only six weeks before being asked by President Kennedy to serve as his Secretary of Defense, for Kennedy was highly impressed by this self-made man.

It was while at Harvard that McNamara embraced the theory of statistical control that he applied so assiduously to decision-making at the Pentagon. Over time this statistical approach proved to be flawed, at least insofar as assessing the progress of the war, because statistics failed to adequately take into account the human element, the human spirit, and the will to prevail. In any case, the body count was not really the most important statistic for the generals running the show.

The most critical statistic for the generals back in Saigon at MACV Headquarters was the kill ratio. After all, this was a war of attrition where there were no front lines or geographical objectives. The goal was simply to wear down the other side by killing as many of them as possible. Of course, our colonels incessantly hammered on us to increase our body count, but the generals back in Saigon were looking at another set of numbers to determine which side was winning or losing the war of attrition; they were looking at kill ratios.

For example, the ROK (Republic of [South] Korea) troops had the highest kill ratio of any troops that were fighting the communists in Vietnam, achieving a laudatory kill ratio of 11 to 1, meaning that the ROKs were killing eleven enemy soldiers for each South Korean soldier killed by the enemy.[1] The Koreans began arriving in Vietnam during September 1965 and they fought until the end of the American presence — into 1973. More than 300,000 ROK soldiers served in Vietnam during which time they suffered 4,687 killed.[2] We Americans, on the other hand, were only killing five of the enemy for each American soldier killed; consequently, with our measly kill ratio of 5 to 1, we were constantly exhorted to do a better job at getting our numbers up. I do not think the NVA were overly concerned about the kill ratio, for they were a very patient people, and whether they were losing five, eight, or eleven of their men for every American they killed; they seemed to feel that this was a tolerable price to pay in order to achieve final victory.

II

Of course, we had dominance of the air, and our strikes included both conventional and napalm bombing. Napalm was simply jellied gasoline that could suck all the oxygen out of the air and turn most everything in its wake into crispy critters. Napalm was invented in a chemical laboratory at Harvard University during World War II, and then manufactured by the Dow Chemical Company in Delaware (which was also the largest producer of the herbicide Agent Orange). Napalm was used in both the European and Pacific theaters during World War II, and its first use in Vietnam was by the French back in 1950.

Ever since the federal government enlisted the support of universities to develop the atomic bomb during World War II, it had continued to provide more and more money to universities for governmental research projects, of which a significant portion was devoted to military applications. Harvard University has been perennially among the top ten universities receiving federal research funds, such that by 1968 nearly 40 percent of Harvard's income was provided by the federal government, and this is saying a lot when you consider that Harvard benefits from one of the largest endowments of any American university.[3] Critics began to claim that many universities had been co-opted by the federal government, as more and more of their government research grant monies were allocated for weapons development programs in concert with defense contractors. Back in 1961, President Dwight D. Eisenhower, in his last public radio speech, alerted the American public and its political leaders to beware of undue influence exerted by a powerful new relationship between defense industries and the military establishment, which he termed the military-industrial complex.

The North Vietnamese did possess some air assets, for they were supplied with MiG-19s by the Chinese and MiG-21s by the Soviets, both supersonic fighters, and they were also supplied with thousands of surface to air missiles (SAMs) that posed a serious threat to American flyers. The MiG-21 was lighter and more maneuverable than the American fighters, although the American McDonnell Douglas F-4 Phantom was generally considered the superior fighter jet during the Vietnam War. MiGs were designed in the Soviet Union by Artem *Mi*koyan and Mikhail *G*urevich, of which they simply utilized the acronym "MiG" for their design bureau.

In any case, the North Vietnamese seemed willing to lose half a million or more soldiers, while we started becoming concerned when our American death toll climbed above 30,000 during May 1968 (reaching 36,956 by the end of the year).[4] Though enemy casualty numbers were difficult to pin down with any accuracy, a senior officer in Hanoi, after the war, disclosed that "nearly a million" North Vietnamese and Vietcong soldiers were killed during the war, along with "millions" of soldiers wounded, and this assessment did not even factor in civilian casualties.[5]

Most everyone with whom I was associated in combat did his duty. I never saw a man break and run, but, then again, where was one to run? In Vietnam, where there were no frontlines, the enemy was all around us. Still, those men who stood their ground under fire gained my deepest respect. It is a challenge to take a young American, who is the most independent person, and instill within him a military discipline. However, once trained, he is a fierce soldier, big and strong, extremely confident, exceptionally aggressive — a very tough adversary.

The military successes of the early Roman Empire were due to its citizen soldiers, and so it was with the American citizen soldiers who tended to fight more tenaciously than any mercenary. This might be a point to take into consideration in assessing the merits of an all-volunteer "professional" military. The Greeks and the Romans aptly demonstrated that one will fight more resolutely for an abstract idea or belief than for tangible pieces of silver. I'm certainly not inferring that the American "professional" soldiers of today are mercenaries, for they are obviously not paid enough for that descriptor. Most European countries still mandate that all their young men serve a compulsory military obligation; in this regard they are actually more democratic than we are, because currently the young men attending elite universities in our country are no longer required to serve in our nation's military; rather, for the most part, they are out advancing their careers and making money, while the ranks of the U.S. military are now generally filled by young men and women from the working class who are looking to feed their families.

Ironically, three-quarters of U.S. forces who served in Vietnam were volunteers, while only 24.53 percent (648,500) were drafted, and yet draftees suffered 30.4 percent (17,725) of the 58,220 deaths in Vietnam, which indicates that many draftees ended up in the infantry. Surprisingly, during World War II two-thirds of those who served were draftees.[6] The Fourth Infantry Division, which assaulted the beaches of Normandy during World War II, was "composed overwhelmingly of draftees," and they indisputably did a pretty good job.[7] However, these statistics pertaining to Vietnam are misleading, because virtually all of the men who received their draft notices or notices for their draft physicals were then offered the opportunity to enlist, and by enlisting for one additional year they could then choose the job they would do, and so many of these inductees enlisted in order to escape the infantry; instead they volunteered to become cooks and truck drivers.

Also, quite a few young men who had run into trouble with the law were given the option of either going to jail or enlisting in the Army, and many of these men elected to enter the military. Additionally, many people might not be aware of the fact that 42,633 men were drafted into the Marine Corps, which prompted quite a few men who had received notices to report for their induction physicals, to quickly enlist in the Army so as to avoid being drafted by the Marines where they faced the virtual certainty of becoming combat infantrymen.[8] As a consequence, scores of men who served in the military during the Vietnam War, in addition to those who were formally classified as draftees, did so because they had received a notice from their draft board or were coerced into joining, and yet all of the soldiers that I knew did their duty.

One way to avoid the draft and the distinct probability of being sent to Vietnam was to join the National Guard, which had historically developed from the days of our colonial militia, or Minute Men as they were called in those days. The National Guard advertises itself as a dual state and federal force, though the Constitution (Article II, Section II, clause 1) stipulates that "the President shall be Commander in Chief of the Army and Navy of the United States, and of the Militia (National Guard) of the several States." Throughout the 1800s the size of the regular Army was very small, which compelled the federal government to rely on the states' militias to augment the Army during times of war. The militia was renamed the National Guard in 1903 and was considered a reserve force of the Army.

During World War I, the National Guard supplied seventeen combat divisions to the war effort, which constituted 40 percent of the American Expeditionary Force in France and included the famed Rainbow (Forty-Second) Division that was an amalgamation of National Guard units from twenty-six states. During World War II the National Guard supplied eighteen combat divisions to the fight, and during the Korean War the National Guard provided eight combat divisions.[9] So what was the story of the National Guard during the Vietnam War?

The National Guard was nearly half a million soldiers strong during the Vietnam War, and yet President Johnson chose not to mobilize the National Guard for overseas service in Vietnam, relying instead exclusively on the draft.

A recent Army War College research paper states, "President Johnson made a conscious decision not to mobilize the National Guard. This was based on his assessment that mobilizing the National Guard would signal intentions to the Soviets and Chinese that might influence their direct intervention in the war. President Johnson did not want a repeat of Korea when China entered the conflict, nor did he want to spark another world war involving both communist superpowers."[10]

Only after the commencement of the Tet Offensive in late January 1968 did President Johnson belatedly activate some National Guard units. However, of the 2,644,000 servicemen and women sent into harm's way in Vietnam (50,000 up through 1964, and then 2,594,000 between 1965 and March 1973 when the war really kicked in), only 7,040 were from the Army National Guard, which constituted a miniscule proportion of the American troops sent off to the war.[11]

Oftentimes the National Guard is referred to as the Governor's Army, because each state has its own Guard units, which the president can order into federal service at his discretion. President Johnson was conspicuously reluctant to activate the National Guard during the Vietnam War, such that many young men, including many college graduates with connections, flocked to the National Guard, knowing that this would preclude them from being drafted into the regular Army and sent off to the war. Perhaps Johnson also felt that calling up the Guard for overseas duty in Vietnam would precipitate bitter debate within Congress over this undeclared war that he was able to expand via increased war-making powers granted to him by the Tonkin Gulf Resolution, for Johnson was well aware of the fact that any public discussion of the war within Congress, as well as the dispatch of hundreds of thousands of National Guard soldiers to Vietnam, would be acerbic.

It seemed sadly laughable to those of us in our under-strength platoons in Vietnam that the Guard was permitted to stay at home, apparently to guard our nation's shores against a highly unlikely foreign invasion. The president and the politicians repeatedly refused the requests of the military brass to call the National Guard into national service so as to supplement the Regular Army that was fighting for its life in Vietnam.

From the perspective of our undermanned foxholes, it seemed to us that the politicians back home were more concerned about safeguarding the promising futures of America's young men of privilege, who were attending our nation's top universities, than those of us who had left school to go out and work for a living. One would have thought that those university men represented the crème de là crème of our country's potential leaders, except in this case they were essentially exempted from having to go off to war so long as they remained in school, or joined the National Guard, which generally required political connections. We in our soggy foxholes no longer considered these young men of privilege the crème de là crème of anything, except the road less hazardous. They seemed so unlike the young men of my father's generation who were impatient to graduate from university so they could rush to join the colors and serve their country during World War II; for it was precisely the university men, our nation's best and brightest, who traditionally formed the cornerstone of our country's officer corps in time of war.

Perhaps this war in Southeast Asia was different. After all the United States had not been attacked, and so when the draft was in effect for the Vietnam War, many young men took full advantage of the college deferment loophole to avoid the draft, and then, when they did graduate, they made concerted efforts to join the National Guard in order to avoid being sent off to the war.

During the Vietnam War, young men with university educations, political connections, and high social standing, could, and did, exert influence to have governors, senators or congressmen sponsor them into their state's Guard units, knowing that this would keep them out of the war. This was the allegation often attributed to Dan Quayle, who served as the vice president under George H. W. Bush, and to Bill Clinton, who successfully ran for president in 1992.

George W. Bush, whose father was a U.S. Congressman at the time, was viewed as a young man of privilege who was able to gain entry into the Texas National Guard (in 1968), and was therefore not subject to being drafted into the regular Army for overseas duty in Vietnam. Even Dick Cheney, who had attended Yale for a short while before ultimately graduating from the University of Wyoming in 1965, applied for, and was granted, 3-A status (deferred because of hardship to dependents) during January 1966, when his wife was in early pregnancy, and thus was not required to serve in the military. Two contemporary politicians, as well as men of privilege, did suit up and place themselves in harm's way: John Kerry (Yale) arrived in Vietnam as a Navy lieutenant a year and a half after me, while Al Gore (Harvard) joined the Army and went to Vietnam four years after me.

Bill Clinton (Georgetown University, then Oxford, then Yale Law School), George W. Bush (Yale), real estate mogul Donald Trump (University of Pennsylvania), and I were all the same age. Actually they were all a little older than I by a couple months or so, though we were each dealing with our military obligations in one way or another, although these men of privilege certainly had more choices than I did, for they were not drafted into the Army as soon as they turned nineteen. Instead, they derived full benefit from their college deferments, and so they had the luxury of postponing their military obligations for several more years, until such time as they had graduated from their prestigious universities around the age of twenty-two.

Actually Bill Clinton did not grow up with the proverbial silver spoon in his mouth, and his father died three months before he was born, but he was so smart that his meteoric rise to the top appeared virtually effortless. I'm not necessarily judging these men of privilege or of innate brilliance, for with all of their gifts I expected them to make a significant contribution to society; I would have been disappointed if they had not. However, of the four of us, I was the only one who could no longer afford to remain in school, and thus I was the only one to leave school at the age of eighteen and head out into the world in search of work. I soon landed a job in the merchant marine, from which I was scooped up by the Army shortly after I turned nineteen. I had already been in the Army for nearly two and a half years, and fighting in Vietnam for more than nine months, before Bill, George, and Donald were even donning their caps and gowns for the graduation ceremonies at their prestigious universities.

It was hard to say how my recently acquired skills in killing would serve me in the future, or how they would affect my re-entry back into the world. In any event, my men and I were not among those privileged few whose futures were destined for lofty heights. Deep in our foxholes, our dreams did not ascend so high; we simply hoped to get out of this war alive. We were just your average Joes, and we were starkly aware of that fact. Still, we felt ourselves no less significant than the privileged few on their ivy-covered campuses. We each had an immeasurable depth of pride from whence we came, and we unequivocally knew that we were in another type of school altogether, being in the Ivy Division was much tougher and less forgiving than any school in the Ivy League. Those Ivy Leaguers may have thought that they had it tough, yet they had no idea of what tough was, for they had never been scared shitless while under fire.

In our school of hard knocks, the most profound lessons of life were being dispensed. In our school, selfish ambition was set aside, camaraderie ascended to the fore, men pulled together for their very survival, and the deepest bonds of brotherhood were forged in the jaws of death, and the death of each one of our buddies felt as though a piece of flesh had been torn from our own living bodies. We knew that back home, many of our contemporaries thought of us as losers, dropouts without much future, such that we no doubt deserved our lot in life, to be huddling out here together in the mud of our foxholes, in the ceaseless rain, with a rifle in our hands. Still, for all of that, we remained proud of who we were. I never heard anyone in my unit use the expression FNG (fucking new guy) in referring to new replacements. We respected anybody who showed up with a rifle in his hands.

We knew very well that many of those ensconced in their comfortable suburbs back home had not the slightest idea of what we were going through; they could not empathize with us at all. They were already distancing themselves from the dispossessed who make up the great mass of humanity. Oh, we were much closer to humanity, virtually nose to nose, such that we had already learned a great deal about loyalty, sacrifice, and camaraderie, as well as the most important lesson of all—that every single life lost diminishes us.

> No man is an Island, entire of it self: every man is a
> piece of the Continent, a part of the main; if a clod

> be washed away by the sea, Europe is the less, as
> well as if a promontory were, as well as if a manor
> of thy friends or of thine own were; any man's
> death diminishes me, because I am involved in
> Mankind; And therefore never send to know for
> whom the bell tolls; it tolls for thee.[12]

Even during our Civil War, there were always young men of wealth or influence who were not inclined to risk their lives in time of war, and who would use their money or connections to have others take their places; this was nothing new. Though there had been conscription as far back as our War of Independence, it was the Confederates who first turned to the draft during the Civil War in 1862, followed shortly thereafter by the Federals during March 1863, and the draft has been invoked in every subsequent American war up through Vietnam, after which the United States relied exclusively on volunteers (professionals?) to fight its wars.[13]

In any event, during the Vietnam War the National Guard was an attractive alternative to those young men confronting the draft who did not want to be sent off to war and face the risk of being killed. Could I really blame them? Many of my acquaintances took this route and joined California's Guard units, and most of them were extremely self-congratulatory about their shrewdness, boasting to me how they would now be exempt from being shipped off to the war and needlessly risking their lives ... for their country. I did not envy them, for they still had been compelled to look in the mirror and face their fears, and they knew the choice they had made, which would trail them throughout their lives. My mind was not clouded, for I had peered into the abyss and confronted my fears. Perhaps I was simply a victim of circumstance, but I was nevertheless willing to risk my life for my country. The U.S. Coast Guard is also an armed force, though it is not part of the Department of Defense; rather it was part of the Department of Transportation at the time, and yet the Coast Guard deployed fifty-six Coast Guard cutters and crews to Vietnam, which approximated the entire Army National Guard contribution.

The draft ended in February 1973, after which the United States transitioned to an "all-volunteer" Army, Air Force, Navy and Marine Corps, sometimes referred to as a *professional* military. I wonder how many rich boys have joined the all-volunteer military. I suspect very few. Let's see: a choice between putting your life at risk for relatively low pay and long hours, or staying back in the world and living the fat life, while driving the big car. Now that certainly seems like a tough decision for the privileged class, when confronted with the prospect of being sent into harm's way.

I suppose one benefit of the all-volunteer military that evolved after the Vietnam War was that there was no longer any qualms about sending the National Guard off to war, but then again the National Guard had always been an all-volunteer force; it's just that during the Vietnam War, with the draft in place, the Guard, for arguable reasons, was not being deployed overseas, and therefore the motivation to volunteer for the Guard was so very intense that even young men of privilege were lining up to join. Nowadays, the Guard, just like the regular Army, is primarily comprised of young men from working-class backgrounds. Some might have college degrees, but I do not suspect there are many volunteers from the elite and private Ivy League universities. In fact, during current times, only four of the eight Ivy League campuses even offer on-campus ROTC (Reserve Officers' Training Corps) programs, and for two of those the training is contracted out to other universities. Even the radical, though public, University of California at Berkeley maintains an on-campus ROTC program.

III

At times my platoon was sent a kilometer (a little more than half a mile) out ahead of the company. My CO called it reconnoitering, but the truth of the matter was that we were being served up as bait. When my small platoon of around thirty soldiers, well below its full strength of forty-four, was sent out of sight and hearing of the rest of the company, we were perceived as easy pickin's by the enemy. The object of these tactics was to encourage the enemy to attack our small unit, which would thus concentrate the enemy in a fixed location so they would be easier to destroy. This tactical theory was based on the assumption that before the enemy could overrun us, the rest of our company was supposed to rush to our rescue and support (reinforce) us.

I knew that I was ordered forward as bait, and my men knew that they were being used as bait; nobody was happy about that, yet those were the orders, and there was no thought of disobeying those orders, at least not overtly. You couldn't say, "Hell no! I'm not doing that," for this was a war zone and any disobedience of orders would enact swift retribution, court martial and all. Still, it was aggravating to be sacrificially placed in harm's way; this was probably somewhat how my soldiers felt toward me when I ordered them to take point. After all, our job was to find, fix, and kill the enemy.

Still, even as an under-strength platoon of thirty soldiers, we felt that we were a bunch of intrepid warriors who would bring down a whole lotta hurt on anyone who tried to mess with us. We had the pride of the infantry; we were ready to kill. We were fearless, believing that the thirty of us could easily hold off an enemy battalion. No one bragged about holding off an enemy regiment, which at full strength for the NVA totaled 2,500 soldiers; then the men were not so braggadocio. I suppose that if our little platoon were attacked by a regiment, then we would probably feel somewhat like Custer, when he found himself surrounded by as many Indians, at which time he probably said to himself, "Oh, shit!"

I've been on the receiving end of incoming artillery, and during those moments I felt even more helpless than when I was caught in an ambush where I could at least fight back. With incoming artillery, the discordant noise of the exploding shells is terrifying and deafening, as the steel-taloned shrapnel rips through the foliage, cutting and slicing its way through the thickest bamboo as well as softer human flesh. The exploding shell fragments become rough, twisted, burning-hot, jagged steel missiles that can have the most devastating effect when they tear through tissue and bone.

Even with our own artillery there was the occasional short round that would spew shrapnel through our own positions, which was why we never called for friendly artillery to be fired directly over our heads unless we were being overrun. There was a story told amongst the infantrymen of an artillery forward observer at our battalion headquarters who was up on his feet observing the strike of artillery rounds that he had called in when, suddenly, a shell fragment tore through the air and ripped through his throat; he died drowning in his own blood, from a shell that he had summoned.

However, with incoming artillery there is only one sensible thing to do, and that is to hit the ground and squeeze yourself into your steel pot (helmet), after which you need to get your own mortars into action, and then it becomes an artillery duel, because the most effective way to suppress incoming artillery fire is with counter-battery fire. However, if we were not able to suppress the incoming enemy artillery rounds with our own mortars, then we would call in our big guns, the 105 and 155 howitzers, and if they could not suppress the enemy fire, then we would call in air strikes, or on a couple occasions, when the enemy was too close to our positions to risk artillery or air, we would call for Puff the Magic Dragon, which was a Douglas AC-47 (antecedent of the venerable DC-3), armed with mini-guns that could devastatingly tear up exposed enemy soldiers.

A howitzer is nothing more than a cannon that is capable of firing shells in a relatively high trajectory. Our standard artillery support consisted of 105mm light howitzers, which could throw a shell nearly seven miles with quite good accuracy, and had pretty much replaced the 75mm howitzers within infantry divisions during World War II. We also relied on the 155mm howitzer that had an even greater range, and had been around since World War I, for it could fire a shell about nine miles; however, we did not consider the 155 to be as accurate as the 105, though perhaps it was simply because the blast from a 155 shell eviscerated an area more than a hundred yards in diameter, which made it somewhat hazardous for close-in support, for which we definitely preferred the 105s. A 105mm shell could kill most anyone standing within thirty yards of the blast, and a 155mm shell could kill most anyone standing within fifty-five yards of its blast. Rarely would we move out from beyond our artillery umbrella, which was the range at which our artillery could cover us, and, in reality, we were even more limited by the range of our prick-25 radios that had a range of three miles when used with the customary three-foot steel tape antenna, though we could relay our artillery requirements through our battalion arty LNO, who had longer range communication capabilities because he was generally in a fixed location. If we were not on the move, in a stationary position, we could employ a collapsible ten-foot fishpole whip antenna that could boost a transmission to five miles, and even as far as seven miles if the atmospheric conditions and terrain were just right.

You don't have much time to hit the ground when you sense incoming artillery. Perhaps you thought you heard the thump of a mortar round being expelled from a mortar tube, and yet you did not want to appear the fool and be the only one to hit the ground in case you had misinterpreted the threat, but if you did not drop, then you faced a higher chance of dying. New recruits were slow to drop, and therefore they were invariably the first to die. This is the reason why many combat veterans returning to the States from Vietnam would invariably flinch or hit the ground whenever they heard a car backfire; it had become a form of instinctive behavior that meant the difference between living and dying. It was as simple as that, and sometimes one's adversity toward appearing the fool, by falling to the ground, resulted in a death that could have been averted.

In war, death is always proximal, hanging over one's shoulder, waiting for a vulnerability to present itself. Perhaps this is the reality of life — that death is always stalking nearby, waiting to claim us in a moment when our vigilance has been relaxed. There are no guarantees in life, and our lives can end at any moment. Consequently, we should live each moment to the fullest, or at least to the point that if we were gone tomorrow, we would have few regrets. I suppose that was the lesson — to make the most of our lives, and to live each moment as though it were our last. We the living are blessed to be here, especially when so many of our comrades have endured the ultimate sacrifice and are here no more.

I knew young men who were killed in Vietnam before they had ever made love with a woman, or been able to legally drink a beer, or even voted; it took another four years before Congress approved the twenty-sixth Amendment to the Constitution that lowered the voting age from twenty-one to eighteen, though twenty-one persisted as the legal drinking age in most States. If I could be drafted into the military at the age of eighteen or nineteen and die in the service of my country, then shouldn't I have the right to vote?

9

The Montagnards

I

I worked from time to time with the Montagnards, the aboriginal tribesmen who inhabited the rugged mountainous interior of Vietnam where some of the mountains ascended higher than 6,000 feet, which did not make them world class, but high enough that it became noticeably cold at night. People in California skied at this elevation at Squaw Valley, but this close to the equator there was no snow at this altitude. The word *montagnard* is of French origin and simply means a mountain person, for the French also apply this word to describe Europeans who live in the mountains. However, the Vietnamese viewed the Montagnards as an inferior race of people, and this was one of the main reasons why the Montagnards were so willing to ally themselves with the Americans. The Montagnards detested the Vietnamese, and they were readily willing to kill Vietnamese from both the North and the South, as they really did not trouble themselves to make the distinction between the two, because they had been persecuted by all Vietnamese, long before Vietnam was split in two. The Vietnamese had come up into the highlands with the French during colonial times, and their highland cities had continued to expand, driving the Montagnards ever further out into the bush.

Many of the Montagnards still hunted and fought with bows and arrows, and wore loincloths, though they were gifted trackers in the jungle, though it's not so difficult to track human beings, for they are messy animals. The Montagnards, who tracked and killed wild animals with bows and arrows in the jungle for their daily sustenance, could easily track humans who oftentimes don't even bother to bury their own feces. Some humans will just leave their shit lying about, steaming in the jungle; I mean, even a cat is not that stupid.

Humans also smoke, and instead of field-stripping their cigarettes, which entails pocketing the filter and dispersing the remaining tobacco, humans tend to simply toss their cigarette butts into the jungle, thus permitting the enemy to come along, count the butts, estimate the size of the force that had passed that way, and plan accordingly. Americans do not always bury their empty food cans, which is another way to track them, though of course this did not apply to the North Vietnamese because they did not eat food out of cans; rather, they just carried a little rice with them, to which they added any protein they happened to come across.

Humans build cooking fires, but do not always eradicate the fire sites before departing the area, thus enabling the pursuing enemy to estimate their number. Additionally, unwashed humans emanate a beastly smell, and they make a lot of noise, even when they are striving to be quiet; they continually cough or sneeze, and they like to open their mouths and talk; in essence, they are the easiest mammal to track and kill. It has been said that humans are the only mammals that can abide living in their own filth. It was truly astonishing that humans had not already become an endangered species, though once they began developing extremely efficient killing tools they were able to take control of the planet to the point where their only natural enemy was themselves.

The North Vietnamese, after more than twenty years of continual fighting, had at least learned how to bury their feces and effectively camouflage their uniforms with foliage to increase their chances of survival. They knew how to conceal their foxholes so they would not become an easy target for a grenade. They had learned the importance of burying their garbage, and they took great care in moving silently through the jungle. Of course, unlike us, they were serving for the duration, while most of us were serving for just twelve months in the war zone.

It generally takes about six months to learn the ropes in any new environment, although in war there is a much greater incentive to learn the lessons faster. An Army private comes to Vietnam with less than a year of training, a little more for an officer; it does not require years to train an infantry soldier, for the skills of the infantryman are fundamental and essentially timeless. One is taught how to fire and clean weapons, discipline is instilled, some basic first aid skills are provided, along with some small unit tactics, and then one is ready to go; the training is not rocket science. So after a little less than six months of training in the States, an enlisted soldier is sent off to the war where essentially he has less than a month to get it together and hopefully survive his first under-fire combat experience, and then after about six months of war, the survivors are considered veterans; this is pretty much how it has been in most all wars. After participating in combat for at least two months, an infantryman, whether officer or enlisted, is entitled to wear the Combat Infantryman's Badge (CIB), fabricated out of silver, consisting of a three-inch-long blue rectangle upon which a silver musket is overlaid, enclosed within a silver oak wreath, to be worn above one's award and campaign ribbons. This was an infantry soldier's most coveted award, for it exhibited, for all the world to see, that this infantryman had been under fire and survived combat.

However, for the North Vietnamese soldier, a year in the war zone was no time at all in a relative sense. I suspect that the North Vietnamese soldiers received about the same basic infantry training as did we before they were sent south. Then after about two to three years of combat experience they probably considered themselves veterans. Perhaps they had more experience of killing and surviving than I, but they were not indomitable, and they were still human beings who still had difficulty keeping their mouths shut; they continued to enjoy cooked food from time to time, and so they too built fires, and like most humans who sweated into their clothing in the hot humid jungle, they stank.

The reek of humans cannot be confused with any other animal. Like a French perfume a human's stench will linger; it can hang in the air for half an hour or more after the human has left the area, if the stink is real ripe. No other animal that walks the earth smells as bad after death as a human. In the case of a dead person, you can smell him a quarter of a mile away, depending on his state of decomposition, and if there are a lot of dead people, then you can smell them up to a half-mile away, and the smell is such a putrid and unmistakable reek that it lingers in the nostrils for hours afterwards, and in the memory cells of the brain for eternity.

II

It seemed sadly tragic that the Montagnards were caught up in this killing business, for they were truly a noble people who would not lie or steal, nor would they permit outsiders to get close to their women. They didn't ask for much, they were not overtly materialistic; they just wanted to live a peaceful life and raise their families. It was a far different experience working with the Montagnards than working with the Vietnamese who seemed to be more materialistic, self-serving, and cynical.

I found the Montagnard women so beguiling in their natural innocence, for though they wore wraps around their loins, above their waists they were completely uninhibited in their bare-breasted nakedness. To be talking and flirting with a young, pretty, half-naked woman, who for eons had known no other way of being, conjured up images of pre-Biblical times, which existed only in the recesses of my imagination, evoking within me some enchanting apparition of the Garden of Eden.

These indigenous peoples of the central highlands were comprised of half a dozen different ethnic groups, totaling around 700,000 people, the largest being the Jarai, numbering around 250,000, followed by the Rhade, Bahnar, Koho, Mnong and, smallest of them all, the Stieng with a population of about 60,000. The mountainous jungle region of the central highlands was their country.[1] By 1967 the Vietnamese population of South Vietnam had reached nearly seventeen million, and yet there were probably less than a quarter million Vietnamese, excluding the military, residing up in the Central Highlands at this time.[2]

These Montagnards from the central highlands were ethnically different from the hill tribes further north, such as the Hmong, whose language is of Chinese origin, while the languages of the central highland Montagnards have been traced back to the Malayo-Polynesian and the Mon-Khmer language groups, which suggests that eons ago these tribes had originated in Indonesia and Malaysia before migrating northward into these verdant mountainous jungles of central Vietnam.

The Malayo-Polynesian (Indonesian) language group included the Jarai and the Rhade, while the Mon-Khmer (Malaysian) language group included the Bahnar, Koho, Mnong, and Stieng. Most of my dealings were with the Jarai, Rhade, and the Bahnar who lived out to the west, along the Cambodian and Laotian borders. The Vietnamese arrived much later and had originally journeyed out of China in various migratory waves. The Chinese had ruled Vietnam for a thousand years before the Vietnamese ultimately gained their independence more than a thousand years ago, in A.D. 938.

Physically, the Montagnards were darker skinned than the Vietnamese, and they did not have epicanthic folds around their eyes. I met a thirteen-year-old Rhade Montagnard boy who carried an old French carbine nearly as tall as he, keeping in mind that carbines are even shorter than rifles, as they were originally designed for use by cavalry who needed weapons that were easier to handle while astride their horses. In any case, the young Montagnard boy and I were talking and I was surprised to learn that he was already a sergeant. His ascendance through the ranks had been based strictly on merit; he had already killed eight enemy soldiers, although I did not think he differentiated between Vietnamese from the north or Vietnamese from the south, for he considered all Vietnamese as foes. I had not individually killed eight of the enemy, except perhaps indirectly from the artillery I had called in, but then this thirteen-year-old sergeant had been fighting a lot longer than I.

It's a fact that most nations prefer to put their young men into uniform. The United States required its young men to register at the age of eighteen, and drafted them into the Army at the age of eighteen or nineteen. These young men were then provided with about six months of training before being sent off to war, where they would fight and die, for that is the indisputable reality of war.

Countries generally do not draft forty-year-old men, or even thirty-year-olds for that matter; fighting and dying for one's country is a duty imposed upon young men, still boys for the most part. Besides, young men of eighteen and nineteen provide the choicest malleable clay from which the most obedient soldiers are formed, and they feel invincible, as only the young can truly feel. By the time a man marries and fathers children, he begins to think too much, realizing that he now has something to lose, and thus he tends to relinquish his inclination to be a hero. Moreover, fighting in hot, clammy, tropical jungle sucks so much out of a person that even those sergeants back in the States who were in their thirties could no longer effectively hump the boonies; they would only slow us down. War is a young man's business.

One afternoon my platoon was sent out on patrol away from the rest of the company. It was so unbearably hot that we had tied our fatigue shirts around our waists, for it was even too hot for the mosquitoes, though I still wore an ammunition bandolier across my chest. After cutting our way through about five kilometers of dense jungle, we broke out into some cleared fields of yams, manioc, and bananas, beyond which we beheld a Jarai Montagnard village, comprised of about twenty traditional wooden houses, built on stilts to ameliorate against the heavy monsoon rains. This was different from the Vietnamese, who even in their highland cities persisted in constructing their houses on the waterlogged ground, out of concrete in most cases. There were also Vietnamese villages, outside the cities in the highlands, where the inhabitants constructed wooden or bamboo hootches with thatch roofs, close to where they tended their rice paddies. We never mistook the Montagnards for the enemy; we always smiled just as soon as we encountered one another; after all, we were both in the business of killing Vietnamese.

The Montagnard villagers invited us to join them in a funeral celebration for a young child who had died of malaria, as there is so much disease in the jungle, for it is dank and damp, and a place where pestiferous miasmas proliferate. Because I was considered the chief of my tribe (platoon), I was invited to squat down with the village chief and esteemed elders in front of a clay jar, about three feet tall, filled with a fermented alcoholic rice and water brew. There was a reed straw that went to the bottom of the jar, and a young, pretty, bare-breasted girl topped off the jar each time one of us chiefs imbibed of the fermentation. The nubile girl refilled the jar with rice liquor from another jar until the level of the brew rose to the stalk of bamboo that was laid across the top of the jar with a splintered piece protruding down into the alcoholic fermentation. Each person was required to drink through the long straw, sucking up the heady brew from the bottom of the jar until the level at the top of the jar gradually dropped below the protruding piece of bamboo; I figured this was about eight fluid ounces.

By the time the chief and elders had performed this drinking ritual two or three times, they were all giggling and having difficulty standing without staggering. The Montagnards insisted that I partake of at least two rounds of drinking, and I did enjoy the taste, the mild high was not unpleasant, and the village chief and elders were happy to see my men and I enjoying the funeral celebration; they were certainly getting into the partying mood.

The Montagnards also intended to slaughter a water buffalo as part of the funeral celebration, and since my troops possessed the only axe, the Montagnards extended to us the honor of sacrificing the tethered animal. Sergeant Tyrone took hold of the axe in both hands and struck the buffalo a deafening blow over its skull, between its huge handlebar horns, with the blunt end of the axe, using full force, but the buffalo just stood its ground, it took another full force whack to bring the buffalo to its knees. Then a Montagnard elder leisurely sauntered up to the animal and casually slit its throat, from which the spurting blood was caught in a wooden bowl, and this liquid life force of the still breathing animal was handed to me, for I was considered the guest of honor, and the chief of my tribe.

I lifted the wooden bowl up to my lips with both hands and partook of the warm crimson ambrosia. I

October 1967, age 21— Drinking rice wine with village elders at a Montagnard funeral, central highlands.

did not hold my nose, or choke when I swallowed, for I had come to understand that this blood sacrifice was a solemn ritual, extending back to mankind's earliest beginnings. Could I feel the elixir's life-charging essence empowering my being? I'm not sure, but I do believe that my participation in this sacrificial blood rite had carried me further up river, further into the primordial darkness of the jungle, and ever further from my California youth.

In the midst of the bleeding process, the buffalo finally keeled over, and we all watched in solemn fascination as its fluttering eyelids ceased trembling, while its life force bled out, and then the butchering of its flesh began. No woman or child cringed at the slaughtering, for they were hungry, and impatiently waiting for meat. It would be fresh meat, without any controlled decomposition to make it tender, but that wasn't really necessary, as this flesh would be consumed within the next twelve hours, before rigor mortis had set in.

Sometimes older Montagnards approached us when we were out patrolling in the jungle. They waved as they approached, and they sometimes were proudly speaking French. They had probably not spoken a word of the language in the highlands during the last thirteen years, ever since the French had pulled out. Yet they were so proud and so certain that we Americans could understand this European language that they had struggled so assiduously to learn, retaining hopes that we had come to help and that we truly cared. Sadly, we simply used these people as a means toward a most tragic end, especially for them, for their persecution continued long after we Americans had departed.

I was frequently the designated translator, because I had taken two years of Spanish in secondary school. My company commander and the rest of the men in my unit felt that my language skills in Spanish would be adequate for translating French. I could ask the basic questions, "How many of the enemy passed here? How long ago? What kind of weapons were they carrying?" Even then I was touched by the heartfelt camaraderie expressed by these noble people toward us Westerners. Of course, the Montagnards held a deep enmity toward the Vietnamese who had the temerity to consider these first arrivals as savages and treated them as such; it was probably not much different from the way that the Anglo-Saxon Americans treated the Native Americans who had preceded them into North America by more than 10,000 years.

The Vietnamese called the Montagnards *moi*, which literally means savage, and now, with the arrival of the Americans, the Vietnamese were taking full advantage of the opportunity to trail along and encroach more and more upon Montagnard lands in the highlands, establishing towns and pushing the Montagnards ever further out into the bush, and yet these noble mountain people still held on, with an unfaltering faith, and always greeted us with warm and genuine smiles.

10

Tet and the Turn of the Tide

I

Not long after the battle of Dak To, my battalion made its way back to the division base camp for several days of rest and refitting, and also to recover from the insidious jungle rot that had efficiently worked its way throughout most of our waterlogged bodies, though the hot dry season was beginning, which would mercifully send the jungle rot into remission. We looked like tattered scarecrows, for we had lost most all of our body fat and we were lean and mean, dusty and sweat-stained. The base camp troops in the rear in their clean, starched fatigues actually came out of the entrance gates and lined up on both sides of the road just to watch us enter the camp.

Back in the States during this time, the Civil Rights Movement was in high gear, though racial segregation still lingered. My platoon consisted almost exclusively of blacks and Hispanics, and so when I was out in the field I lived mostly in a black world. Nevertheless, all the men in the platoon got along, though the black hand-slapping culture predominated, which we all found quietly amusing, even amongst the black soldiers who recognized that the whites and Hispanics were adopting their ways. Whenever we were in the rear, which was not very often, my men and I listened to Motown music. We sat around playing 45 vinyl plastic records of Eddie Floyd's "Knock on Wood," the Temptations' soulful lament "I Wish It Would Rain," and "Black is Black" by Los Bravos. In those days there were no compact discs (CDs), as that technology wasn't available in the U.S. for another sixteen years.

After about a week in the rear, we once again headed out into the boonies. However at the end of November, after nearly three months as a platoon leader, my company commander informed me that he had recommended me to serve as the commanding officer (CO) of the Fourth Infantry Division Mortar Battery in the heart of the populated urban area of Pleiku. This was just two months prior to the onset of the Tet Offensive that would erupt throughout many of South Vietnam's cities, including Pleiku. I was pissed off that I was compelled to leave the men of my platoon. My CO was surprised at my reaction, as he considered my new position to be a highly coveted assignment, since I would gain the prestige of being a commanding officer in wartime, which is exceedingly rare for a second lieutenant (O-1).

Being a commanding officer in wartime was the culminating aspiration of all of my fellow infantry officers, especially the West Pointers. A platoon leader, who is a lieutenant, leads a platoon; however, this is not considered a commanding officer position. Generally, the lowest level of commanding officer is at the company level, in the person of the company commander, who is formally recognized as a commanding officer, and this position is traditionally filled by a captain (O-3). There are also positions for which colonels and generals are designated as commanding officers, and yet there are officers who have attained the rank of colonel, or even general, without ever having been a commanding officer. They may have been an executive officer (XO), which is tantamount to being second in command, or they might have been staff officers, serving as operations or intelligence officers for the brigade or division, but if they did not directly command the entire unit, then they were not a commanding officer.

I commanded a little more than a hundred men, and I had four M-30 heavy 4.2" (107mm) mortars and eight M29 81mm mortars and mortar crews under my command at the division base camp, while I also commanded two 81mm mortar detachments located outside division base camp, on the other side of Pleiku. Within two years the Army replaced the M29 81mm mortar with the M29A1 81mm mortar that was heavier and could fire more powerful rounds.

Mortars were weapons carried by an infantry company and used to provide indirect (high trajectory) fire support against attackers, except for the "heavy" 4.2" mortar, which weighed 675 pounds and was thus too heavy to lug out into the jungle. Still, mortars belonged to the infantry; these were our weapons, and we manned them with great pride. My battery sergeant was a Sergeant First Class (E-7), and all of my section leaders were E-6s (staff sergeants); this was a notch above the sergeant ranks that I had encountered out in the jungle. And in the military, rank means a lot. My battery provided protection for the Fourth Infantry Division Base Camp, the city of Pleiku to our north, and Hensel AAF (Army Air Field) to the southeast. My two 81mm mortar detachments outside of division base camp were located out in Montagnard villages to the north of Pleiku, and were tasked to support various units in their vicinity, such as the MACV compound, a maintenance battalion, and the Pleiku Air Base that was used by the South Vietnamese Air Force, so at least I still had the opportunity to get out of base camp and into the field to some extent.

Unlike the jungle, where one simply dug a hole out in the vegetation with one's entrenching tool to take a dump, back in base camp we were required to use latrines, which were essentially outhouses in which soldiers sat on wooden boards, with a hole cut out, and they voided their bowels into a 55-gallon oil drum that had been cut in half. Enlisted soldiers were detailed to pull these shit-filled drums out from the rear of the outhouses each day, pour diesel fuel into them, and then set them ablaze until the feces burned down into a soggy disinfected coagulated glob. The smell of the burning excrement was almost as bad as that of dead bodies, but not quite.

Back at the division base camp there was more noise than I had ever heard in the jungle, where silence had been the key to survival. I found the ceaseless cacophony abrasive and unsettling. In base camp the soldiers wore field jackets at night to protect themselves against the highland cold, and they had ponchos for the rain, as well as sleeping bags, blankets, and even pillows; they slept on cots inside of roofed bunkers. They even had personal possessions like large framed family photographs, and magazines sent from home. Troops in base camp received the *Stars & Stripes*, which was a Department of Defense-authorized daily newspaper that was already a couple days old by the time it made its way up to us from Saigon, and though it didn't provide much detailed information about the war, it had a decent sports section and devoted a full page to the comics.

On the seventeenth of December 1967, President Johnson called for a month-long bombing halt of North Vietnam and sent out peace feelers to Hanoi. However, Hanoi was already in the final stages of planning for the Tet Offensive that was to commence in just a little more than a month, and so Hanoi simply fanned false hopes by responding that it was willing to negotiate, but only if the United States included the NLF in the negotiations as well. Of course, this pronouncement presented insoluble problems for the U.S. in its dealings with the government of South Vietnam, and though nothing came of these preliminary peace feelers, Hanoi now knew that the United States was seeking a way out, by its willingness to negotiate, and therefore sensed a vulnerability that it might later exploit during the Tet Offensive that was to begin on January 30. A little more than three months into the Tet Offensive, the United States, in an even weaker position, relented and entered into peace negotiations with the North Vietnamese in Paris, France.[1]

As the holidays approached, some of the base camp troops had even obtained little Christmas trees that they decorated with tiny ornaments. Bob Hope came up to Pleiku with his USO Christmas show, accompanied by Raquel Welch, and I had the opportunity to attend the show, which was pretty much for the base camp troops, as the soldiers out in the jungle were too busy to attend.

The base camp soldiers also possessed battery-operated record players on which they incessantly played their 45 vinyl records (seven inches in diameter with one song on each side). For the most part, the troops seemed to be listening to either Grand Ole Opry or Motown music over the Armed Forces Radio station beamed to us from Saigon, even though I also enjoyed the music of Bob Dylan and the Beatles. I'm not saying that Bob was singing about drugs when he sang "Mr. Tambourine Man" (1964), or that the Beatles were singing about LSD when they sang "Lucy in the Sky with Diamonds" (1967), but they were certainly opening the doors of perception to my generation.

About a year and a half earlier, back in May 1966, while I was in advanced infantry training at Fort Ord, California, I was given a weekend pass and had traveled up the coast to visit an old high school friend of mine, named Todd, who was living in the Santa Cruz Mountains to the south of San Francisco. Todd was attending San Jose State University, and thus he was exempt from being drafted into the Army. Todd was already smoking pot and dropping acid (LSD) by the time of my visit. I recall that when I walked into his apartment he was listening to the songs from Bob Dylan's *Blonde on Blonde* album that had just been released.

In those days, all the stoners that I met were biker dudes who hung out with people like Ken Kesey, and the Merry Pranksters who were driving around in their psychedelically painted bus. These were still the early days before there were even hippies wandering around the streets of San Francisco. I think that it deeply disturbed Todd that I would inevitably be going off to war, for it was clear that he did not ever expect to see me alive again.

In base camp I was able to eat fresh oranges from time to time, which enabled me to fend off scurvy, though fresh oranges were not available to the troops out in the jungle who were eating exclusively out of cans. Still, the division base camp held its own unpleasant aspects, for since the camp was a static location, inhabited by several thousand troops, it attracted rats. I regularly saw quite a few soldiers in the dispensary each morning who had been bitten by rats while they had been on guard duty in bunkers along the base camp perimeter, as they were patiently lining up for their rabies shots, which were injected through the abdomen via a very long needle, on a daily basis for three weeks; none of those in line were smiling or laughing. Those poor unfortunates were probably the last to undergo this painful procedure, for a new vaccine, human diploid cell rabies vaccine (H.D.C.V.), was just being developed, which was administered via a simple series of shots in the arm to those who had contracted the rabies virus.

Sleeping on a canvas cot in a sandbagged wooden bunker with a screen door in base camp was considered the height of luxury when compared to sleeping in a muddy foxhole in the jungle, wrapped in a shelter half to fend off the rain. Base camp was a lot safer too, even though it was subject to sporadic mortar and rocket attacks as well as sapper attacks by enemy troops intent on penetrating the concertina wire, particularly where our mortar battery was located, since no walls were constructed in this part of the base camp in order to enable us to depress our mortar tubes to their minimum elevations for long range fire. Consequently, we were compelled to put out coils and coils of concertina wire in front of our mortar emplacements to deter the bad guys.

I, along with every other soldier, had been issued a field jacket that was made of nylon and cotton, and which served as a cold-weather jacket. Virtually all officers had their field jackets tailored, to which they then affixed their rank and insignia; however, I never bothered to tailor my field jacket, nor put any insignia on it. Infantry troops out in the field went without field jackets because they were too heavy and bulky to carry, and so I refrained from ever pulling it out of my duffle bag the entire time I was in Vietnam.

Around this time I had acquired my own jeep, and I can assure you that I never met another lieutenant in Vietnam who had his own jeep and driver. I had traded some 60mm mortars to a Special Forces captain for the jeep, which I desperately needed so that I could inspect my 81mm mortar detachments on the other side of Pleiku. The Special Forces troops were happy, as they tended to prefer the lighter 60mm mortars that we did not utilize.

The range of our much heavier 4.2" (107mm) mortars could be augmented by propellant increments that looked like thin square wafers with a hole through the center so they could fit around the protruding primer; we even broke the wafers down into quarters, and stuffed the small pieces between the other wafers. The four-deuce (4.2") mortar could fire a twenty-seven-pound high-explosive (HE) round out to a range of more than three and a half miles, which could take out enemy mortars and kill most anyone standing within thirty yards of the blast, the same effect of a 105mm howitzer shell.

II

The Tet Offensive of 1968 consisted of three phases and persisted for eight months, into September of 1968. The first phase (intended to strike at numerous cities throughout South Vietnam in order to spark a general uprising among the population) began on January 30 (January 31 in most instances); the second phase of the Offensive was scheduled to begin on the fifth of May (intended to strengthen the position of the North Vietnamese at the peace talks that were to begin on the tenth of May in Paris), and the third, and proclaimed decisive, phase was to begin on August 17 and continue into late September.[2]

For the first phase, the enemy marshaled 84,000 North Vietnamese and Vietcong troops for a massive number of coordinated attacks against thirty-six (of forty-four) South Vietnamese provincial capitals, five autonomous cities (South Vietnam had six autonomous cities: Saigon, Dalat, Hué, Da Nang, Cam Ranh, and Vung Tau), sixty-four (of 242) district capitals, as well as fifty hamlets. In the face of this onslaught stood the South Vietnamese military, supported by regional and local militias, while the United States order of battle consisted of two Marine Divisions (First and Third), seven Army combat divisions (First, Fourth, Ninth, Twenty-Third, and Twenty-Fifth Infantry Divisions, First Cavalry Division (Airmobile), and 101st Airborne Division), five Army combat brigades that were all formed or reactivated during the 1960s (173rd Airborne Brigade, the Eleventh, 196th, 198th and 199th Light Infantry Brigades; in modern parlance "Light" generally means that the unit is not mechanized and lacks heavy anti-armor capability), and a couple squadrons of the Seventeenth Cavalry, as well as Special Forces and two tank battalions (First

Battalion, Sixty-Ninth Armor, and Second Battalion, Thirty-Fourth Armor). During the first phase of the Tet Offensive, the Third Brigade of the Eighty-Second Airborne Division arrived in Vietnam (during February) and served in the lowlands, while the remainder of the division was held in the U.S. as the Army's strategic reserve.

During the initial outbreak of Tet, the Marines were up along the DMZ, while stationed in the south, around Saigon and in the Delta, were the First, Ninth, Twenty-Fifth Infantry Divisions, the 101st Airborne Division, and the 199th Light Infantry Brigade. Down in the lowlands, along the coast to the north of Saigon, were the Twenty-Third Infantry Division (Americal), the First Cavalry Division, the Third Brigade of the Fourth Infantry Division, the Eleventh, 196th, and 198th Light Infantry Brigades, as well as our Allies (the Australians, New Zealanders, Philippinos, Thais, and the Koreans). Up in the central highlands, there was the equivalent of only one American division (First and Second Brigades of the Fourth Infantry Division along with the 173rd Airborne Brigade and one armor battalion).[3]

On January 30 (first day of the Vietnamese New Year), Pleiku became the focus of enemy attacks in the central highlands. Although most everyone knows of the intense fighting that took place in the old imperial capital city of Hué, and around Saigon—in the Chinese section of Cholon as well as on the U.S. Embassy grounds itself where nineteen VC gained entry and fired away with rockets and small arms until they were all killed—many people may not be aware that during the first eighteen hours of the Tet Offensive, "II Corps [the highlands in particular] received the bulk and intensity of the enemy attacks." Fighting raged in the highland cities of Pleiku, Kontum, Ban Me Thuot, and Tan Canh (near Dak To). Out along the coast (in II Corps) fighting broke out in Nha Trang, and there were also early enemy attacks further up the coast in I Corps at Hoi An and Da Nang (fifty miles south of Hué).[4]

Around 1:00 in the morning on the thirtieth of January (most of the enemy attacks throughout South Vietnam commenced more than twenty-four hours later—on January 31), Pleiku began receiving enemy 82mm mortar rounds, as well as B-40 (RPG-7) and Russian-made 122mm rockets, of which numerous 122mm rockets were fired at the Air Base, ripping apart a maintenance hanger and several barracks buildings. I was apprised that a Local Force VC battalion and a Sapper battalion (elite suicide commandos) had quickly followed up the artillery bombardment of Pleiku with a ground attack.

I had my men up and manning the tubes, for which we were receiving target coordinates from the artillery observer atop Artillery Hill that loomed high above us. This was different than leading an infantry platoon where you could generally see the enemy, for now I had to rely on the judgment of an observer posted on top of a hill above me. Nevertheless, we complied with his commands and pumped out rounds for nine days, until the fighting around Pleiku subsided around February 7. During those days, I averaged just three or four hours of sleep each day, though I recall going without any sleep at all for the first forty-eight hours, and then I still felt guilty when I was compelled to catch some sleep during the ensuing days, while infantrymen out forward were not enjoying that luxury. However, my men continued to man the tubes around the clock, even though they, at prescribed times, were taking turns sleeping at intervals.

Our ARVN allies, the Twenty-Second ARVN Ranger Battalion and the Third ARVN Cavalry Squadron were initially engaged in battling the attackers, supported by a U.S. tank company (normally comprised of eleven or more tanks) of the First Battalion, Sixty-Ninth Armor Regiment, after which some Special Forces strike force companies were added to the mix. They were later reinforced by additional elements of the Fourth Infantry Division.

Here I was at division, supporting South Vietnamese units battling the enemy around Pleiku. Their forward observers relayed their requests for indirect fire support through the artillery observer perched atop nearby Artillery Hill, because we lacked Vietnamese language capability, and he then passed the fire coordinates on to me, and I apprised my men as to the firing missions, while also transmitting firing coordinates over the radio to my men in my outlying mortar detachments.

My battery took no incoming mortar rounds, as most of the fighting occurred to the north of us, within the city of Pleiku and around the Air Base on the other side of the city, though we were provided target coordinates that were within range of our 4.2" mortars, as well as my two mortar detachments that were out in the vicinity of the Air Base, and so we supported South Vietnamese and U.S. ground forces for more than a week, at the end of which time I was apprised that around 200 of the enemy had been killed in the fighting. When you're firing mortars and artillery, you don't have the occasion to view the bodies of the enemy killed. I don't believe the fighting in Pleiku received much media attention back in the States, because our ARVN allies had done most of the fighting.

In most instances, the fighting throughout South Vietnam fizzled out after about a week or so, except in the case of Hué where the fighting raged on for more than three weeks, ending with the recapture of the city on February 25. The NVA and VC troops battling the Marines in Hué massacred 2,800 Vietnamese civilians whom they contended were supportive of the South Vietnamese, a stark reminder that we were in the midst of a civil war, as the communist assaults clearly did not arouse the South Vietnamese to rise up and join their cause.[5] Prior to the creation of the DMZ in 1954, Hué had been just about in the center of Vietnam, but after the partition, Hué was in the extreme north of South Vietnam, only fifty miles south of the DMZ. There are some who contend that the first phase of the Tet Offensive continued all the way into spring, ending only when the seventy-seven-day siege of Khe Sanh was finally broken on April 8.

By the time the smoke had cleared toward the end of February, around 45,000 of the attacking troops had been killed, though, at the time, we in Pleiku were only aware of the fact that we had simply beaten off another enemy attack in the highlands. The magnitude of the country-wide assaults quickly spread by word of mouth, though we ultimately learned more about the Tet Offensive by reading issues of *Time* Magazine that found their way into base camp than by any information filtering down to us from division headquarters. Still, those infantrymen we supported around Pleiku were very grateful for our assistance in dealing out death upon the attackers.

The VC, in particular, had suffered quite a thrashing and were severely crippled, but this did not mean that the NVA were ready to fold up their tents and call it quits. They still manifested a formidable will to win, and they zealously believed that time was on their side, for in the minds of the North Vietnamese there was never any perceptible lack of resolve in achieving their ultimate objective of driving the foreign devils from their soil and ending the artificial separation of their country.

Besides, the NVA didn't really care that much about winning battles; their sole intent was to win the war, and they believed they would eventually prevail, because they believed they had more patience than Americans who continued to delude themselves that body count reports conclusively demonstrated that they were winning the war. My mortar battery had expended several thousand shells during the fighting around Pleiku, and just like in the Mel Gibson movie (based on the Moore and Galloway book, *We Were Soldiers Once ... and Young*), we pissed on our mortar tubes to cool them off when they began to overheat.

It wasn't until February 8 before I was able to drive into the city of Pleiku on my way to inspect my mortar detachments on the other side of the city. As my driver and I maneuvered our way through the dirt and gravel streets of Pleiku lined with drab, squat concrete buildings, I observed that some sections of the city were pretty chewed up after being subjected to extensive mortar and rocket fire, though the bodies had been cleared away, and an eerie silence prevailed. I was informed that the ARVN troops had gathered up the bodies of the enemy dead and placed them on display in the soccer field if I cared to review them, but I didn't bother to stop by; rather, I drove over to the Air Base that my mortar detachments had been supporting, and I observed the 122mm rocket damage to the hanger and a number of fair-sized craters caused by 122mm rockets that had fallen short.

After a week of furious fighting, it seemed that everything had settled down, and my men at our outlying detachments, who had been supported by South Vietnamese infantry, had suffered no casualties. My damage assessments took more time than anticipated, such that I found myself heading back to division base camp in darkness, after the imposed curfew, and so my driver and I were racing southward through the streets of Pleiku, and then along the deserted stretch of road leading to the camp. We had our headlights on in order to increase our speed to around fifty miles per hour, though the road was dusty and pock-marked, yet speed was more important than concerns about a bumpy ride or our jeep being lit up like a Christmas tree, as the enemy would have much greater difficulty trying to hit us with an RPG round while we were moving at full speed.

When we pulled up to the front gates of Camp Enari, the brilliant spotlights of the gate towers were flashed on to illuminate our vehicle, so that I had to shield my eyes from the blinding light. Two enormous timber gates were swung open to allow us entry, and, as we proceeded into the camp, I was hoping we wouldn't be stopped and written up for violating curfew, but the guards just waved to us as we passed on through. The two mammoth wooden gates were slammed shut behind us, and the spotlights were extinguished. Darkness resumed outside the camp to become once again the domain of the enemy, who owned the night.

Paradoxically, the enemy had turned a tactical defeat into a strategic victory, because their sacrifices during Tet had resulted in a perceptible loss of confidence among the American people in the ability of our military to win the war. It was akin to the demoralizing effects inflicted on the British by the voyage of the American colonial man-of-war USS *Ranger* (eighteen-gun frigate) during our War of Independence, when John Paul Jones took the fight to the British Isles in 1778, and literally to the front door of his adversaries when he even raided the manor house of the Scottish Earl who had ruthlessly ruled over his subjects, including John Paul Jones' own father. Afterwards, he went on to capture the British HMS *Drake* (twenty-gun frigate) off the coast of Northern Ireland, which constituted the first defeat of a British warship by a ship of the colonial Navy, and so terrorized the British people, who never imagined that the colonists were capable of carrying the war to their shore, that many British began to harbor doubts about the price they were willing to pay to suppress the rebellion in their North American colonies, and some British began to contemplate granting the colonies their independence.[6]

Similarly, after the first phase of the Tet Offensive, the perception began to grow in the minds of Americans that the enemy possessed the capability to strike at will, not only against the major cites of the South, but that the enemy also had the audacity to come right up to our front door when they stormed the U.S. Embassy in the heart of Saigon. The televised scenes of grisly street fighting and an impromptu execution additionally turned public opinion against continuance of the war.

Shortly after the commencement of the Tet Offensive, I was promoted from second lieutenant to first lieutenant. I contracted malarial fever at this time, even though I had been religiously taking my malaria pills. I all of a sudden got chills that started my body shaking right in the middle of the sweltering hot day. I staggered over to my cot and covered myself with as many blankets as I could stack on top of myself. My sergeant hovered above me, calling for more blankets, but I still kept shivering beneath the mountain of covers, with my teeth chattering together. Then, after a short while, the chills subsided, and I was overwhelmed by the sweats, and then my body became so hot, and my head so feverish, that I became dizzy and had to lie down on my cot once again, and I ripped off my long-sleeved fatigue shirt, saying to hell with the mosquitoes, but then after a short period of time, I again turned so cold that I covered myself once again with up to six layers of blankets, and yet I was still shivering from the cold, while the soldiers around me were sweating from the scorching midday heat. I started pissing brown urine and felt too sick to even smoke. Brown urine is one of the less common yet most dangerous complications of malignant malaria, resulting from the extensive destruction of red blood corpuscles by malarial parasites, of which the corpuscles' iron-containing protein (hemoglobin) is excreted in the urine, which therefore becomes dark, somewhat like the color of cola.

My temperature climbed so high that I was finally rushed to the base hospital where even the nurses seemed in a panic as they stripped me naked, without providing me any fig leaf, and then they hurriedly rolled out a basin beside my bed that was filled with large chunks of ice and alcohol, a mixture that rapidly decreases the body's heat by evaporation. The nurses rigged up a big fan at the foot of the bed, which they turned on full blast, and then they started washing me down with towels soaked in the ice and alcohol mix in their frantic efforts to bring my temperature down before my brain began to boil. I recall a doctor coming by with a clipboard who asked me in an oily voice to please tell him which of the two pills I had not been taking, so that he would know how best to treat my particular form of malaria. I told him I had been meticulously taking both pills as prescribed, which was absolutely true. What audacity on his part; he was looking to write me up for malingering.

My body, which had been feverishly hot, was now violently shivering from the ice and the alcohol, and my teeth were clattering together. The freezing cold, caused by the icy evaporating alcohol, was near to unbearable. Yet the doctors and nurses had weighed the trade-off of permitting my skin and my body to turn blue with cold, in order to save my brain. I don't think I clearly understood the urgency in their eyes, but they knew quite well that my brain was cooking, and that if they did not take immediate and drastic measures, I could die. I had relapses from this malarial fever for nearly three years following the war, after which time the fevers finally subsided.

III

After the first phase of the Tet Offensive, General William C. Westmoreland, Commander of all U.S. Forces in Vietnam, asked for an additional 206,000 troops to fight the war, but the tide of popular opinion in America had turned, and the United States soon reduced, not increased, the number of its troops in Vietnam.[7]

Although the U.S. military vociferously proclaimed that they had won a major tactical victory during Tet, they failed to realize that they had suffered a devastating strategic defeat, because the will of the American people had been broken, and the people no longer had confidence in the ability of the U.S. military to win the war, in no small part because the military had exhibited such excessive hubris just two months prior to Tet when General Westmoreland addressed Congress and overly optimistically avowed that the enemy "could not resist much longer."[8] But our military leaders served under civilian politicians, who were well aware of the fact that they were losing the support of the people. The attrition tactics of search and destroy had resulted in too many casualties, which the American people were no longer willing to endure.

Less than five months after the commencement of the Tet Offensive, General Westmoreland, the principal proponent of search and destroy, was replaced by General Creighton Abrams who introduced the concept of "clear and hold" that would bring the troops in from the jungles to secure the hamlets, as well as place greater emphasis on training and upgrading the South Vietnamese military. This was a move away from the attrition tactics of *search and destroy* that had been employed for the last three years with a great deal of bloodletting, but without resounding triumph.[9] It should be noted, however, that Westmoreland himself, three months after the onset of the Tet Offensive, began to apply euphemisms such as "combat sweep, reconnaissance in force, and spoiling attack" to replace the phrase "search and destroy," which began to assume sinister connotations, not because it conjured up images of killing, but rather because it had begun to generate images of burning Vietnamese hootches and the wanton destruction of property in the minds of many Americans.[10]

In most of America's wars, the object was to defeat the opposing army; this was the strategy in our War of Independence, our Civil War, and World War II, but during the Vietnam War, our mission was to *defend* South Vietnam and thus we were precluded from deploying ground forces north of the DMZ. As a consequence, the Vietnam War had simply become a war of attrition, more akin to the horrific trench warfare of World War I, when the term attrition was commonly used to describe a war in which nations were willing to absorb heavy casualties in order to wear down the other side, and this was in fact the U.S. military strategy for winning the war in Vietnam. Our leaders felt that this was a viable alternative to a war of annihilation (fought with nuclear weapons). However, Americans are by nature an impatient people; they want wars to end quickly, and they have little patience for long and sanguinary conflicts. Ironically, Vietnam became America's longest war, along with our War of Independence, and this is considering only the eight years that combat ground forces were engaged in Vietnam.

Additionally, this was a *limited* war, whereby the United States defended South Vietnam, but did not use ground forces to invade North Vietnam, due to its very real concern that this would prompt China to enter the war.[11]

I made the acquaintance of a Vietnamese Army captain, named Nguyen Thu Huong, who was providing security for one of my mortar detachments out in the field, and one day he introduced me to his wife and children who operated a laundry in the city of Pleiku. They insisted on doing my laundry for free, so, in order to reciprocate, I occasionally brought a case of beer to the laundry, which I'm sure they turned around and sold. One afternoon Nguyen invited me and three of my sergeants to take lunch with him at his officers' club. This was quite special, to be received as a guest in the officer's club of another nation in a wartime environment.

I remember sitting at the head of the table, while all of us raised our beers and toasted to our victorious future. I noticed that we were drinking the bitter Tiger Beer, derisively called "Tiger Piss" by Americans who swore it contained formaldehyde. Additionally, there was "33" beer (also called Ba Muoi Ba [thirty-three in Vietnamese]), a rice beer, which was our preference. The name "33" was derived from the fact that the beer, when initially produced around the turn of the century for the Legionnaires, came in the rather small 33-centilitre (one-third of a liter, or 11.2 fluid ounces) bottles that were unusual in those days when beer was generally produced in larger bottles.

One day, about a week later, I was on my way back from inspecting one of my mortar detachments in the field, I stopped by the laundry and was visiting with Captain Nguyen's wife and children, when an American Army staff sergeant burst into the laundry and pulled out a 45-caliber semi-automatic pistol, into which he frenetically slammed a clip, chambered a round, and then he started waving the pistol around. Let's face it, this is a huge bullet to come out of the barrel of a pistol; it's almost the same diameter of a 50-caliber machine gun bullet, and it will tear a hole through flesh and bone that cannot be easily mended.

Apparently, this volatile soldier believed that he had been ripped off in some deal to purchase pot, and he appeared quite intent on shooting someone, for Pleiku, like many Vietnamese cities close to American Army bases, seemed rife with drugs and prostitution. He waved his pistol in the face of Nguyen's wife, and so I stepped forward and counseled the soldier to calm down. The sergeant regarded me with the most crazed look in his eyes, and then he swung his pistol around and pointed it right in my face with shaking hands. I found myself looking down the barrel of the gun. I said to him in a gentle tone, "Hey, soldier, I'm not the enemy." I looked into his eyes, and he seemed to be far away, then he blinked a couple times, as though he was trying to pull himself together, after which he finally holstered his weapon. We left it at that, though I could just have easily had him brought up on charges and thrown into the stockade — my choice, but this soldier was an E-6, and I could tell by looking

February 1968—*Top:* The author (right) with his battery sergeants (unnamed) in front of the Vietnamese Officers' Club in Pleiku, central highlands. *Bottom:* Enjoying a few beers with their host, Nguyen Thu Huong (standing), a captain in the Vietnamese Army.

at him that he had seen some dark things, so I let it go. Usually when any enlisted soldier threatens an officer, in any way, whether drunk or sober, he will find himself up in front of a court martial, and he will do some long, hard time, for the Army shows little tolerance for this kind of behavior.

It was around this time that I confronted my only racial incident in Vietnam. Only about a dozen of the one hundred men in the division mortar battery were black, and, unlike out in the boonies, all of my sergeants were white. From time to time, we were required to pull all of our ordnance out of the ammo bunkers to check for expired mortar rounds that were cited on lists delivered to me periodically from division headquarters, as expired rounds had a tendency to fall short and could result in friendly fire mortalities, and the mortar rounds were stored in large heavy wooden cases.

One afternoon, Staff Sergeant Atkins, from Macon, Georgia, one of my section sergeants, came up to me with a quizzical look on his face, as though he was confronting an unfamiliar situation. He had assigned half a dozen men to take the cases of ordnance out of the ammo bunkers so he could inventory the numbered lots. All the men he had selected were black, as the men in the battery tended to stay together in their racial groups to a large extent. One of the men, Tucker, a black private from St. Louis, outspokenly complained that Sergeant Atkins was racially biased in assigning the detail, and this had sparked a spreading contagion amongst the other soldiers in the detail.

I walked with Sergeant Atkins across the battery, past our mortar tubes, to the ammo bunker where Tucker and the rest of the detail were standing around. I knew Sergeant Atkins was a professional soldier, who was not an overt racist, though he tended to issue orders without providing much explanation. He didn't feel the need to be popular among the men. I could see that everyone was looking toward me to adjudicate the issue.

They knew I was from out West, without a southern accent, which seemed to count for something among the black soldiers from northern American cities, and they felt that I would be fair. I did not want to countermand Sergeant Atkins' orders, for he was a good NCO upon whom I relied. Still, I listened to Tucker and the others in the work detail while they voiced their frustrations, which helped them to calm down a bit. I didn't mention anything about race, but rather turned to Sergeant Atkins and asked him to augment the detail with another six men from Sergeant Schmidt's section (who were all white). That seemed to be the end of it; they all appeared satisfied with my resolution, and nobody's dignity or authority was impinged.

During March 1968, after I had been in Vietnam about six months, a platoon of C Company, First Battalion (of the Twentieth Infantry Regiment), Eleventh Light Infantry Brigade, in country less than four months and assigned to the Americal Division (so named because it was formed on the island of New Caledonia during World War II, though after the war it was re-christened the Twenty-Third Infantry Division), under the leadership of a twenty-four-year-old lieutenant named William Calley, massacred defenseless Vietnamese women and children in the village of My Lai out along the South China Sea in the southern half of I Corps, about eighty miles south of Da Nang. I was unaware of this atrocity at the time since it happened far away, and because it was hushed up for a year and eight months.

The Tet Offensive shattered President Lyndon Baines Johnson hopes for a negotiated settlement to the war and, during March, after nearly losing the New Hampshire primary to the anti-war candidate Senator Eugene McCarthy, he called for a second halt (the first being three months earlier, during December) to the bombing of North Vietnam, and on March 31 he announced that he would not run for a second term. He also dispatched two diplomats (Averell Harriman and Cyrus Vance) on a quest to try to come to terms with the North Vietnamese. Intensive American bombing of North Vietnam during the last three years had not shaken the will of those tenacious people, and to make their point, the NVA embarked on major offensives throughout the South immediately after the bombing halt. It was just as well that Johnson elected not to run for a second term, because he was becoming paranoid about criticism, taking most of it personally, and he was given to bouts of depression; the weight of responsibility had worn him down.[12]

The next month, Martin Luther King, Jr., was assassinated in Memphis, Tennessee, on the fourth of April 1968. We were shocked. Here we were, far from home, fighting a war on foreign soil, while it appeared that there was another war going on back home.

Senator Robert F. Kennedy provided a heartfelt eulogy to the nation in an effort to temper any ensuing racial violence, though by 1968 King's preaching of nonviolence was losing support to more impatient organizations, such as SNCC (Student Nonviolent Coordinating Committee) and the Black Panthers, which were endorsing a more activist approach, causing King to become despondent over this turn toward violence. People were becoming impassioned for change; they wanted greater equality and an end to the war, and more and more elements of society were embracing violence as a viable means of achieving their ends.[13]

At the other extreme, April was the same month that Stanley Kubrick debuted his film, *2001: A Space Odyssey*, which depicted a manned space flight to Jupiter, after the discovery of a monolith on the moon that indicated we might not be alone in the universe, and that, perhaps, a more evolved and peaceful intelligence, beyond ours, is out there, though the special effects were unmistakably hallucinogenic. The world back home was indeed changing.

IV

While I was in base camp, the men from my old second platoon frequently stopped by to visit whenever they were in the rear. During early May, after eight months in Vietnam, at the beginning of my second monsoon rainy season, the men from my old platoon stopped by to let me know that their platoon leader had been medevac'd, so there was now a vacancy. They just assumed that I would jump at the opportunity. But I had to stop and think.

I would be giving up my cot, my jeep, cold beer, saluting senior officers, smelling shit burned with diesel fuel, the Vietnamese city environment with its occasional carnal pleasures, as well as the nurses and the Donut Dollies. Yes, as a young lieutenant with my own jeep in the division base camp, with its hospital nurses and Donut Dollies, I had the opportunity, on a couple occasions, to escort a young round-eyed lady back from her hospital duties to the WAC barracks, on moonlit nights, and on those nights I didn't need my driver.

On the other hand, it was unpalatable to me to know that the men of my old platoon were facing greater hardships and dangers than I, while here I was, enjoying the comforts of division base camp. It was almost as though the intensity of life could only be experienced when one was closer to death — in the frontlines. And so I walked across base camp to Second Brigade headquarters and spoke to the colonel, confiding to him that I had heard there was a vacancy in my old platoon in Company B of the Second Battalion, and that I deeply felt that I needed to be with my troopers out in the field. I told him that I could not stand the smell of burning shit in base camp any longer, which made him laugh. Two days later I was apprised that I would be returning to my old infantry platoon at the end of the week. There was virtually no standing in line, or much of a wait, for those volunteering to go out into the boonies with an infantry unit.

Just before I left my command of the Fourth Infantry Division Mortar Battery, the sergeants with whom I worked came to collect me one night. They were headed to the non-commissioned officers (NCO) club, which was not for officers, but for the non-commissioned officers ranked from E-5 up to E-9.

In the Army, the enlisted ranks progress from E-1 all the way up to E-9. E-1 through E-3 are privates (an E-3 being a Private First Class [PFC] who is entitled to wear one chevron), then comes a corporal who is an E-4 and wears two chevrons, and is the lowest ranking non-commissioned officer, followed by five ranks of sergeants, starting at E-5 (generally referred to as a buck sergeant who wears three chevrons), followed by an E-6 (Staff Sergeant), an E-7 (Sergeant First Class), an E-8 (First Sergeant or Master Sergeant), and then an E-9 (Sergeant Major, Command Sergeant Major [established in 1967], and Sergeant Major of the Army [established in 1966]).

As non-commissioned officers (NCOs), corporals and sergeants were extended some leadership authority. An Army infantry platoon at its full strength of forty-four would generally be comprised of thirty-two privates, four corporals (serving as fire team leaders when a squad was broken in two), two specialists (RTO and medic), four buck sergeants in my platoon (serving as squad leaders), and one staff sergeant in my platoon (serving as the platoon sergeant), all led by one officer who was a lieutenant. A Marine rifle platoon had roughly the same complement of around forty soldiers, also led by a lieutenant.

In any case, everyone conceded that the NCO club was the wildest and most rambunctious club on base. However, this was division base camp and not Saigon, so the clubs were simply large sandbagged bunkers with lighting supplied by diesel generators. Still, from time to time, some USO group would fly up to the highlands from Saigon to entertain the troops.

At the officers' club, everyone would passively sit around and clap sedately for the cabaret singers or the country western band, but at the NCO club they knew how to party, and they even had strippers from time to time! Now, if an enlisted man ever attempted to impersonate an officer, there would be hell to pay, but for an officer to impersonate an enlisted man — well, it was simply inconceivable.

Officers were barred from entry into the mythical NCO club, and even in the NAM, there was a partition at the NCO club, with staff sergeants (E-6) and above having free run of the club, while buck sergeants (E-5s) were relegated to a specified area. Nevertheless, my sergeants came to collect me at my bunker so they could escort me over to their NCO club. I chuckled at their invitation, for I knew very well that the bouncers at the door would take enormous pleasure in kicking an officer's butt down the stairs. My sergeants had even come up with an E-6 staff sergeant's fatigue shirt for me to wear, which concerned me a bit because most E-6s were in their late twenties, while I was only twenty-one, so I felt I had a better chance of getting away with looking like an E-5, but my sergeants didn't want me confined behind any restrictive partition; rather, they wanted to ensure that I would have free run of the NCO club.

My sergeants proceeded to accompany me across the base where the bouncers at the door gave us a serious look, which caused me to momentarily regret that I hadn't bothered to grow a mustache, yet, to my surprise, they allowed all of us to pass into the sacred club. We partied like mad men, and I was fully aware that my sergeants had paid me the ultimate compliment by considering me as one of them — for a night. I mean this was truly a very big honor.

11

Back to the Boonies (May–July 1968)

I

When I returned to the boonies, the soldiers of my old platoon were happy to see me, though my platoon was now integrated, for I now had a squad of white troops who were predominately from the South, but they carried their load and got along with the blacks and Hispanics, though the squads remained racially segregated by choice. Even though racial tensions had been steadily increasing across America during the last two and a half years, beginning with the Watts Riots in Los Angeles back in August 1965, I perceived no racial disruptions out in the field during 1967 or 1968, where we all worked together to increase our chances of survival.

My men knew that I had volunteered to return to the field and that I truly cared about them, and that I would do all that I could to look after them; still, they all thought that I was certifiably insane to voluntarily leave the comforts of division base camp to crawl back into a jungle foxhole. Many of my men made lots of jokes about what each of them would be willing to give up, if they could only trade places and secure a position for themselves in the greater safety of division base camp. Frequently, they said that they would willingly give up their left nut (testicle) simply for the base camp comforts of hot showers and a cot.

The NVA were not making any conciliatory gestures as a result of the bombing halt following phase one of the Tet Offensive. Their cities had been subjected to aerial bombing for the last three years, but they were not deterred; in fact they were actually stepping up the pace and proceeding with phase two. The central highlands were considered a critical area by both sides, for whoever controlled the highlands could virtually split South Vietnam in half. American intelligence indicated that two full NVA divisions (the First and the 325th) were operating in the highlands, where the Fourth Infantry Division and a brigade of the 101st Airborne were presently stationed. At this time all three of our brigades were in the highlands, and my battalion, along with the rest of the Second Brigade, was deployed to the west of Pleiku.[1]

11—Back to the Boonies (May–July 1968)

Other than the period 30 January to 25 February (the onslaught of the Tet Offensive) during which Americans suffered more than 2,300 deaths, the second bloodiest month-long period of the war was May 1968, during which there were also more than 2,300 American deaths; these were the only two monthly periods in which the American death toll ever exceeded 2,000 during the entire war.[2] In fact, the generals at MACV referred to this period as "mini–Tet" (although the communists considered this period as simply the second phase of the Tet Offensive), during which time the enemy was striving to follow-up on the psychological triumph they had achieved during the first phase of the Tet Offensive. This was also the month that the monsoon season began once again, and the rains were already cascading from the skies, and we soon fell victim to the insidious jungle rot. This was the time of year when the enemy preferred to close with us in battle, as they knew that we could not regularly call in air support or re-supply during the heaviest rains.

II

I know it sounds strange, but during my time in Vietnam I don't think I ever took the war personally, by which I mean that I went through the war with a certain degree of detachment. I did not go through the war filled with rage. I always viewed the enemy soldiers as someone's son, brother, or husband. I did not take out my anger on those we captured. Nevertheless, I saw things. I observed our South Vietnamese allies torturing the enemy for information; I saw American soldiers handle captives roughly. I did not tolerate that kind of behavior and I tried to intercede whenever I saw it occurring.

I don't agree with those who say that one has to learn to hate the enemy in order to be an effective warrior. If one observes superior athletes, in most cases one will see that they don't feel the need to get angry or dispute a call, for they have supreme confidence and high self-esteem, and they don't need to make themselves angry or brutish to be successful. Hatred and anger only diminishes a person, so far as I can tell.

On one occasion, my platoon, while out in the jungle on patrol, had surprised a small enemy reconnaissance detachment and taken three of them prisoner. We brought them back to our company perimeter adjacent to a Montagnard village. Our captain got on the radio to battalion, and shortly thereafter a helicopter arrived with about a half dozen South Vietnamese soldiers onboard, all dressed in crisp clean fatigues. Our allies assertively strolled over and took the prisoners from us, and then they roughly dragged the prisoners over to a village hut for interrogation. I saw them bring out a standard car battery that had two wires with alligator-clip electrodes at the ends, and the battery had been modified to accommodate a hand crank. They proceeded to strip the prisoners naked, and then they attached the electrodes to the prisoners' genitals. I walked away, but I could still hear the screams; so much for any adherence to the Geneva Conventions concerning the treatment of prisoners.

Even when the French were fighting in the highland battles of 1954 and the horrific battle of Dien Bien Phu against the Vietminh, both sides honored the exchange of wounded prisoners.[3] However, during the American phase of the Vietnam War, this display of humanitarian conduct was sadly lacking. We were told not to expect much mercy from the NVA, so perhaps both sides had kicked it up a notch.

We Americans tend to dehumanize and villainize our enemies by calling them japs, chinks, dinks, krauts, or gooks, and in so doing we tend to consider them less human than ourselves, thus enabling us to contravene the Golden Rule and dispassionately go out and kill our foes. For we soldiers were in the killing business, make no mistake about that, and yet this tendency to villainize our enemies also seemed to affect the way that we treated prisoners of war (POWs), who, one would think, should be treated in the same manner that we ourselves would expect to be treated if we happened to fall into enemy hands. Also, by dehumanizing one's enemies, one fuels over-confidence, and yet anyone bothering to read about the battle of Dien Bien Phu would quickly surmise that the French had nothing over the Vietminh who defeated them with superior tactics, artillery, and generalship. Any army that can win a war against a modern Western army without possessing much of an air force should not be underestimated.

After the interrogations were over, our allies literally dragged the three prisoners, kicking and screaming, out of the hut and onto a waiting helicopter with the prisoners' hands tied behind their backs. In the process of cramming the prisoners onto the chopper, one of the prisoners became so terrorized that he soiled his pants, which provoked an explosion of derisive laughter amongst his captors, for though none of us was a stranger to the vicissitudes of war, it was nonetheless considered unmanly to soil one's pants.

I had not yet shit my pants in combat, but I know what it's like to have one's sphincter pucker; you can feel it, when terror and the threat of death are confronting you, and you cannot run away because it would destroy your self-esteem, so you stand there and face the terror, and you can distinctly feel the fear in your sphincter, which twitches and puckers, and I suppose that it's just one more step before you lose control. It's akin to the experience we had as small children when we had done something wrong that incurred the wrath of a big person, against whom we were defenseless, and we found ourselves at the mercy of the big person and their visceral anger, as well as their intimidating physicality, which made us feel so afraid that we would literally shiver in our skin.

These prisoners had never been airborne in their lives, and when you're riding in a helicopter, it feels like you are more outside than inside the aircraft because it is open on both sides, and the prisoners were absolutely terrified that the interrogations were going to be continued aloft. I had heard stories of interrogations conducted in the air, during which the first prisoner, grabbed at random, was tossed out of the chopper before he was even asked a single question — at about 1,500 feet above the ground. Then the captors sat down next to the second bound prisoner and began asking questions. If they did not get the information they wanted they continued tossing prisoners out of the chopper, while working their way down the line to the next prisoner. I had never witnessed this act; perhaps they were just tall tales told to add to the macabre atmosphere that is so pervasive in wartime, but the terror in the eyes of those prisoners, as they were hustled aboard the chopper with their hands bound behind their backs, was so strong that I could smell it, and it wasn't just the shit.

Though I had been outranked by my company commander, I was livid, and I resolved never again to allow any prisoners of mine to be subjected to electric shock interrogation, even if it meant defying my company commander. When I observed the sardonic and pitiless expressions on the faces of the interrogators, I indubitably realized that this is what happens to people when their country has been continually at war since before they were born — a certain callousness incontrovertibly sets in. Would any of this callousness rub off on me?

Just to be exposed to war forever changes a person, even the children and the non-combatants. People who are compelled to live in a war-torn environment develop a different perspective on the way they look upon life; it's a harsher, more brutal view of life than that to which most Americans have ever been exposed.

Is it possible to rise above one's environment and appreciate the beauty and the poetry of life? Perhaps, but let's face it, innocence is lost due to war, and innocence once lost cannot be regained, only feigned; this is the price one pays for looking behind the velvet curtain.

It's unfortunate that when we are young we cannot also be wise, for then we would exercise more care in parceling out our innocence. If I could do it again, I would expend my innocence parsimoniously, in measured increments, so that it would last me awhile. As I grow older, I can see that it is the innocence of youth that is so attractive to those who have lost theirs. Losing one's innocence makes it more difficult to regain one's youth, though not impossible.

I was taught in the Army that the Vietnamese communists cared less about dying than we Americans, and woe to those of us who happened to fall into their hands. Do our militaries encourage this kind of hate in order to anesthetize the soldiers they are sending off to war, so as to make the killing more impersonal? I think our military wanted us to kill without remorse; I'm certain that they did not want us standing around feeling all sorrowful about the killing we had done; rather, they wanted us to get on with the job of dealing out death until it was time to return home to our loved ones on Elm Street. The fact is that the military teaches soldiers to kill, not to love; love is something you get at home, if you're lucky.

III

Frequently, as we moved through the profuse jungle of the mountainous highlands during the rainy season, we found ourselves on the grassy banks of deep and fast-flowing rivers that we were required to cross, and these swelling rivers generally extended about twenty yards to the far bank as they came rushing down from the higher mountains. We tied a couple of ropes around the waist of one of our strongest swimmers, who stripped down naked and dived into the river, and swam frenetically for the far shore, while fighting the powerful current that was rapidly sweeping him downstream. Even though this was a high-risk endeavor, there was something intrinsically comical about watching someone thrashing their arms like mad in an almost fruitless effort to battle the powerful current that was rapidly carrying him downstream, which made us all laugh uproariously, though we had scouts posted up river to alert us for trees that were frequently swept down river in the raging torrent and which could pose a distinct and terrible threat to our swimmer.

When our naked swimmer reached the opposite bank, he walked back upstream amongst our taunts that he'd better hope that he didn't encounter the enemy in that state, as he would no doubt scare the hell out of them. When our nude swimmer was opposite our unit, he then tied the two ropes to a tree, one above the other, about four feet apart, and we would do the same on our side of the river, as we pulled the ropes taut. We then proceeded to cross the river on this extremely crude rope bridge by walking on the bottom rope, while using the top rope as a balance.

We took great care to keep our weapons dry although we were burdened with our seventy-pound backpacks, which resulted in a precarious balancing act. The last man across on our side also stripped naked, untied the ropes, and we then dragged him through the waters of the fuming river over to our side, while still laughing our heads off. Crossing rivers in this fashion, in full battle gear, could be quite hazardous, though fortunately we never lost a man to the river, although we did lose a couple weapons, which was almost as bad.

Though morale remained generally good, this was the first time that I observed soldiers who had endured all they could take of combat, and who were willing to shoot themselves in the hand or the foot in order to get out of the field; these self-inflicted gunshot wounds were not uncommon, they occurred from time to time in most every battalion, though I had not seen this type of behavior the first time I was out in the field. Some of my men, from the old days, confided to me of their apprehensions, and I kept mute. Yes, I did. It was their decision. They had been out in the boonies, in continual combat, for ten months or more; for them, that was enough.

Maybe I was a little crazy after all, for I was clearly glad to be back with the soldiers of my old platoon, even though the risk to my life had increased exponentially. Besides, I was a young man of twenty-one, and still too young to be thinking seriously about death and dying. I believe there is a very strong attraction to being on the front lines. What could ever surpass this feeling? It's as powerful as sex, even though we all complained. But to be out here, with your band of brothers, was so fulfilling that anything else was less. You truly felt guilty if you were back at the aid station being treated for a small piece of shrapnel, while your comrades might be in need. I could never truly feel happy about sleeping on a clean cot at base camp when I knew that my men were out here, sleeping in a hole they had dug out of the earth. Perhaps I was born to suffer, or I wanted to suffer, but I sure as hell felt a lot happier being back in the jungle with my men. I guess that was it. I was not really here to rid the world of communists; I mean, that's not what I was willing to die for. I was here because of these men, considered by many to be social outcasts and losers, and yet here they were, willing to put their lives on the line for their country. Well, who would not be in awe of such men? We were willing to die for each other and, brother, let me just say, "That's the long and the short of it."

Sometimes I would see photos of Marines at their fire bases of Khe Sanh and Con Thien up around the DMZ that separated North Vietnam from South Vietnam, and they all seemed to be wearing flak jackets, because they were continually subjected to big-gun artillery fire, while I only had to contend with enemy mortar and rocket rounds, and our own artillery that occasionally spewed some shrapnel through our positions when we brought it in real close. In any case, flak jackets were too heavy and impracticable to be worn day after day in search-and-destroy missions through thick tropical foliage; though I recognized its utility in providing additional protection, my men and I never wore flak jackets while we were out humping the boonies.

It is remarkable that any NVA infiltrated into the South across the DMZ when one considers all the Agent Orange herbicide (a 50/50 mix of two herbicides, 2,4, dichlorophenoxyacetic acid and 2,4,5 trichlorophenoxyacetic acid) that had been dumped into that area over the years, and no major battles, to my knowledge, took place within the DMZ itself. Approximately 19 million gallons of herbicides (of which Agent Orange was the primary one) were sprayed over Vietnam from 1962 to 1971, of which more than half was dispensed over III Corps (in which Saigon is located); however,

I Corps came in second, where Agent Orange was applied mostly around the DMZ.[4]

Even the airborne soldiers, who were air mobile with their helicopters, had their home bases to which they returned. There was only one combat parachute drop by American forces in Vietnam, made by a battalion of the 173rd Airborne Brigade during February 1967, the rest of the time they relied on helicopters to get them to their jump-off points, from which they then set out humping the boonies.[5] The Special Forces soldiers with their Green Berets generally worked out of villages to which they occasionally returned, and yet Airborne soldiers and Special Forces were the glamour guys, while we straight-leg infantry soldiers were not glamorous, though it seemed that we spent an inordinate amount of time living and sleeping out in the jungle. Many infantry soldiers in my battalion spent less than thirty days away from their jungle foxholes during their entire twelve-month tours.

My infantry company spent most of its time in the boonies, rarely returning to base camp, maybe once every three to four months, and then for no more than a week, and we weren't even the glory boys. Even the *long range reconnaissance patrol* guys (LRRPs), who didn't have it easy, seemed to spend more time in base camp than we did, and in my dealings with LRRPs, I found that quite a few of them were assigned to these patrols as punitive assignments to atone for some indiscretion. Most every time I talked to LRRPs, I rolled my eyes at their tall tales, because I knew that their assignment was to sit and listen and watch, but it was not their mission to engage the enemy and fight. No, that was our mission. I'm not referring here to the formation by the Army of Long Range Patrol (LRP) into Ranger companies of the Seventy-Fifth Infantry Regiment that began in February 1969; rather, I'm referring to the earlier days, when General Westmoreland authorized the creation of LRRP units among most infantry divisions in 1966, though some divisions had already started creating LRRP units back in 1965, and I recognize that LRRPs suffered a high number of KIA throughout all the years they were active in Vietnam.

When I first arrived in Vietnam I had this incredibly frightening and lonely feeling that the umbilical cord had been severed, even though this was not the first time that I had been away from home. Before entering the Army I had been to Mexico, the Philippines, Tahiti, and Australia, but even in those far distant places, if in trouble or in need, I could have communicated with my parents, but in Vietnam there were no telephones and no place to run in the event I became too terrified.

We relied on our buddies for survival, a long, long way from home. Sometimes you will hear Vietnam vets refer to their buddies, or make reference to camaraderie. Think of it! You live in the jungle, sleeping in a foxhole with one or two other guys. You depend upon one another for your very survival. In the field, when you need to relieve yourself, you grab your entrenching tool and dig a hole and you relieve yourself while your buddy stands guard. Even married couples are not that close; when they argue, they can go into the other room and shut the door, but in Vietnam, out in the jungle, when you got pissed off at someone, there was no place to go; you were always there, always together. This is what most civilians cannot truly understand—this concept of wartime camaraderie, this very deep, undying loyalty to one another.

Yet at the same time we shied away from becoming too close, for then we agonized too much when someone got killed. So we always held ourselves back from delving to the deepest personal depths; there were no tears in Vietnam; we would just suck it up. We never really told anyone our life stories, though we were all so young that our life stories were transparently short. Perhaps romantic love would one day enable me to penetrate to the deepest recesses of another's soul. Still, in Vietnam we needed each other so desperately; we called it camaraderie.

IV

U.S. representatives participated in preliminary peace negotiations in Paris, commencing on the tenth of May, a little more than three months after America's commitment to winning the war had begun to falter, following the enemy's audacious attacks throughout South Vietnam during the first phase of the Tet Offensive. Conducting peace negotiations in the midst of a war caused me to think of the bitterness felt by German soldiers during World War I, who believed that their politicians had sold them out while they, the soldiers on the frontlines, still retained the will to fight.

Governments do worry about potential reactionary actions perpetrated by bitter and angry war veterans returning home from a lost cause. The United States does not have much of a history of losing wars; in fact, Vietnam was the first war that America clearly lost, though one could scarcely consider the Korean War a victory. It was somewhat embarrassing, something not to be talked about, certainly nothing to brag about. This was the wellspring of the bitterness felt by soldiers who were still expected to fight and to die, while their political leaders were losing the will to continue the fight and were looking for some way to extricate themselves from the conflict without utterly losing face. Eventually, the soldiers out in the jungle looked for meaning in their sacrifices, of which they found very little, except loyalty to their comrades, and they came to realize that sacrifice does not require victory to lend it value.

I better appreciated the speech that General MacArthur gave at West Point after he had been relieved of command during the Korean War. In his closing remarks he said to the young Army officers of the future, "The world has turned over many times since I took the oath on the Plain at West Point, and the hopes and dreams have long since vanished. But I still remember the refrain of one of the most popular barrack ballads of that day, which proclaimed, most proudly, that 'Old soldiers never die. They just fade away.' And like the soldier of the ballad, I now close my military career and just fade away — an old soldier who tried to do his duty as God gave him the light to see that duty."

After Korea, Eisenhower expressed serious doubts about using American conventional forces to fight a land war in Asia, but succeeding presidents either did not share Eisenhower's concerns, or failed to take heed of lessons learned, or of history for that matter.

V

One rainy afternoon in May, my platoon was crossing some rice paddies in single file. Wading through foul water in socks and boots was not pleasant, but our boots might mitigate against the stab of a pungi stake, and perhaps save our lives. The foot soldier does not get to choose the battleground; the politicians and the generals make those choices. Why couldn't we fight on nice sandy beaches? But I suppose that had already been tried at Iwo Jima and other beautiful sandy beaches, but that was no picnic either.

Jim, a twenty-year-old soldier in my platoon from North Carolina, stepped on a pungi stake while we were wading through the paddies. The stake stuck him through his boot and drove itself right up through the heel of his foot, the part of his boot that was not protected by the mid-sole steel plate. We lifted Jim up out of the rice paddy, called in a dust-off (medevac chopper), and then waited around, smoking and talking. Even Jim was smiling, though his foot was throbbing and he was bleeding profusely, for it appeared that he had received the million-dollar wound; he was leaving the jungle and deadly combat, and he hadn't even lost an arm or a leg. As we heard the chopper approach, we popped a purple smoke grenade so it could identify our position on the ground, and then the dust-off swooped in and picked up Jim and carried him away, back to the MASH unit at division base camp.

We proceeded to climb out of the paddies with the muddy water draining from our jungle boots through the nylon-uppers, which only brought closer the realization that we now had to continue marching in our soaking-wet socks through the fungi-laden foliage, while the ensuing jungle rot proceeded to consume our flesh to the point that it could turn one's stomach. Prolonged exposure of the feet to warm water could result in tropical immersion foot, akin to trench foot, except that trench foot is caused by prolonged exposure of the feet to cold water, so it was critical to change socks regularly by putting on a dry pair at least once a day.

I owed Jim five dollars from a poker game. Yes, I would occasionally play cards with my men, for, after all, we shared the same foxholes. This was not the dress-white Navy where officers and enlisted did not even bother to eat together, and where the officers were served food on fine china plates by white-jacketed messmen. We in the Army infantry squatted down in our dirt holes together and ate our food out of cans. I sent Jim the five dollars the next day, passing the money in an envelope to a chopper door gunner who was heading back to the rear, and who promised me that he would drop by the hospital and give it to my wounded soldier. Now you might think that a five dollar debt was no big deal, but in war, one always paid one's debts right away. You never wanted to leave a debt unpaid; you did not want to die owing anybody, and you did not want someone to die to whom you owed an outstanding debt, for you knew that guilt would follow you, and since you could be killed on any given day, you repaid your debts at the earliest possible opportunity.

About a week after Jim had been medevac'd, I made some inquiries and was told that he was okay, but that he had contracted a fever, which the doctors diagnosed as a touch of malaria. A week later some more of our troops returned to the field, and I asked them about Jim. They told me that Jim had died yesterday, from blood poisoning as a result of the pungi stake wound. Jim was twenty years of age when he died. Think of that — to die in the service of your country before one had even experienced romantic love or parenthood. My trooper is now one of the more than 58,000 soldiers whose names are inscribed on the Wall.

People died, but the world did not stop spinning. Even when people were killed in the morning, by mid-afternoon one was hungry and it was time to take a bite to eat, then dig in for the night, grab a few hours sleep, then awake before sunrise to go to work again. Work, of course, meant hunting and killing other human beings, though we called it search and destroy instead of hunt and kill.

In the mountains of Vietnam, where triple-canopy jungle predominated, an impression of dusk prevailed, even during the middle of the day. The sun sometimes filtered down through the tall trees and onto the jungle floor in the form of smoky silver lances, creating a cathedral-like atmosphere, though for the most part, it was a world of mist and rain. There were many days when aircraft could not fly in such all-consuming cloudy conditions. Hence we were not always assured that we would be re-supplied, or that we could get choppers in to take out our wounded or dead, and on one occasion we were compelled to sleep with our dead, and then awake in the morning and carry our dead along with us, while waiting for an opportunity to clear an LZ (landing zone) so that choppers could come in and lift our comrades out of the jungle for their final journey home.

VI

My battalion, though dismounted upon its arrival in Vietnam, became the Fourth Infantry Division's first mechanized infantry battalion, which meant

June 1968 — The author and the unnamed privates riding on one of the armored personnel carriers (APC).

that we were the first to be issued armored personnel carriers (APCs), which we used about a third of the time. Of course, none of us were foolish enough to ride inside one of these contraptions, for a round from a RPG (rocket-propelled grenade launcher) could easily penetrate the light-skinned armor of our APCs and ricochet around inside, tearing up flesh and bone, so everyone piled up on top.

The RPG rocket-launchers used by the NVA had been modeled after the German anti-tank weapons of World War II that were far superior to the bazookas (2.36" rocket launchers) used by the Americans during that war. The RPG was a shoulder-fired rocket launcher that could accurately fire armor-piercing rounds over a distance of three hundred yards. Still, we were happy to have transportation that was additionally armed with intimidating 50-caliber machine guns.

Another difference in leading the platoon from the hatchway of one of our four APCs was that instead of being positioned about one-third of the way back from the front, as was the case when I was on foot, on an armored personnel carrier I invariably led from the front. This was not done to be tactically more effective (in fact, my superiors continually exhorted me to sit in the hatchway of the second vehicle); rather, I chose to ride in the lead vehicle so that if we happened to run over a landmine in the road, then my APC, being in the lead, would take the hit.

Let's face it, I was best able to comply with battalion's unrealistic orders at times, when speed was of the essence and we were afforded no time to check the road for mines; instead we were compelled to just race down the road, hell bent for leather, and I could not expect any of my other three APCs to brave that kind of risk. Though most of the time we simply used our armored personnel carriers to carry us to a destination from where we then debarked and proceeded to hump the boonies on foot.

I noticed that the white Southerners in the other platoons frequently flew Confederate flags off the backs of their APCs. My great-grandfather had fought in the Civil War on the Union side and survived, though I had spoken to one of the white soldiers in the first platoon from North Carolina who had lost a total of five family members at the Battle of Gettysburg. I suppose that war was not so easy to forget in his family.

On a couple occasions we pulled convoy duty on Highway 19, for trucks making the 109-mile journey from the coastal port city of Qui Nhon up to Pleiku; it has been said that whoever controls this road controls the highlands, and whoever controls the highlands controls Vietnam. The French had suffered a horrific defeat on this road, about twenty-five miles to the east of Pleiku, at Mang Yang Pass, back in June 1954, one month after the Battle of Dien Bien Phu. Along the route we were compelled to pass by some rubber tree plantations that were operated by the French, which we were prohibited from entering or despoiling, and as a consequence, these rubber plantations essentially afforded sanctuary to the enemy, from whom we frequently received sniper fire. However, our Rules of Engagement stipulated that we could not despoil or intrude into these plantations; rather, if fired upon, we could only respond with desultory return fire while we simply increased the speed of the convoy as we passed by.

If you ask infantry soldiers about the Rules of Engagement, whether enlisted or officer, they will tell you that these are rules put together by a bunch of lawyers that make the life of an infantryman even more hazardous than it already is. However, I understood some of the rules that applied to troops in heavily populated urban areas where there were lots of civilians, which restricted soldiers from firing unless they were fired upon, but we had a bit of difficulty understanding why we could not rip into those French rubber plantations and tear the hell out of the enemy that was firing away at us with impunity and killing Americans.

By late summer, in the midst of the third phase of the communist Tet Offensive, the CIA–established Phoenix Operation was in full swing. This program was initially created to facilitate inter-agency sharing of intelligence as well as to utilize infiltration, capture, or assassination, to neutralize the VC infrastructure; however, the common view held by the troops in the field was that it was a program intended to strike terror into the enemy by assassinating suspected VC leaders throughout South Vietnam. Army infantry types were sought as volunteers to train and supervise Phoenix Vietnamese cadres.

During the Phoenix program's three years of operations, more than 20,000 people were killed, though some contemptuously called it murder. Now both sides were using assassination as a part of their military strategy. There was a fair amount of controversy regarding the Phoenix program, as many of the targets were fingered by so-called Vietcong defectors. The war was becoming murkier, but the enemy was undeterred and continued to unleash attacks throughout the summer and fall of 1968.[6]

On one occasion my platoon was tasked with providing security for a week at a bridge that crossed a river in the remote reaches of the highland jungles. Our mission was to ensure that the truck convoy route remained open, as well as to protect a group of Army engineers who were responsible for maintaining the pontoon bridge they had constructed, which essentially floated on the water, though it was tethered to pilings on each side of the muddy river that was nearly fifty yards wide.

There was a Montagnard village on the far side of the river and the villagers were cordial, and they were sometimes willing to trade their simple but elegant copper bracelets for cigarettes. It struck me as interesting that copper was the very first metal to lift mankind out of the Stone Age and catapult him into the age of metals. And even though copper is a relatively soft metal, when heated together with tin it forms bronze, an alloy that is much stronger than either of its two components, and it was bronze that sparked mankind's quest for ever stronger metals. The creation of metalworking rapidly expanded beyond bronze to the forging of iron, a metal much more plentiful than copper and tin, in addition to being even harder and stronger than bronze; and thus it was iron that ultimately permitted humans to make the giant leap forward in the development of metal tools that truly enabled man to plow the earth behind his domesticated animals. Of course, the Iron Age also illustrated man's continual progress in developing ever more deadly weapons. One was tempted to wonder which would predominate — the plowshare or the sword?

We all looked upon this bridge assignment as nice, relaxing duty, even though we were out each morning on the dirt road, accompanying the engineers who were out with their metal detectors looking for any land mines that the enemy had planted near the approaches to the bridge during the night; when detected we cleared around them with our bayonets and then destroyed them with C-4 plastic explosive. Now that my platoon had four APCs, I frequently sat up in the hatchway of the command vehicle astride the 50-caliber machine gun, as our mechanized platoon could now put out sufficient fire to secure both ends of the bridge.

Each morning I walked down the dirt road from our bivouac area to the river to bathe. The Montagnard women also were out early and they gathered for their morning bathing ritual just a short distance upstream on the far side of the river. The young, nubile, bare-breasted women appeared so entrancing as they washed one another's hair, and I could hear their laughter as it airily

11—Back to the Boonies (May–July 1968)

floated across the river, which was in sharp contrast to the world of war that was all around them; though even in the midst of war, I suppose, there is still a place for laughter and the levity of youth. I observed that the pretty Montagnard women kept their wraps on around their loins, even when they were bathing.

On one particular morning I found myself sitting on the pontoon bridge as the first vestiges of an amber dawn pierced the retreating darkness, with my feet dangling in the water, and I was talking to one of the engineers, a nineteen year-old kid from somewhere in the Midwest who was planning to return to the States in about six weeks. He talked of how much he missed his family and of the big celebratory meal that they were all planning for him upon his return home.

The engineers had it made in my mind, for they were not frontline infantry, and these guys had built themselves impregnable bunkers into the steep banks on this side of the bridge. The young engineer said that he had pulled guard duty during the night and that now he was tired, so he was going to hike up to his bunker and catch some sleep. We shook hands and then he walked off the bridge and up to his bunker.

I remained sitting on the pontoon bridge, with my fatigue pants rolled up, and my legs still submersed, while little rivulets formed around them, and I was trying to see if I could spot any fish in the muddy brown water. I could already sense the impending oven-like heat of the day that would soon sweep down upon us. Not more than twenty minutes elapsed since the young engineer had strolled away before I heard an ear-splitting crashing explosion that made the earth shake.

At first I thought that perhaps a B-52 had dropped a 750-pound bomb nearby, but then I could see people running, and I looked up toward the river bank and became somberly aware that a huge tree had inexplicably ripped itself free from the earth and come crashing down, directly on top of one of the engineers' bunkers; it turned out to be the bunker of the young man with whom I had just been speaking.

I went high-tailing it off the bridge and up the hill, gathering my men along the way, and urging them to bring along their entrenching tools. My medic was already at the mouth of the bunker; he looked at me and said, "Sir, he's alive. I can hear him breathing." I had all of my men digging furiously into the bunker, though it still took us nearly twenty minutes to dig our way to the young engineer. By the time we reached him, his head had been squeezed to half its original size.

We gently brought him from out of the bunker and wrapped him in a shelter half, while I got on the radio and called for a dust-off (medical evacuation chopper). When the medevac people learned that our casualty was dead, they informed me that a re-supply chopper, in our vicinity, was being redirected to our location. When the helicopter arrived it was already loaded with wounded from another engagement, and so we were compelled to tie the young dead engineer to one of the outside skids of the chopper so he could begin his final journey home without any further delay. We took our time with the ropes, meticulously ensuring that the dead engineer was firmly lashed to the skid.

Afterwards, I stood in the dust of the road, under the hot sun, and watched the young engineer rise with the chopper, which quickly gained altitude, and then it hovered above me momentarily, before it streaked off eastward, toward division base camp. I looked to see if the shelter half would continue to enfold the young engineer when the chopper accelerated, and was relieved to observe that we had done a good job at ensuring that the young soldier was well secured, and that he would now have a safe ride home. We all gave the young engineer a crisp salute as he headed home.

For hours and for days afterwards, I was angry at the vagaries of fate. Still, upon reflection, I came to realize that the digging of the bunker itself had probably caused the weakening of the tree's root structure, as though the young engineer had unknowingly been digging his own grave.

During the Vietnam War, according to the official DoD figures, Americans suffered 47,434 hostile deaths, comprised of four categories: killed in action (40,934), died of wounds (5,299), missing in action/declared dead (1,085), and captured/declared dead (116); while an additional 10,786 deaths (18.5 percent) were non-hostile, meaning they died from other causes besides combat, which included illness, accidents, missing/presumed dead, and even homicides. It is these two categories (hostile and non-hostile) that comprise the total of the 58,220 troops who died in Vietnam.[7] It should be noted that 18.5 percent was the lowest percentage of non-hostile deaths in all of America's wars, except for the Korean War. During World War II, for example, non-hostile deaths accounted for 28 percent of that war's total American military deaths.[8]

I examined one soldier who appeared to have been killed by friendly fire (the ultimate oxymoron) for inadvertently stepping into the line of fire of one of our own machine guns during an ambush, though I couldn't be absolutely certain, as there was a lot of firing going on. Still, I did not report that I suspected his death to be a result of friendly fire, believing that the soldier might not receive a hero's burial if it was determined that he did not die from enemy fire. All I knew at the time is that if the soldier did not sustain a wound by the enemy, he would not be entitled to receive a Purple Heart. I do not believe that I was the only officer who simply reported that the soldier was killed while performing his duty in hostile action against the enemy. It wasn't until 1985 that award of the Purple Heart was finally authorized (Public Law 99–145) for wounds received as a result of friendly fire.

At the end of our bridge security assignment, my platoon was relieved by some tanks. This was the first time that I had ever seen a tank in Vietnam, as this was predominately a jungle country and not particularly conducive for tank warfare, and, to my knowledge, the enemy had only just starting using

11—Back to the Boonies (May–July 1968)

some light reconnaissance Russian tanks up around the DMZ about four months earlier, during the onset of the Tet Offensive, so I wasn't sure what was the role of armor in this war, except perhaps for performing road security.[9] During World War II the U.S. Army fielded four armored divisions for every seventeen infantry divisions, essentially a one-to-four ratio of tank units to infantry units, while in Vietnam, up through the spring of 1968, there were only two U.S. armor battalions in Vietnam, amongst approximately eleven infantry divisions (Marine and Army). These were M48A3 upgraded Patton tanks, fitted with powerful 90mm turret guns, capable of firing Canister and Bee-hive rounds against enemy infantry.[10]

I could see the tanks approaching as I was standing amongst my men. I suppose we all looked pretty much the same in our dirty, tattered jungle fatigues, and, like the rest of my men, I wore no identifying insignia. The lead tank came racing over the bridge, then it appeared to accelerate up the slope as it headed in our direction, before coming to a screeching halt, all fifty-two tons, virtually at our feet, spewing dust over those of us standing nearby. The hatch flipped open, and a young blond-haired officer stuck his head out. I could tell he was an officer because he had his second lieutenant's fabric bar sewn onto the lapel of his fatigue shirt. I must admit that he cut a dashing figure, and I could swear he was even wearing a yellow silk scarf to denote that he was in the cavalry.

Instead of asking for the officer in charge, the young armor officer started giving orders to my men, so I wandered over to this impudent officer to inquire about his orders and his mission. He continued to stand in the hatchway of his tank turret, while adopting the classic George Patton pose, with jutting jaw and the knuckles of each balled-fist resting on his waist, elbows pointing outward, addressing me and my men in a condescending fashion.

I had to check to see whether he was wearing ivory-handled revolvers, but his torso was too far down in the hatchway for me to get a clear look. When I informed him that I would be giving the orders to these men, he shrieked, "Who the hell are you?" At the time he was not yet aware of the fact that not only was I an officer as well, but, being that I was a first lieutenant, I outranked him. When he realized that I was the ranking officer, his demeanor changed dramatically, from insufferable arrogance to one of utmost geniality. Still, he could not believe that someone in such dirty, tattered jungle fatigues, sporting no insignia, could be the ranking officer. Welcome to the infantry!

I had been back in the jungle for about a month when it was announced that Democratic presidential nominee Robert Kennedy had been assassinated in Los Angeles on June 5. What was the world coming to? Only two months earlier Martin Luther King, Jr., had been assassinated, and now Bobby Kennedy? We were stupefied; we seemed to be losing all of our heroes.

VII

Even when we were out in the jungle, we were still required to shave. We turned our steel helmets upside down on the ground, poured in about half a canteen of cold water, and then started shaving, without shaving cream. We carried no mirrors, because they were too fragile and they reflected light, which could attract the enemy. The resupply choppers, weather permitting, continually provided us with loads of ammo, food, and cigarettes, but for some inexplicable reason they never brought us enough razor blades, such that we had to share a single double-edged blade amongst a squad of seven to nine guys for a week, at the end of which time I felt as though I was sandpapering off my whiskers. Maybe the supply guys in the rear felt that eighteen- to twenty-one-year-olds, being so young, didn't really need to shave all that much. I promised myself that when I returned to the States, not only would I forever appreciate clean sheets and hot showers, but I would also indulge in nice relaxing shaves, with warm lather and a brand new ultra-sharp double-edged razor blade each day, and that I would avail myself of the finest badger-haired shaving brush and shaving soap that money could buy.

Occasionally, whenever we found a relatively clean stream or river, we bathed, for even in the midst of the torrential monsoon the rain was insufficient to rinse the soap and shampoo off of a soldier standing naked out in the open, though we had certainly tried. Sometimes two weeks or so passed before we had the opportunity to bathe, at which time our fatigues were sweat-stained with visible salt markings, and our bodies stank. And just like dealing with leeches in the muddy rice paddies, we took turns bathing, while those not bathing provided security for those in the water.

In Vietnam, while out in the jungle, we could write letters home on anything at hand, affix no postage, and still the government delivered them. We wrote letters on pieces of the cardboard packaging of our C-rations, or made a small postcard from an inverted cigarette package, and they were delivered as bona fide pieces of mail through the U.S. Postal System. At the time, I thought this was pretty cool, receiving special treatment because I was living in a foxhole, though in my case, I had no wife or children to whom I could write. I didn't even have a steady girlfriend, so I never had to worry about receiving a "Dear John" letter apprising me that she had tired of waiting for my return and fallen in love with some Jody who had stayed behind. The Army uses marching cadences called jodies that refer to a mythical Jody, a civilian who remains at home and attempts to take advantage of your girlfriend. Of course, I could have written my mother, father, or my older sister Penny in Africa, but what was I going to write about? How many of the enemy we had killed that day? I did not write much; there was nothing to write home about, certainly not for the calm and stolid world back in the States; my letters would only upset and worry them; best to keep my fears and feelings of anxiety to myself. Why burden others?

11—Back to the Boonies (May–July 1968)

In 'Nam, I experienced a broader spectrum of emotions and feelings than those to which I had ever previously been exposed. In the war I felt terror, hunger, and thirst. Well, I was not dying of thirst, but I still felt this deprivation to a greater extent than at any other time in my life. During the dry season, for example, we would be so desperate for water that at times we filled our canteens with muddy water from a truck's tire depression on a road, and then we dropped a couple of halazone tablets into the canteen, shook it, then drank it. Halazone (p-N,N-dichlorosulfamylbenzoic acid) is a chloramine water-disinfecting agent that has a very strong and unpleasant chlorine smell.

During my time in the war zone, I felt exhaustion and fatigue, terror and grief, soaking wetness, cold, and sweltering humid heat, but oddly enough I felt no jealousy. I found that there was no jealousy out in the jungle. Of course, jealousy isn't really an emotion as a French professor later pointed out to me, "*Jalousie n'est pas une émotion, jalousie est un sentiment* (Jealousy isn't an emotion, jealousy is a sentiment)." Emotions, from the French viewpoint, are basic and instinctual such as the emotions of fear, love, sorrow, and rage, whereas sentiments are not instinctual, rather they are learned; we are not born with them.

In the States, life was so comfortable that people seemed to feel very little. Oh, they might talk about living for the moment, because there was always the possibility that they might be run over by a bus while leaving the bar at the end of the evening, but they were just posturing, for they knew very well that, in all likelihood, they would be waking up the next morning.

In 'Nam, we literally did not know if we would live to see another day, for we were always besieged by danger, and its collateral emotion—fear. Sometimes it almost seemed to me that back in the States the only intense sensation that people ever felt was sexual, which frequently fostered jealousy, because this was the one intense feeling that they could still experience in their prosaic world that was virtually devoid of emotions or other feelings of any gripping intensity.

Perhaps this is why we veterans of war have this mystical melancholia concerning our war experiences. Not that we would ever willingly volunteer to repeat the experience, but nevertheless we came to miss the intensity and breadth of emotions and feelings that we had experienced while struggling to survive in the jungle, and, most of all, we evinced a melancholy yearning for those rare insights into the meaning of life that had been afforded to us when we were under fire. It was as though we stood closer to the truth in war; an epiphany of sorts, that revealed itself only when one was facing death, expressed by the luminary tautology, "So, this is what it feels like to be truly alive!" And this was the gift that we brought back from the ordeal.

All of us, I am sure, slip into the somnolent passivity of taking life for granted at times, but still, there are periods when our appreciation for life is renewed, and I am certain that most survivors of war have more of these moments than they ever had before the trial of war. This is the discovery — that pure joy is nothing more than simply being alive. In other words, don't sweat the small stuff; you don't have to prove anything anymore.

VIII

We occasionally participated in helicopter assaults, which were always adrenalin-pumping experiences. We assembled on the tarmac in full battle regalia during the early pre-dawn hours, which in the tropics is the most magnificent part of the day, when the misty freshness of the air emanates a certain perfume that portends a renewal of the world, or a momentary perception of heaven.

We were all standing around with our weapons in hand, smoking cigarettes, while the weight of our heavy backpacks had not yet bent us over, as we waited for the choppers to arrive. We were assembled near our company or battalion perimeter, while the choppers had to come out from division base camp where they had been parked overnight. However, since we were heading out into combat, we did not talk much; rather, it was a time of silent personal communion, for we knew that we would soon be set down near a suspected enemy troop concentration, resultant from some gathered military intelligence; most likely one of our LRRPs had observed a sizeable enemy force in the vicinity during the night.

The whoop-whoop-whoop of the chopper rotors signaled their approach, just as the tropical pastels of light invaded the pre-dawn darkness, before the onset of the sapping humid heat that would soon be unleashed upon us. As the "slicks" (Bell helicopters powered by jet turbines, with the seats removed to accommodate more troops, designated UH-1 [utility helicopter], which the troops simply referred to as a "Huey") touched down on the tarmac, we hustled aboard while struggling under the weight of our heavy packs and ammunition. Each slick could accommodate a squad of about eight soldiers. Usually, we did helo assaults as a company of about 125 soldiers, though on a couple occasions the entire battalion assembled together for an air assault. This was something to see, as there were hundreds of troops, all loaded up with equipment, ammo, and three days' supply of food, in the early dawn light, ready to go, ready to kill. On occasion there were constraints brought about by the limitation of available helicopters, in which case we were compelled to go out in waves. If we were fortunate, we also had Bell AH-1G Cobra gunships as escorts, armed with 70mm rockets and Miniguns or 20mm "Gatling-style" cannon.

Once aloft, some of the men sat on their steel pots to protect their balls from being shot off by enemy ground fire. There were door gunners at each side of the slicks, who all wore flak jackets, blasting away with their M60 machine guns that fired .30 caliber (7.62mm) rounds at a rate of 550 rounds per minute, while the shell casings were bouncing all over the interior of the chopper.

I squatted in the open doorway and observed dozens of helicopters to my left and right, flying low over the emerald green jungle-canopy in the direction of the Laotian border, with the sun rising behind us, and then up ahead I could discern an open grassy breach in the jungle, as the choppers began to swoop down, preparing to drop us off.

The choppers swung in low, and the lush meadow, that appeared so inviting from a distance, had transformed itself up close into six-foot-high clumps of razor-sharp elephant grass, which posed a menacing obstacle for soldiers, yet provided an ideal habitat for tigers.

We all slid forward on the slick stripped-down deck of the chopper, until our boots were resting on the outside skids, as the chopper began its descent; with one hand we grabbed hold of the steel grips on the metal flooring of the chopper, while holding our rifle in the other hand, and as the chopper hovered about twenty feet over the ground we got ready to jump, and then when the chopper hovered about six feet above the ground, we jumped free of the skids. As we hit the ground, the weight of our heavy backpacks added to our momentum and sent us sprawling.

We furtively looked around to determine whether the landing zone was hot with enemy fire. If so, then we would pop a red smoke grenade to warn off the approaching choppers. If the LZ was not hot, we would pop green smoke to apprise the gunships and approaching helicopters to bring in the rest of the troops. The chopper pilots and door-gunners then returned to division base camp for the night, while we, the infantry, were left out there, long after darkness had descended, endeavoring to survive, for it was our job, unlike any other branch of the Army, to close with the enemy at close quarters and kill them before they killed us.

IX

The infantry, armor (tanks), and artillery comprise the three combat arms of the Army. Each branch had its own color that was exhibited on their dress uniforms. We in the infantry wore blue trim down the seam of our slacks and on the jacket sleeves of our dress uniforms; the armor (the old cavalry branch) wore yellow trim, while the artillery wore red trim. Originally, the cavalry were fighting horsemen, but horses had become obsolete by the time of World War I, and were replaced with motorized armored vehicles (tanks), and thus the armor, with its tanks, carried on the tradition of the cavalry. The First Cavalry Division, which had absorbed the Fifth, Seventh, and Eighth (horse) Cavalry Regiments back in the 1920s, left their horses behind when they went into battle in the Pacific during World War II.

Then, around 1965, with the expanded production of the helicopter, the First Cavalry Division became the Army's first airmobile division with more than four hundred helicopters, and its three brigades were deployed to Vietnam essentially as infantrymen.[11] The Second and Third Brigades were airmobile infantry, while only the soldiers of the First Brigade were airborne infantry (fully parachutist-qualified), though by late 1966 they too reverted to being airmobile infantry after it was determined that the use of parachute drops in Vietnam had become a remote possibility. These soldiers were entitled to wear the Combat Infantryman's Badge (CIB), for we in the infantry still considered tank drivers to be the modern-day (horseless) cavalry.

By the end of 1967 the number of U.S. military personnel in Vietnam had climbed to nearly 486,000, rising to more than 536,000 during bloody 1968. Nevertheless, the communists, via recruitment in the South, as well as infiltration from the North, were committed to keeping pace with American troop increases. There were a total of 16,899 American deaths (hostile and non-hostile) in Vietnam during 1968 of which 13,005 were killed in action (KIA). The total number of combat troops during this time was approximately 117,920 (22 percent of the more than 536,000 troops in country), and although the 13,005 KIAs (an average of more than thirty-five killed each day) were not all infantry, unquestionably the infantry suffered the preponderance of these deaths. These are high numbers, and are simply intended to illustrate the risks faced every day by the infantryman in his foxhole. And this only takes into account those killed in action; it does not even include the other three hostile (combat) death categories (died of wounds [1,630], missing in action/declared dead and captured/declared dead [272]).[12] The Army suffered 65 percent of all the hostile deaths in Vietnam; the Marines suffered 28 percent, while the Air Force and Navy suffered 4 percent and 3 percent respectively.[13] Within the Army, 70 percent of all hostile deaths were borne by the infantry (21,578), followed by Aviation (helicopters) (6 percent), and then Field Artillery (4 percent).[14]

The U.S. Department of Defense states that 153,303 U.S. troops were wounded in Vietnam, which equates to 3.7 soldiers wounded for every soldier killed in action, although this number only counts those who required hospitalization, in essence, those considered to be most seriously wounded; it does not count the other 150,332 additional soldiers (acknowledged by DoD, but in a separate category), who received flesh wounds from shrapnel or from small-arms fire and received treatment at field aid stations, and were then sent back to their units, which boosted the total number of U.S. soldiers wounded in Vietnam to 303,635, all of whom were entitled to award of the Purple Heart.[15] I sometimes wondered why two sets of books were kept on the wounded. Perhaps our leaders did not want the public to know how many soldiers were really bleeding in this war. If you consider that 2,644,000 servicemen and women served in Vietnam, of which 581,680 (22 percent) were in combat roles (if we were to take the total number of Army, Marines, Air Force, and Navy together,

11—Back to the Boonies (May–July 1968)

this conservative "combat role" percentage would be reduced even further), and if you add the 303,635 wounded to the 47,557 who suffered hostile deaths, then you begin to perceive the incredibly high percentage of combat troops who shed blood for their country in Vietnam. During 1968, at the height of the carnage in Vietnam, the odds of an infantryman being killed or wounded were the highest of the entire war, considering that there were 46,797 wounded (who required hospitalization) and 14,930 hostile deaths, of which infantrymen comprised the vast majority.[16]

I have heard people say that there are no atheists in foxholes, but I'm not so certain. I did not find God in my foxhole, just the opposite in fact, for death appeared to me to be completely arbitrary; good guys and bad guys would die, few were spared. I asked the inevitable rhetorical questions: Where was God? What was his purpose amongst all of this savagery? I understand that people need something beyond themselves for moral sustenance, something which attempts to explain the vagaries of existence. Voltaire once said that if God did not exist, it would be necessary to invent him, and I understand that people need something, larger than self, to grab hold of, be it religion or philosophy. I do not believe I am the only veteran of war who has forsaken religion. The more one sees of the horror and brutality of life, the more one questions the sense of it all. Is there any meaning to the madness?

There was a popular Vietnam War movie, *Platoon*, that came out in 1986, eleven years after the war had ended, that attempted to capture this very period of the war, as the filmmaker, Oliver Stone, arrived in Vietnam the same month as I (and was also born in the same month and year as I). Though he served with the Third Battalion of the Twenty-Second Infantry Regiment, which was part of the Third Brigade of the Twenty-Fifth Infantry Division at the time (on August 1, 1967, the Fourth Infantry Division and the Twenty-Fifth Infantry Division swapped Third Brigades). I felt that Oliver did a masterful job in putting this film together.

12

Last Six Weeks
(August–September 1968)

I

After more than ten months in Vietnam I finally took my one and only R&R (Rest & Recuperation) trip, intended to provide a respite from the stress of combat. Some soldiers, mostly those in the rear, arranged to take two, or even three, R&Rs during their tours, but soldiers in the field got only one trip. Though most soldiers were eligible for R&R after six months in Vietnam, I purposely scheduled my R&R toward the end of my twelve-month tour, in order to lessen any thoughts I might have, once away from the battlefield, of failing to return to the war.

We could choose from ten locations: Hawaii (which my brigade headquarters told me was reserved only for married guys), Sydney, Tokyo, Hong Kong, Manila, Singapore, Taipei, Penang (Malaysia), Kuala Lumpur (Malaysia), or Bangkok. Due to travel distances, R&R in Hawaii and Australia was for seven days, while for all other locations it was for five days. I had been to Australia when I worked in the merchant marine before the Army, so I decided to choose Bangkok, because I wanted to go some place where I could really lose myself in a foreign world. I came in from the field to base camp and pulled my class B service uniform out of my duffle bag, which was a khaki uniform that resembled the class A service uniform, but without the coat, and I shined up my brass belt buckle with some Brasso, and got ready for my flight out of the war to Thailand.

The Thais are a people who were driven out of China more than a thousand years ago, during which time they migrated to the south and established their kingdom in modern-day Thailand around 860 A.D. In Bangkok I found a bar where I was able to drink absinthe, the bitter, strong, licorice-flavored, emerald-green liqueur that turns milky when water is added. Absinthe is an extremely potent drink containing 68 percent (136 proof) alcohol; it also contains wormwood, which is a wild herb that grows in Europe. The production of absinthe was banned in France during the 1920s because it was believed that absinthe users were prone to paranoia, madness, and suicide; it was considered as dangerous as opium or cocaine.

12—Last Six Weeks (August–September 1968)

Wormwood is no longer used in the production of licorice-flavored drinks like pastis, but it was still available in Bangkok, like every other seductive opiate. I drank absinthe from the time the bars opened in the morning till they closed late at night. Perhaps I had been in the jungle too long, for it seemed that most of the soldiers on R&R were smiling, laughing, and enjoying the typical carefree pursuits of R&R, yet the battle-hardened warriors amongst us were more somber, and tended to gather in dark places. Perhaps we were more tenaciously endeavoring to forget—yesterday, as well as the day before yesterday.

Most all of the soldiers on R&R went straight to the public massage parlors where the young women were all behind glass, wearing numbers pinned to their bras, and the soldiers would pick out the number they wanted, and they would have that woman for their entire time in Bangkok, twenty-four hours a day. A fair number of us infantrymen were more interested in forgetting the war through alcohol and opiates, and so I did not take a woman for the week; rather, I just took a woman on a daily basis, when I was in the mood, though it got harder and harder to get a pretty girl, as the Thai women did not favor one-night stands; they called us butterflies.

In my absinthe-induced phantasmagoric hallucinations, I envisioned myself surviving the war and making it all the way back to "the world," but then I would succumb to imaginary fears that the world had changed in my absence, and there was no longer any place for me, and then my anxieties would subside, but then they would resurge once again, and I would become fretful that the world had not changed at all; rather, it was I who had changed, and I had changed to the point that there was no place for me back in the world.

> And sipping of my Pernod, and a-knowing what I know,
> Sometimes I want to shriek aloud and give away the show.
> I've lost my nerve; he's haunting me; he's like a beast of prey,
> That Spanish man that's watching at the Café de la Paix.[1]

II

After my return from my five days of R&R, I was informed that I was to serve as the S-3 Air for the battalion during my remaining five weeks in Vietnam. This was a staff position (generally filled by some unfortunate captain). I would be the officer-in-charge (OIC) of air-operations for our infantry battalion. Essentially, I would be spending virtually all daylight hours up in helicopters serving as the battalion forward artillery observer, even though I was an infantry officer, and I would otherwise assist our four infantry companies on the ground.

This also happened to be the time when the third, and proclaimed decisive, communist offensive phase was to kick off (17 August 1968), and continue for about five and a half weeks. More than 2,000 Americans were killed in action during the months of August and September 1968.[2] During this third phase, the NVA, in lieu of the VC (as in the first phase), did most of the fighting. Nevertheless, the communists suffered another tactical defeat, as was the case during the first and second phases, and yet the strategic victory they had unexpectedly garnered during the first phase of the Tet Offensive was sufficient to achieve victory.

Now that I was back at battalion headquarters, I was required to wear my officer's fabric insignia on my uniform, including my CIB above my heart and my Fourth Infantry Division patch on my left shoulder, though I didn't know why all this was required, since I was still out in the boonies; perhaps this was done so that occasional VIP visitors from brigade or division could easily discern our ranks at a glance, and not mistake me, at the age of twenty-one, as a private or a corporal; perhaps I should have grown a moustache after all.

This assignment was nearly as hazardous as being a platoon leader, for if any of our four infantry companies on the ground came into contact with the enemy, then I was required to remain aloft, calling in artillery and air strikes. Now I had become the poor son of a bitch who had to hover above the fighting during daylight hours, until such time as battalion could coerce some unfortunate captain into filling the slot. There was, however, one not so small consolation: I wouldn't have to hump a seventy-pound backpack around the boonies all day long.

I have been shot at in virtually every type of helicopter that was flown in Vietnam; sometimes I flew in the little OH-6 two-seater light observation bubble helicopter, manufactured by the Hughes Aircraft Division, often referred to as the "Flying Egg," though it could kick it up to nearly 150 miles per hour. This was indisputably the time when I upped my daily dosage of Camel cigarettes to four packs a day. To go from no cigarettes to four packs a day in less than a year probably indicates a certain degree of stress. I suppose that before Vietnam I hadn't a frigging clue as to what stress really was; four packs a day to cope with stress is beyond the pale, beyond what one could possibly face in a civilized environment, for this was the stress of terror and killing. Actually, with only about six hours of sleep a day, this equated to less than five cigarettes an hour, which didn't seem like a whole lot to me at the time.

I smoked quite a few Camels while waiting on the tarmac — alone, for the arrival of my helo at first light each morning. The helo had to come out from division base camp to pick me up in a jungle clearing that was hacked out of the thick jungle foliage alongside our battalion headquarters. During those moments I wanted so much to say, "No thank you, I'd prefer not to do this today." However, there was no one to whom I could appeal; those were the orders, and so I just had to grit my teeth and do my duty, and climb aboard the chopper.

We were all a bit crazy by this time, including the chopper pilots who flew so low and fast that we were literally tree-hopping in order to minimize the

12—Last Six Weeks (August–September 1968)

enemy's opportunity to shoot us down. I had become a "double-digit midget" about two months ago, insofar as my remaining days in Vietnam were concerned, and I was now considered a short timer. We began to chide those soldiers with triple digits by saying, "I'm getting so short, I have to look up just to look down." Or, "I'm so short; I have to reach up just to tie my shoes." Becoming a double-digit midget was the first major breakthrough on the road to becoming a single-digit midget, and the realization that one would soon be departing the war and heading home.

I recall a time when our battalion commander was leaving the field to return to the land of the big PX (meaning the United States), and I happened to be accompanying him as he went for his last traditional goodbye helicopter ride in Vietnam. The pilot took the chopper straight up to around 10,000 feet; it could rise to over 14,000 feet but we were limited by our oxygen dependency; still, at 10,000 feet, I could feel the frigid cold through the sizzling heat of the tropics. Then the pilot stalled the chopper, and we began to free-fall back toward earth while experiencing a stomach-churning sense of weightlessness as we rapidly careened toward the ground, and all the while the pilot was attempting to regain control of the chopper by autorotation of its rotors.

This was a white-knuckle experience that brought our stomachs up into our throats, though of course we were all too macho to display any fear, so we all pasted tight-lipped grins on our faces. Personally, I did not think this was so cool at the time, but I was not really pissed off either. I don't think we cared so much about dying at that point; we had seen so much death that it was really no big whoop, so we just grinned and endured the ride.

III

War is not Hollywood. In the movies, soldier-actors attempt to portray indomitable courage, which they conceive as standing up and firing away at the enemy while bullets are bristling all around them. However, movies are a form of entertainment; they rarely capture the stark terror of staring death in the face. No person can see in advance how he or she will hold up when death is stalking nearby. War deepens the personal understanding of the survivor; for a man who has never had to face a bullet, meant to kill, cannot fully understand this inexorable fear, and this was simply survival—the first step. One could take other steps, at one's own risk, which could take one ever further away from home and from one's own sanity. Other steps led all the way to heroism. I never aspired so high, because I was afraid, but not so fearful that I failed to do my duty.

I knew a few soldiers who appeared to be fearless, who would stand straight up on their feet and just blaze away at the enemy; not many, maybe one or two out of fifty. I certainly thought they were a little dinky dau (crazy), for it truly was abnormal behavior, that's undeniable. I was not one of them.

War is the act of extinguishing lives to preserve one's own, while under severe stress and fatigue, and in this sense it is truly primordial, reflecting the most primitive and bestial nature of humankind from which we apparently have not yet transcended. I have seen soldiers who, while under fire, have been unable to control their bowels, and I can understand their fear. I have seen men, who, while in the jungle, have had nervous breakdowns which revealed themselves in bizarre physical manifestations akin to epileptic fits, during which we hurriedly looked for something to place in the sufferer's mouth in order to keep him from swallowing his tongue while he was going through convulsions, until the seizures passed; this was a level of fear that few people rarely experience during their entire lives. I mean, who would voluntarily submit themselves to this degree of terror? I'm sure there are thrill-seekers back in the world who love bungee jumping and other death-defying activities; nevertheless, there is a level of fear that one experiences in combat that is beyond the imaginings of the ordinary person, where even your parents cannot reach you.

August 1968, age 21— The author serving as battalion S-3 Air, after eleven months in the war.

There was a scene in the (1978) *Deer Hunter* movie, when the soldiers were being held prisoner in the tiger cage, and they were hyperventilating from terror, and though this was simply an imaginary scene that never really happened, except on the silver screen, they did a fine job of conveying an approximation of this sense of wartime fear, though even this exceptional acting was somewhat exaggerated, because some degree of denial is essential in order to function, in order to survive.

Does art imitate life or does life imitate art? Undoubtedly, in the beginning, art imitated life, for one only has to look at a Hardin spear point from the Early Archaic Period (around 7,500 B.C.), following the last ice age, to recognize that this hunting tool, with its sharp point and well executed flaking that had shaped its razor-sharp serrated blade edges was a formidable killing tool, crafted for man's very survival.

Yet this spear point was also exceptionally beautiful in its practical aesthetic and has forever after been imitated in the world of art, for the tool itself is undoubtedly a work of art, derived almost by accident from practical necessity.

However, there have been times when the artist shapes life itself, when a literary genius like Shakespeare could actually rewrite history in the *Tragedy of King Richard the Third* that vilified the last king of the House of York, thus paving the way for the Tudor royal line that ruled England during the time of Shakespeare, or, when a gifted painter like Pablo Picasso could influence people to see the world in an entirely new way during his cubist period, by portraying space and dimension without resorting to the illusion of perspective, thus prompting the viewer to rely on his intellect, rather than his senses, to discern the true reality of things.

John Wayne, Charles Bronson, and Steve McQueen were the cinema heroes of my adolescent days, and I enjoyed their action movies, although these celebrated actors never really fought out of a foxhole; rather they were simply actors attempting to portray real-life people. Yet, is it not conceivable that real-life people, in turn, strive to emulate the actions of their cinema heroes?

Did I grow up watching John Wayne movies and then rush out into the world with a vision of emulating John Wayne and his way of handling tough situations? Perhaps, in the beginning, but it did not take me long to realize that John Wayne had never actually found himself in the face of a fusillade of bullets, looking imminent death in the face, for if he had, then he would have revealed some perceptible degree of fear, for even the most courageous of heroes must exhibit some emotive reaction whilst standing in a hailstorm of bullets, be it only the squinting of the eyes in a futile, but unconscious, attempt to ward off the approaching projectiles.

I sometimes read Civil War history books that depicted the apparent flagrant disregard of danger exhibited by infantry officers who were leading their men into the attack, but even they, I'm sure, evinced some emotion, even with their stoic fearlessness that was intended to reassure and calm their men. Still, I am convinced that they displayed something, whether it was a tightened jaw, a pulsating heart, or a rush of pure adrenalin. When I watch the cinema war heroes stand up on the celluloid screen in the face of enemy fire while displaying no discernable human frailty, I question the credulity of the scene.

Is it the experience of the real-life person, or the depiction of the cinema actor, that most successfully captures the hearts and the minds of the audience? Are we drawn to reality, or to romantic fantasy? I think the answer is obvious, because I too was John Wayne, until my first encounter with deathly war and brutal reality. Movie actors tend to depict war as heroic, but war, from the perspective of the foxhole, is anything but heroic, it is an abominable struggle for survival; it is the application of the primordial kill-or-be-killed mentality. We had become animals and little more.

The Lou Rawls rendition of the song "They Don't Give Medals To Yesterday's Heroes" holds particular meaning for me, because one might very well be a hero on one occasion, or even on several occasions, but that does not necessarily mean that one will not succumb to the stress of battle fatigue on yet another day. In World War II, during the invasion of Normandy, the planners arranged for fresh units without a great deal of combat experience to assault the beaches, for they were well aware of the fact that soldiers who had previously run head on into burning-hot, lethal metal soon realized that death is indiscriminate, and they thus became less and less inclined to expose themselves to enemy fire.[3]

Being shot at is petrifying. Real life means applying a tourniquet and hoping that the wound can be treated before the limb needs to be amputated. Real life means plugging a sucking chest wound with the cellophane wrapper from your cigarette pack so the lung will not deflate. Real life is scary shit.

IV

In Vietnam I was required to coordinate all activities by my watch. We officers set our watches for troop movements and for coordinated assaults, to the point where I was sick and tired of wearing a watch and keeping track of time. Toward the end of my tour I gave my watch away to a Montagnard who had befriended me. I hoped that I would no longer have any further need for a watch.

Generally, infantry lieutenants only spent six months in combat, and then they were pulled back to the rear and assigned to some staff job; this was the common practice. I suppose the Army considered that six months under fire was the limit, in terms of the stress, that an infantry officer should reasonably be expected to bear. However, I was an exception in that I spent virtually my entire tour in combat leadership roles, except for the S-3 Air assignment, but that was also on the frontline, so essentially I spent my entire twelve-month tour in harm's way, which was rare for an infantry lieutenant, though it was not rare for an enlisted infantryman. Privates, corporals and sergeants spent their entire year in a combat environment; they were the true heroes. Some soldiers during World War II served for more than four years in combat units, but they still had established frontlines and places in the rear where they could be pulled out of the fighting to rest and recuperate, but in Vietnam there were no clearly defined frontlines and so the soldiers in their foxholes were continually under threat, and thus for them, eleven to twelve months of combat seemed interminable.

During my five weeks as S-3 Air, we frequently took sniper fire while I was riding in the Bell UH-1 "Huey" chopper, which was your standard assault helicopter, and on those occasions the door gunners just blasted away with their M60 machine guns, but when I was in the Flying Egg, there were only two of us, the pilot and me, so the pilot kept on flying, while I would lean out of the chopper and return fire with my M16. Fortunately for me, during my five weeks in the air, I was not involved in any battalion-size engagements, and thus spent most of my time assisting the artillery, located on a hill several miles behind me, in plotting and registering their rounds around our infantry companies when they were digging in toward the end of each day, in case they were attacked during the night and needed to call for artillery support.

On 21 August 1968, the Chicago police beat and tear-gassed a crowd of 10,000 anti-war demonstrators during the Democratic Convention. The initial front-runner, Bobby Kennedy, who had won the critical California primary, had been assassinated a little more than two months ago and was no longer in the running, which left about a half-dozen lackluster candidates running for president, of which Richard Nixon, a Republican, appeared to be ahead in the polls. Nixon had served as vice president under Eisenhower from 1953 to January 1961, at the end of which time he had run for president, but lost against Kennedy in the November 1960 elections. Two years later, in 1962, Nixon ran for governor of California and lost again, but now he was back, saying that he had a plan for stopping the blood-letting in Vietnam, yet Nixon held his cards close to his chest and deferred from revealing any details concerning his plan.

On the very same day that the Chicago cops were beating in the heads of protestors, Soviet tanks rolled into Prague, Czechoslovakia, and smashed the liberal reform government of Alexander Dubček. The United States was too bogged down in Vietnam at this time to become embroiled in events taking place in Eastern Europe. Students around the world during this year — in Berkeley, in New York at Columbia, in Berlin, Paris, Rome, Warsaw, Tokyo, Mexico City, and Prague, protested vociferously against the United States (for its involvement in the Vietnam War), as well as against the Soviet Union (for its invasion of Czechoslovakia).[4] Young people around the world wanted an end to the Cold War, of which Vietnam and Czechoslovakia were simply offshoots, and the young people also wanted an end to the incessant, bellicose bickering between the United States and the Soviet Union. Their slogan was, "Make love not war!"

At the time of the Democratic Convention in Chicago I was twenty-one years of age and scheduled to depart the war within three weeks. These students were my contemporaries, though, by remaining in school, they had not been required to serve in the military like me, and yet I was the object of their vituperation. Did I have any right to be angry? Would I be able to relate to them? I would try. Meanwhile, I had more pressing concerns — namely survival.

In the Army, the infantry is referred to as "The Queen of Battle." This was meant as a compliment to the infantry, which prompted the respect of all the other branches of the Army, because only the infantry had the most hazardous mission of coming face-to-face and closing with the enemy. We, as infantrymen, not only had tremendous pride in being in the infantry, we truly believed we were the best in the Army, and nobody in the Army was bleeding more than the infantry.

The other branches of the Army no doubt thought we were out of our minds to join the infantry, yet they grudgingly admitted that we bore the brunt and the horror of war. Generally, the artillery was several miles behind the infantry, on some fortified hilltop, supporting us when we were under attack. As previously mentioned, if an infantryman had been in combat for a specified period of time, then he was entitled to wear the CIB (Combat Infantryman's Badge) on the left side of his uniform, above all of his other ribbons and medals. Only an infantryman who had been in combat and under fire was entitled to wear this badge of distinction. Additionally, the CIB was not intended for general officers, because the recipient must be serving in the frontlines, in an infantry unit no larger than a battalion. There is the story often told of General Douglas MacArthur, who had won so many medals, including the Medal of Honor during World War I, yet still he craved a CIB, which he never did receive, because by the time the War Department established the criteria for the Badge in 1943, MacArthur was already serving far above battalion level.

PART III: 1968–1970

13

Homecoming (September 1968)

I

After completing my year in the war zone, I was leaving the jungle highlands of Vietnam during the first week of September. This was it: I had become a single-digit midget; my time was up. Still, anyone leaving the jungle was beset with mixed emotions. We were truly sad to leave our fellow comrades, but those of us departing put on forced smiles as we shook the hands of those remaining behind. We had done our duty for our country, not much more could be expected. We were the fortunate few, with a sense of pride in our fellow soldiers and ourselves.

The war would go on without me, but I would not forget, certainly not these men, my fellow warriors, some of whom fought in these Highlands through the summer of 1969. There was no formal goodbye ceremony out in the jungle, and by this time my unit had moved south of Pleiku in the direction of Ban me Thuot, the southernmost city of the central highlands, an area where wild elephants can still be found. A supply chopper, making its rounds, took me and a couple others back to division base camp where I had to wait around for my Bronze Star ceremony, which was finally conducted on the very day of my twenty-second birthday. I stood in a line with about a half-dozen other soldiers, while our brigade commander read our citations and passed out our medals. The next morning I headed over to the nearby Air Base where I walked out onto the tarmac and boarded a barebones C-130 and strapped myself into one of the jump seats, along with about a dozen other soldiers who were also departing the highlands.

I had spent my entire year in the highlands with the Second Brigade of the Fourth Infantry Division and its Mortar Battery, operating in an area no more than 130 miles south to north (stretching from Ban Me Thuot in the south to Dak To in the north, with Pleiku near the middle), and no more than forty miles east to west, though this still encompassed an area of 5,200 square miles (about the same size as the State of Connecticut), much of which was shrouded in thick jungle interspersed with numerous rivers and rice paddies, with few roads, and where most travel was done along jungle footpaths or by simply cutting our own paths with our machetes, thus making our area of operations (AOR) a fair-sized expanse for our under-strength brigade of around 1,600 fighting infantrymen to cover. Yet during my time in the central highlands, there were seldom more than three American brigades (equivalent to one division) patrolling the highlands at any one time, which was less than 5,000 frontline infantrymen.

The 173rd Airborne Brigade, elements of the First Air Cav, and the Third Brigade of the 101st Airborne, served in the highlands at times, but being air mobile they were frequently moved around and saw much more of the country than we did, though I don't know if they considered all that air travel as a plus. Nevertheless, we straight-leg infantrymen did not move around as much as the airborne soldiers. Did our leaders really expect us to win the war with no more than a division-sized force in the highlands?

This was our last flight over enemy territory, as we interminably made our way down from the mountains to the coast and the port city of Cam Ranh. Many of the soldiers were making macabre jokes about what a hell of an ending it would be if we were shot down on our very last day in the combat zone, after surviving for an entire year in the fetid jungles below us.

I actually got stuck in Cam Ranh for two nights before I was able to board a commercial jet for my flight back to the States. Unfortunately, I got involved in a poker game on my last night, during which I lost most all of my pocket money.

I had been to Cam Ranh Bay previously, a little more than three years ago, when I was working as an ordinary seaman on troop transports in the merchant marine, during which time my ship had transported the First Brigade of the 101st Airborne across the Pacific Ocean and into this port during July 1965. At that time there was nothing at Cam Ranh except a couple of dilapidated old piers that jutted out into the South China Sea. Now the port facilities were extensively developed and looked a lot like the port of San Pedro, California.

While waiting for my commercial flight out of Cam Ranh, I had simply assumed that I would be returning to Travis Air Force Base near Sacramento from where I had departed for the war, and which was only a two-hour bus ride from home. However, it was not until the last minute, prior to departure, before I was informed that I was flying into Fort Lewis near Seattle, more than eight hundred miles from home. When I landed at Fort Lewis and was going through (military) customs, the MPs (military police) were saying to me that I could just grab my duffle bag and catch a taxi right outside the door to the commercial airport. I realized that I could have stowed a couple weapons and grenades in my duffle bag, as the MPs did not even bother to open an officer's bag.

I asked the MPs how much was the taxi fare to the commercial airport? They all laughed, because they could not believe that an officer ever lacked for money; however, I wasn't laughing, for I was trying to figure out whether I could even afford the taxi fare after having been fleeced in last night's poker game.

13—Homecoming (September 1968)

When I arrived at the Tacoma-Seattle Airport, I dialed up my mother's home in the San Francisco Bay Area, but no one answered the phone (she had flown down to Southern California to visit family, as she had no idea when I would actually be returning from the war). So I proceeded to telephone Mrs. Hursh, the mother of my high school friend Gary, and asked her if she could wire me some money so that I could complete the last leg of my journey home from Seattle, for these were the days before there were any ATMs or extensive use of credit cards. It was nine years before the first full-service ATM was installed in a bank in Ohio (in 1977), and although some Diners Club and American Express credit cards were in circulation, it really wasn't until 1976, after BankAmericard changed its name to Visa, that people began to frequently use credit cards as a matter of course. And there were no cell phones at this time; another fourteen years passed before the Federal Communications Commission (FCC), authorized the usage of commercial cell phones in the United States in 1982.

Fortunately, Mrs. Hursh agreed to wire me the money via Western Union. However, the money would not reach me until the following day, so I proceeded to spend my first night back in the States sleeping across several plastic seats in the arrival lounge at the Tacoma-Seattle Airport, though at least now I could legally enter the airport bar and order a beer. I had turned twenty-one during the week I had arrived in Vietnam, so I had not much opportunity to legally drink at a bar in the United States until now.

People whom I had known prior to Vietnam, or whom I had encountered in Vietnam, had some bizarre comments about how they perceived I had been affected by the war. For example, I had attended high school with a guy named George; we were in the same high school class and even spent time hanging out together during our school days. After the Battle of Dak To, when my battalion had returned to division base camp, some of the guys in my platoon actually knew George, who was a truck driver in the rear, and so they invited him to come over and join us infantrymen for a beer.

It was good to see my old high school friend, though it had been three years since we had last seen one another. I felt that we had a nice time during our visit, drinking some beers together and catching up on the past. However, when I returned to the States nearly nine months after our base camp reunion, I ran into someone who had talked to George upon his return, and he told me that George had mentioned running into me in 'Nam, and that George had depicted me as a "psychotic and fearsome wild man." Perhaps George was right. But then again, I was an officer, though I was in the infantry where officers and enlisted men shared the same foxholes, and I remembered, during my early training days, how we had all been struck with terror whenever an officer appeared, and so perhaps George just tripped out because he was not used to hanging out with officers; I mean it's a possibility, because I cannot believe I was that bad.

I thought back to the time when I had first gone out into the boonies after arriving in Vietnam and all the soldiers out in the jungle seemed to talk incessantly about war, and killing, and dying, and perhaps over time I had become just like them. I had probably unsettled George when I talked about killing in the jungle. My mother once showed me a letter I had written to her from Vietnam, and even when I was reading the letter, it was hard for me to recognize the author as myself.

II

I was the favored son; I did not lack for love growing up. My parents were products of the Great Depression, though they were just reaching their teens during those harsh times. My father was born on his family's horse ranch in Oregon in 1917, but the family was ultimately compelled to sell the ranch during the Depression and move to Pasadena, California, where my grandfather struggled to eek a living selling real estate, while his wife ironed bed linens in an old folks' home. Both of my parents picked up the prevailing values from those hard times. They were conservative and hardworking, and they were imbued with a deep appreciation for education. My father continued to read classical literature and could quote Shakespeare extensively into his eighties. My parents exhibited a perceptible depth and strength of character, and they possessed all of the laudatory qualities of those Depression days—abject honesty, an unquestioning work ethic, the deepest compassion, devout loyalty, and the highest moral and spiritual character.

My father only physically disciplined me on two occasions: once for talking back to my mother, and another time when I uttered the word *damn*. We did not swear in my family. And yet, when I returned from the war after living exclusively with men for a year in jungle foxholes, I had begun to use rough and coarse language; it just slipped out, and oftentimes in mixed company, unfortunately.

Undoubtedly war is brutalizing. I had lived like an animal for a year, and now I was trying to fit back into society. I was expected to just slip back into the comfortable world that I had inhabited before I was sent off to the war, and forget all about the recent bestial and horrific past.

My uncle John, who had served in the South Pacific during World War II, couldn't wait to sequester me at a family gathering upon my return from the war. Our encounter was like a Norman Rockwell painting, where two men, one older and one younger, had gathered together in the garage, away from the women. And the young man was in military uniform, and the two men were speaking, almost with an air of solemnity, and I discerned that Uncle John couldn't wait to hear my war stories, engendering heroic images of Iwo Jima, except that he could see in my eyes, right away, that there was no bravado, and that I really did not want to talk about the war. Uncle John had been a diver in

13—Homecoming (September 1968)

the Navy out in the Pacific during World War II, which was a high-risk occupation, although he had not been under fire, and so he was perplexed by my reluctance to recount stories of war.

One afternoon I was taking lunch with another old high school friend, named Larry, who was working as a certified public accountant (CPA) in San Francisco's Financial District, and during our meal Larry confided to me that when I first returned from the war, the one thing that he clearly, and hauntingly, remembered was that I "had the shakes," that my "hands were constantly shaking." I was truly amazed by his observations, because he only mentioned this to me more than thirty years after my return from the war.

Okay, maybe I had been a little crazy back in 'Nam, but I was certainly better now, wasn't I? After a year of struggling to survive in the kill-or-be-killed environment of Vietnam, returning to the States was like returning to another planet. People seemed so secure in the Land of the big PX. They were comfortable in their certitude that they would sleep soundly during the night and awake the next morning. They were not in death-defying professions where they were expected to go out and kill each day.

Their understanding of life was incomplete. They were unaware that the law of the jungle still prevailed in many places on this planet. I was less naive, for I knew that my human species (*Homo sapiens sapiens*), after nearly 200,000 years of existence, had not ascended very high up the evolutionary ladder.[1]

I realized upon my return from the war that I was different. The world appeared the same, but it seemed that I had changed. After my return, I had less fear, and it was not because I was naively fearless, for I had seen death aplenty in Vietnam; rather it was more of a kind of "I don't give a shit" kind of fearlessness, which is the really scary type. I had less fear of bullies on the street, of intimidation, of failure, of everything—except love.

> Cowards die many times before their deaths;
> The valiant never taste of death but once.
> Of all the wonders that I yet have heard,
> It seems to me most strange that men should fear;
> Seeing that death, a necessary end,
> Will come when it will come.[2]

Upon my return to the States I was authorized thirty days of leave, which is the military word for vacation. What did I do? Not much. I spent most of the time with my mother and my father who lived about 400 miles apart from one another. I smoked a lot of cigarettes; I went to bars in San Francisco with my old high school friends (with my shaking hands), now that we were all of legal drinking age. We had very little to talk about; as though we epitomized two worlds colliding—one being the world filled with brightness and the levity of youth, and the other world filled with darkness, struggle, and death. Did people really expect that my demons would just fall away?

One day, while I was on leave in California, just two weeks out of the war,

I found myself in Los Angeles with my stepsister Rebecca, as my father had remarried while I was in Vietnam, and we were in a rough part of town, and two big, tough-looking black men saw us from across the street and proceeded to cross the street at an angle to intercept us.

I could see them out of the corner of my eye, and then there they were — right smack dab in front of us, blocking our way. They were both much bigger than I, and here I was, a white guy in a t-shirt — in their neighborhood, smoking a cigarette just as casually as you please. The two aggressively challenged me with their eyes, and I gave them just a regular look, which nevertheless appeared to cause something to germinate in their eyes, like a palpable fear of portending darkness, which produced a startling change in the belligerent demeanor of these two street toughs.

Perhaps I had also said, "Fuck off," although I cannot recall saying anything at all. It was just the look, of which I was not even aware, that stopped them dead in their tracks, and then they even docilely stepped aside, as my stepsister and I walked between them. Even my stepsister commented on my behavior, which momentarily frightened her, as it had also frightened the two thugs, as though some residual emanations from my wartime exposure to death were radiating from off of my body, like invisible tentacles, and squeezing the hostility out of those two bullies. They could clearly sense my "I don't give a shit" attitude, and so they kept their distance.

I felt more apathy toward life after my return from the war; most endeavors seemed mundane and meaningless. Had I become a callous soul? Was I no longer capable of finding true love and happiness? What would become of me over the next thirty years? Would my life become an enlightened uphill journey, or a downward desolate slide? Although at the time I really did not give a hell of a lot of thought to the next thirty years, I just wanted to get away, even though I still had nearly six more months to do in the Army.

While on leave in California I had no exciting homecoming adventures, no love affairs — nothing. I felt alienated from everybody, from friends, from family, perhaps even from myself. I felt alone, the way we are when we enter this world, and the way we will be when we leave this world — alone. I did not consider this realization frightening; I recognized it for what it was — life. The doors of perception had opened, and I had absolutely no recourse but to walk on through, or perhaps I was pushed, but wherever I was going, it seemed better than remaining in this insulated environment where people appeared to be incessantly chattering away about nothing in particular, but chattering away nevertheless, in their frantic attempts to fill the frightening void of emptiness, that surrounds us all, with pointless noise.

Most people believe that the experience of war has a beginning and an end, like a chapter in a book, which is followed by another chapter pertaining to school or work, but life is not that simple. The chapter concerning war, where one was involved in killing other human beings, has no end. It is an

13—Homecoming (September 1968)

experience that one carries around for the rest of one's life, like a nagging weight on one's back that one can never entirely shake. We come to find that we are condemned to lug our morbid wartime yesterdays throughout all of our todays, and all of our tomorrows. In any case, I was relieved once again to get away, even if only to some army fort in the Deep South.

I purchased a sports car while I was on leave, a sleek blue Triumph GT-6, and I headed eastward across the country, enroute to my last Army assignment at Fort Polk, Louisiana, reputed to be the armpit of the Army.

I drove across the country on Route 66, which was nothing more than a four-lane highway in those days, before it became a freeway. Whenever Route 66 entered a major city, like Albuquerque or Oklahoma City, I was compelled to drive from stoplight to stoplight, and there was always a diner, with a bleached blond buxom waitress on the other side of forty who still made decent tips from serving coffee to lonely and horny travelers.

I stopped over in Albuquerque, New Mexico, for a couple of days to visit with my sister Penny and her husband John; they had not been married long. I had missed the wedding because I was in Vietnam. John was now working as a Marine recruiter. I had not seen much of my sister during the last four years, so we particularly enjoyed our visit together.

Less than three months after my visit, John was stricken with spinal meningitis, which left him paralyzed from the waist down and confined him to a wheelchair for the rest of his life. He no longer fit the image of a Marine recruiter, and ended his military career on full disability. I visited him at the Veterans' Hospital in Long Beach, California, where I pushed him around in his wheelchair, and we sat out in the little garden area and talked together, mostly about pain and suffering, and the meaning of life.

Veterans' hospitals are such sobering reminders of war; perhaps that is why they are hidden away from the general public for the most part. In these hospitals I encountered battle-scarred veterans of Vietnam, and also some lingering casualties of Korea and even World War II. There I saw the multiple amputees, the paraplegics, and the quadriplegics, none of whom would ever find their way onto a recruiting poster. Even family visitors appeared to be infrequent callers on these gruesome reminders of the horrors of war. I considered these veterans' hospitals to be such truly depressing places, because they were habitually filled with young men, who made up the bulk of the patients, though I also observed that quite a few of these patients, from earlier wars, had grown old and gray, and forgotten, in these hospitals.

14

Stateside Army

I

I spent my last five months in the Army at Fort Polk, Louisiana, which like every other Army fort in the South to which I had ever been assigned was named after some Confederate general; at least those old Confederate warriors undoubtedly would have understood us Vietnam vets a lot better than the people north of the Mason-Dixon Line, for those old Confederates indubitably knew something about defeat. I don't know if victory would have made me feel any better, for I have come to realize that everyone who goes to war comes back a casualty.

It was difficult returning to stateside garrison duty, as every veteran knows. I was back in the world of G.I. (Government Issue) haircuts and spit-shined boots. I no longer cared about such things, and yet I was an officer who was expected to set the example.

I could understand why some soldiers willingly volunteered to return to Vietnam for a second tour, because no one cared about spit-shined boots in the jungle, and men did not have to salute in the field; in fact that's the last thing I ever wanted any of my men to do in the boonies, salute and thereby identify me as the officer in full view of the enemy; might as well just pin a target on my back.

Spit-shined boots and a snappy salute, what purpose did they have in the daily struggle for survival in the muck and the grime of the jungle? In war, frivolous bullshit is kept to a minimum, while outside of war, the world seemed piled high with frivolous bullshit.

Fort Polk was not the most desirable of stateside Army posts, to say the least, for it was situated in hot, muggy swampland, not unlike the sweltering, sodden paddies of 'Nam. I drove over raised roads with swampy bayous stretching out on either side, and mangrove trees growing right out of the water, as though a body could get lost out here and never be found.

I finally found my way to the fort where I located a barracks latrine in which I could change into my lieutenant's uniform, on which I pinned my Combat Infantryman's Badge above my Vietnam campaign ribbons that included my Bronze Star, but not my Purple Heart (as my wound was minor, caused by a small piece of mortar shrapnel that required only about twenty stitches, so I deferred from wearing it out of respect for those more seriously wounded), and then I headed over to the command building to report to my new commanding officer. All the buildings on the fort were old ramshackle wooden buildings from pre–World War II days.

The last time I reported to a CO was in Vietnam when I became the S-3 Air for the battalion and my CO was a lieutenant colonel in a tent, who was wearing an olive-drab t-shirt and who offered me a cup of coffee, without salutes. This was different; my new CO was a short chubby major, sitting in an immense office, behind a large mahogany desk, who regarded me with serpentine eyes as I approached. I could discern from the ribbons on his class A service uniform that he had never been to war.

I came to a halt in front of his desk, snapped to attention, saluted, and barked, "Sir, Lieutenant Lawrence reporting for duty!" I held my salute, as I waited for the overweight major to respond. As the junior officer, I would initiate the salute, and then the senior officer would return the salute, and only after the senior officer dropped his arm could I then drop my arm. So there I was, holding my salute until the major, after taking an inordinate amount of time just to pull his fat ass out of his chair, finally gave me a desultory limp-dick response to my crisp salute.

I dropped my arm and then adopted the position of parade rest, with my arms clasped firmly behind my back, and my legs spread the prescribed eighteen inches apart. The major looked at me, and then he adversarially chided, "I didn't say parade rest!"

So I snapped back into the position of attention, with my heels locked together. The slovenly major looked at me and abrasively spewed, "Lieutenant, let's get one thing straight! I don't care for Vietnam vets! Do you know why?"

I responded, "No, sir."

He screamed, "Because Vietnam vets have shitty attitudes! You're back in the States now, lieutenant, and I'll expect you to keep yourself squared away! Is that clear?"

I replied, "Yes, sir, very clear, sir!" But I had redirected my gaze, and now, instead of looking straight ahead at some fixed point on an imaginary horizon, I was looking him dead in the eyes, thinking to myself, "What an asshole."

The major uncomfortably registered my ominous look and rapidly concluded the welcome ceremony, for he comprehended, at that very moment, that he knew nothing about killing. He had committed a cardinal sin in my mind by exhibiting absolutely no respect for me, without knowing the first thing about me. Okay, I was his subordinate all right, but he had not the slightest clue that the chain of command worked in both directions. You cannot be much of a superior officer if you're unable to cultivate the support and respect of your lieutenants.

There were quite a few officers like this major, who had not gone to Vietnam and resented those who did, because we had passed through the mystical crucible of war and survived, while they had not yet been put to the test. We veterans of war were more independent of spirit, for we had existed for a time outside of conventional constraints, and, as a consequence, we were freer than those who had always lived within the confines of the straight world, with its rules and regulations that induced compliance by the application of fear and intimidation.

We veterans of war had lost most all our fear, as though we had been liberated from a prison in which we had passed most of our lives; a prison where conventional behavior was strictly enforced. It was the worst kind of prison, because it was a cultural prison as well, in which we had been told what to think from the time we entered school, during which time our minds had been strictly molded into the standard shape intended to make us into productive citizens, and where any dissent or rebellion was immediately squashed by those in authority. After returning from the war, I realized that I had escaped; "Free at last! Free at last! Thank God Almighty, I am free at last!"

As a consequence of our liberation, we Vietnam vets were naturally feared and resented by those who were still in shackles, especially by our superiors, for they could sense our irreverence toward their pretence of superiority, which they labeled authority. The major was pissed off that he had not been tested, and thus he struck out at me. Yet, at the same time, he was conscious of the fact that he was too afraid to volunteer for combat, and so he continued to hide behind his huge mahogany desk, condemned to forever push his guilt away, yet all his efforts would prove futile, and in the process he would turn into an angry and bitter man.

I came to find that serving out the remainder of my military obligation was less than thrilling. Dealing with my new superiors left me with a sense of melancholy, verging on depression, but not so depressing that I thought of going AWOL, though being back in the stateside Army, I felt that I was back in the land of bullshit, where people who had not put their asses on the line were abusing the power of their rank. On reflection, maybe the major was right; perhaps we veterans of war did not have sterling attitudes. What did our society expect? They had put us into uniform and sent us halfway around the world to kill other human beings, and then they wondered, upon our return home, why their intimidation tactics no longer appeared to strike fear in our hearts, which they devoutly believed was the time-tested method for achieving strict obedience.

We had been in the war, and we would frequently say, when our superiors threatened us, "What are they gonna do? Send me to Vietnam?" Still this major was a jerk, that was clear enough, and I was no longer fearful of authority. I had become unpredictable and therefore a dangerous animal. Still, when you're in the Army, the government owns you, 24/7 (twenty-four hours a day, seven days a week).

I had hoped to get a plush assignment upon my return from Vietnam, like at the Presidio in San Francisco, but I wasn't an Academy grad, or even ROTC; rather, I was an OCS officer and therefore low on the totem pole for receiving any special consideration. Instead I was assigned to the Deep South, though perhaps this was not such a bad thing after all, because in the South, people still held the military in high esteem, as opposed to many cities in the North where vets would sometimes be spat upon and berated for participating in an unpopular war.

But we were just young men, not policymakers, though we were closest at hand, and therefore the easiest targets for their vituperation, which I innately knew was not really directed at me; rather it was directed at the politicians who had sent us into harm's way to carry out their policies. I understood the sanctimoniousness of these angry people, but I also knew that it was easier for them to pontificate from their pristine porcelain thrones than to fearfully dodge a real bullet. For the most part the protesters were young and innocent, and I did not want to dishearten them.

I certainly did not dispute their right to disagree with the bombast of our elected politicians. I have never much cared for the virulent rhetoric that attempts to depict critics as unpatriotic. An American has every right to express his opinions, even in the midst of a war, especially a war as controversial as this war, in which young Americans were sent overseas to defend the puppet regime of South Vietnam based on some whimsical rationale that this would prevent communism from reaching our shores, at which time I suppose the National Guard would finally leap into action and battle the raging horde.

II

At Fort Polk I was tasked to provide infantry soldiers with their last three weeks of training before they were sent off to the war. These young soldiers were all very well aware that some of them would be killed and some would suffer ghastly wounds, but they were naively unaware of the fact that even if they avoided being killed or horribly wounded, they would nonetheless all be scarred by the experience. I knew that none of them would return home without some injury, for even those fortunate enough to escape bodily harm would still suffer psychological wounds that would be undetectable to the casual observer.

They had all completed their Advanced Infantry Training (AIT), and had received their orders for Vietnam, so they were all keenly motivated to learn anything additional that could improve their chances of survival on the battlefield. Yet they were in the infantry, the branch that sustained 70 percent of all Army combat (hostile) deaths in Vietnam. They knew that they were in for it.

Now that I was back in the States, I wore starched tailored olive-green garrison fatigues, as did all infantry officers, so that we could convey to the troops that sharp, crisp look that was intended to set an example for the men. I almost felt like a dandy after the jungles of Vietnam; however, the young soldiers could see my Combat Infantryman's Badge, and they knew that I had been there, and so they trusted me — the survivor, and thus they paid rapt attention to everything I uttered, as though I was offering them a sacred mantra for survival, and I did not have the heart to disillusion them.

I worked in a state forest, about fifty miles to the north of Fort Polk, where it was my responsibility to teach these soldiers, who were still teenagers for the most part, what they needed to know in order to survive, and yet I knew that some of them would die. I had only recently turned twenty-two, but in their eyes, I was a grizzled old veteran of war.

I spent most of my days and nights in the forest working with these young soldiers who already held reserved seats on their scheduled flights to Vietnam. I stayed up into the morning hours with them; I tapped them on their helmets with a piece of wood if I caught them asleep at their listening posts, because in real life, they would have had their throats slit.

I tried to teach them the real-life lessons of war, rather than just the classroom prognostications. I taught them how to dig foxholes with sufficient overhead cover to protect themselves against the mortar rounds that would inevitably rain down upon their heads from the overhead jungle canopy as blazing shards of flesh-ripping shrapnel. It was not just a question of how deep you could dig, but whether you had covered your foxhole with adequate overhead cover, which meant tree limbs of sufficient size to impede the cascading shrapnel. I taught them the importance of camouflaging their foxholes, which was the finishing touch that was not generally taught stateside, but which could prompt the enemy to hesitate for just that critical moment, during which time our man could get off the first shot.

I taught them how ambushes were conducted in the jungles of Vietnam; for it requires great patience to wait for other men, with weapons, who do not want to die, to walk into a death trap. At the Infantry School we were taught to align ourselves into an "L" shape, with a trigger man at the heart of the kill zone, just about where the two lines of the "L" come together. The trigger man would patiently wait — allowing the enemy to walk down the line of the L, coming toward him, until the lead enemy soldier was nearly within spitting distance, as we wanted all of the enemy to enter the trap; we wanted them all inside the kill zone, at which time the trigger man would initiate the ambush, and then the rest of us would blow our claymore mines, throw our grenades, fire several automatic bursts from our M16s, and then we would all beat feet and disperse into the jungle, and then reassemble at a rally point about a kilometer away.

Well, that was the school solution, but in reality the average American soldier does not run off into the jungle and then reassemble again half a mile away with the rest of his comrades. No, what actually occurs in this school approach is that you have eight to ten soldiers lost in the jungle. In Vietnam, in real life, after we triggered the ambush, we formed a perimeter; essentially we circled the wagons, and then we would stay and fight. If necessary, we called in artillery. Only at first light did we move, and then we moved out together. The John Wayne lone cowboy approach did not work in the harsh reality of the jungle fighting in Vietnam; rather, cooperation and teamwork were the keys to survival and success.

The soldiers to whom I provided training were sent to Vietnam between October 1968 and February 1969, so some were fighting in the war up through February 1970, and during those seventeen months more than 10,000 American soldiers were killed in Vietnam.

Did I help anyone to survive? It's one thing to teach a classroom course and then grade the students as to what they have learned by assigning As and Bs; however, it's another thing altogether to teach a group of soldiers who are heading off to war immediately after class, with the intent of putting into practice the survival lessons they had learned from me. It was no longer just a group of soldiers; rather, it was the red-headed boy from Missouri with the high-pitched laugh, and it was the tough black kid from the mean streets of Detroit, and it was the country boy from Arkansas who talked a little slow, but whose mind was not. It was these young boys of eighteen and nineteen who were being sent off to war, and it broke my heart. I suppose, at twenty-two, I was still a young man, but I was no longer a boy, that's for sure.

When I was in 'Nam, I was one of those officers who believed that it was not just enough to give the orders to my men, but that it was also beneficial, whenever feasible, to ensure that the soldiers understood the rationale for the orders. Not all of the officers whom I encountered shared this point of view, and it seemed that the old-timers, especially the colonels with whom I spoke, didn't have the slightest clue as to what I was even talking about. Give an explanation to the troops? What for? Many officers simply issued the orders, and felt the troops needed no further explanation. I believed those officers were short-changing themselves and their units, because they obviously did not exhibit much respect for their men. In effect, they were abusing the privilege of rank, and, unbeknownst to themselves, they were obtaining only perfunctory compliance and obedience.

People are not stupid. If one truly respects the men whom one commands, then there is nothing those men would not do for their leaders and their unit. They will give everything, even when their lives are in great peril. I considered the soldiers whom I commanded to be intelligent, thinking individuals who merited an explanation, which I devoutly believed would make them and the entire unit more effective. Perhaps I thought like this because I did not have much formal education myself. In that respect, I was more like my men than most officers, for I never had much occasion to feel superior.

III

People talk about returning from Vietnam and being plagued by nightmares. I must say that when one is in 'Nam, living out of a hole in the ground, listening for the slightest sound in the foreboding jungle, while continuously exposed to sudden mortar attacks, one certainly develops a reaction to unexpected noises for one's very survival, and this instinctive vigilance fades slowly, and lingers for some time after one has returned from the war.

One hot, muggy weekend afternoon in Louisiana, shortly after my return from the war, and after spending the entire night out in the forest working with the troops, I was exhausted and immediately fell asleep as soon as I returned to my little Louisiana clapboard rented house with its squeaky front porch and screen door.

I was dead asleep in the humid heat of the afternoon, without air-conditioning, when, all of a sudden I heard a noise, and as I raised myself slowly up in my bed to peer out the window, I observed several North Vietnamese soldiers, with AK-47s at the ready, creeping cautiously up toward my house.

I could also sense them, and hear them, but it seemed as though I was trapped in my bed and unable to move, though they were stealthily drawing closer and closer. They were so well camouflaged with leaves and greenery that they seemed to melt into the lush Louisiana foliage. At moments they appeared almost as a blur, as though perhaps my eyes were deceiving me, but no, there they were, at the extremity of my peripheral vision, stepping up onto my wooden porch, slipping cautiously up to my screen door, and then they attempted to open the screen door, but I had a little latch in place to keep the door from blowing in the wind, and so the door snagged, and therefore I had a moment to take some form of evasive action. But then the enemy soldiers were now pulling violently at the door, and in an instant they would be rushing in upon me, and I was struggling so frantically to escape that I could actually feel the sweat streaming off my body, and yet it seemed as though I was dog-paddling through quicksand, and so I was compelled to exert all of my strength to break free, and then ... I awoke!

When I looked around, I saw, in astonishment, that I had ripped the bed sheets to shreds, while in my sleep, and I was soaked in sweat, and then I again heard the squeaking of the screen door, followed by the sound of someone knocking. It was the next-door neighbor girl who had come by to visit. I did not have too many dreams like that after the war, but I had a few, and that was not the only time that I tore the sheets to shreds in my sleep, which, for a time, caused me anxiety about having anyone else share my bed.

A recent *Psychiatric Times* article supports the National Vietnam Veterans' Readjustment Survey of the 1980s, which found that 15.2 percent of male Vietnam War veterans suffered from post-traumatic stress disorder (PTSD), "though rates were highest among units that had more exposure to combat."[1]

Although the Army, Marine Corps, Air Force and Navy each had different percentages of people in combat roles, it is reasonable to assume that this 15.5 percent PTSD figure could apply to at least 70 percent of those Army troops in Vietnam (22 percent) who were in combat roles, of which the infantry roughly made up half. One could make a strong argument that this 15.2 percent figure for PTSD amongst all those who served in Vietnam was grossly understated when it came to the infantry.

It should be noted that Title 38 of the United States Code prohibits veterans from suing the government for injuries suffered while in the military, which includes afflictions from PTSD, Agent Orange, or other causes, although sufferers are entitled to receive treatment at their local VA hospital.

Among Civil War veterans, PTSD was called "soldier's heart," for World War I vets it was called "shell-shock," for World War II vets it was called "combat fatigue," and for Vietnam vets it was initially called "post–Vietnam syndrome." Whatever the name, sufferers have a tendency to become easily startled, to succumb to drug and alcohol abuse, to be quick to anger, to become withdrawn from family and friends, to be depressed, to suffer recurrent nightmares (recurrent memory of a traumatic event), to experience sleeplessness, and to be inclined to acute anxiety. Something happens, I'm certain, to many who have survived war, such that a particular sight or a sound can certainly trigger the resurgence of terrifying wartime memories.

I also adopted a rather peculiar nocturnal routine that I adhered to for more than four years after my return from the war. I think it had something to do with living in a foxhole for so many months while being exposed to the elements of nature, which included sleeping in the pouring rain. I remained awake for one thirty-six-hour period each week. I awoke, for example, at 6:00 in the morning on a Monday, and then I did not go to sleep again until Tuesday evening, at which time I slept soundly. In this way I experienced the entire twenty-four-hour cycle of a day. I observed the sunrise, the sunset, the starlit night, another sunrise, and then the day again, whether it be rainy, clear, or cloudy. I believe this was a means of remembering—the war, when we were required to be awake at odd hours, without much sleep, yet during which time we developed an expanded appreciation of life through the day's miraculous cycle. Perhaps I had also developed a comfort in the night while I was in Vietnam. I don't know whether this was considered to be abnormal behavior or not, for nobody seemed to understand my unusual routine, not even me.

The most favorable aspect of my new assignment was that the forest in which I worked was far away from Fort Polk, which enabled me to rent an apartment in the small college town of Natchitoches, home of Louisiana Northwestern State University. Natchitoches is in the northwestern quadrant of Louisiana, only about forty miles from the Texas border. During the Civil War, Natchitoches was as far north as the Federals were able to penetrate into Louisiana, which contains some serious bayous and swamps, as they pushed up from the south in their unsuccessful attempt to reach Shreveport, just sixty miles further north, which during those days was the capital of the Confederacy for all rebel lands to the west of the Mississippi River (which included Louisiana, Arkansas and Texas).

And though the Mississippi River flows through the city of New Orleans, most of the state of Louisiana lies on the Texas side of the river. Both the Missouri and Ohio rivers feed into the Mississippi before it enters Dixie, after which this engorged river separates the states of Arkansas (on its western side) and Tennessee (on the river's eastern side), before the river proceeds southward to separate Louisiana (on its western side) from Mississippi on the far shore, but then, when the river reaches the final third of Louisiana, it enters into the state and makes its way through the cities of Baton Rouge and New Orleans before it flows out into the Gulf of Mexico.

Huey Long, "the Kingfish," was born on a farm not more than thirty miles from Natchitoches. Huey went on to become governor of Louisiana and then represented the state as a U.S. Senator during the Depression years. Huey stood for the common man and lashed out against corporate wealth, while ruling over Louisiana's political machine until an assassin's bullet brought him down.

Natchitoches is particularly well known throughout Louisiana and eastern Texas for its Christmas season light display, during which the townspeople string Christmas lights throughout the trees lining both shores of the Natchitoches River, which meanders through the center of town, and people came from far and wide to view this holiday spectacle.

I made friends with some university students, as well as some of the professors. I had only recently turned twenty-two years of age, so I seemed to fit in, even though my friends were receiving a lot more formal education than I possessed. They were even making career plans, while I was not. We frequently congregated at the local pizzeria, eating pizza and drinking beer by the pitcher, then standing around the jukebox, singing "Hey, Jude," along with the Beatles. Nobody really knows what the song is about, except Paul who wrote the lyrics. Some people thought the song was about shooting up heroin; others thought it was all about pursuing love, while others believed that Paul wrote the song to cheer up Julian Lennon when his father left his mother to pursue Yoko Ono. Whatever the meaning, it was a perfect song for a bunch of sad drunks to sing, with their arms clasped around one another's shoulders, while standing around a jukebox in a forlorn pizzeria just around closing time.

The students were fun and they threw some great parties. I even gave a party or two. One night I was hosting a party at my apartment and a bunch of students were brewing up an alcoholic mixture they called Purple Goddamns, for which they took 190-proof (95 percent) Everclear grain alcohol and mixed it with Welch's Grape Juice. People were drinking this concoction, then going into the bathroom and passing out, while sitting on the toilet! People were dancing, the music was cranked up, and then the doorbell rang.

I opened the door, and two menacing Louisiana policemen with short-sleeve shirts and beefy arms were standing in front of me, asking whose apartment was this. I replied that it was my apartment; they gazed at me, while listening to my alien Californian manner of speech, and then they said in their northern Louisiana drawl, "Neighbors are complaining about the loud music and suspect that there might be underage people drinking alcohol here, which if true, means we'll have to shut this party down, and you'll have to come along with us to the station." It wasn't sounding good, but then a young, pretty, dark-haired Louisiana co-ed named Leah spotted the two policemen, and she sashayed right up to them and called them by their first names, while giving each of them a hug, and then she invited them inside to sample our Purple Goddamns—they enjoyed the party.

When I was in 'Nam, slogging around the jungle and the paddies in my filthy, tattered, sweat-encrusted uniform, stinking and tired, I said to myself that when I returned to the States I would forever appreciate clean sheets, hot showers, and nice relaxing shaves with warm lather, a nice shaving brush, and a sharp new razor blade for every shave. However, over time I came to find that one tends to lose one's heightened appreciation for these luxuries of life, and it wasn't too long after my return from the war that I began to take clean sheets and hot showers for granted.

However, I have always avoided caraway seeds, ever since the war, and I did permit myself one pleasurable extravagance. I purchased an expensive badger-haired shaving brush and a mug of shaving soap, and I treated myself to a hot luxurious shave each morning, using a new double-edge razor blade for each shave, after which I just tossed the blade in the trash and unwrapped a new double-edged blade for my next shave; it was the height of indulgence. I continued this practice for nearly ten years, until the razor manufacturers stopped making double-edged razor blades and compelled everyone to use the more expensive cartridge blades.

Two pretty, young professors of English at the University, named Jennie and Sally, lived in the apartment below mine; they were both a little older than I, but we became friends. Sally had a boyfriend in New Orleans, and so the three of us occasionally drove down to New Orleans from Natchitoches on weekends to link up with Sally's boyfriend Bo, and the four of us would do the town. I recall that Bo escorted us to Brennan's Restaurant, which is a New Orleans' legend, located in the heart of the French Quarter. Brennan's was well known for serving French and Creole cuisine, and Bo brought us there for the Sunday brunch and the eggs benedict, which is essentially a breakfast meal that consists of two halves of a toasted English muffin sitting side-by-side, upon each of which is placed a grilled slice of Canadian bacon, on top of which is placed a poached egg, which is then ladled over with Hollandaise sauce (a rich, egg-based sauce flavored with lemon, butter and a hint of cayenne pepper).

IV

When I was around Fort Polk, I was in an integrated military environment, and when I was in Vietnam I had lived predominately within a black world, so I had a fair number of black friends with whom I worked at Fort Polk who were also Vietnam vets, and most of them were from the North, and they would often tell me how difficult it was to meet ladies in Louisiana.

Being as how I was connected to students at the university, I asked my white friends to assist me in arranging a blind date between two black ladies from the university and two of my black friends from the Army. It took a little effort, but it was finally arranged, and on a Friday night the two black ladies knocked at my apartment door. They were pretty ladies and I invited them in, and I put on some music, and offered them a glass of wine. They were different from what I expected, or at least they seemed different from what I had observed in northern girls. These girls were exceedingly attractive, yet quite conservative; there was no shuck and jive here, and they were exceedingly well educated, and exhibited a sophisticated taste in jazz as well as classical music.

Much to my chagrin, my Army friends did not show up. They had stood up these two pretty girls, and I was feeling like a real jerk. On reflection, I realized that my black Army friends really did not want to venture out too far from the safety of the integrated Army fort, certainly not to enter the Deep South. In desperation, I escorted the two young ladies down the stairs to the apartment of Jennie and Sally. I could see that their lights were on and music was playing, and so I knocked at their door. Jennie opened the door and regarded me and my two lady friends. I explained to Jennie that my two Army friends had not showed up, and I noticed that Jennie gave me somewhat of a rueful look, but with her gracious southern hospitality, she invited us inside. Upon entering, I could see that Jennie and Sally had four other friends in their apartment, three guys and a woman, and so the nine of us passed an enjoyable evening together. All of Jennie and Sally's friends enjoyed talking with the two black female co-eds, and the evening ended with everyone having a good time.

The next day I saw Jennie, and I was talking to her about the enjoyable time had by all the previous evening. Jennie gave me the same rueful look that I had seen last evening, and then she said, "Yes, Bert, that was an enjoyable evening, but you know, you cannot bring people of color around here again," clearly implying that our landlord would find some excuse to evict us if we continued to have inter-racial social gatherings—the year was 1968.

Though much civil rights legislation had been passed during the mid-1960s, much of the South was still visibly racist in 1968, more so than I had observed out west in California, though there was noticeable racial tension in most large cities across America during the late sixties.

Slavery was abolished in America more than a hundred years ago, back in 1865, following the end of the Civil War, yet at war's end, Southern whites feared that blacks, who constituted the majority of the population in the region, would become the dominate culture and ultimately govern over a white minority. As a consequence, Southern whites made concerted efforts to nullify the potential political power of blacks by disenfranchising them from voting, which was accomplished by compelling blacks to pass examinations for which they were destined to fail, or restricting voting rights to only those who owned property, and so for one hundred years following emancipation the Southern white minority vigorously enforced segregation between the races by zealously retaining political control. These conditions rigidly persisted until the Civil Rights Act was finally passed four years prior, in 1964, but changes were proceeding slowly.

V

Working in the state forest, I got to know the game warden who befriended me. He accepted me because I had patriotically served my country by fighting in Vietnam and, because I was from California, he could not quite pigeonhole me. He didn't exactly consider me a Northerner, even though California fought on the Union side during the Civil War.

Sometimes the game warden invited me to accompany him and a couple of his buddies as they went out squirrel hunting with shotguns, and the squirrels eventually found themselves into a pretty tasty stew. My friends in Natchitoches were amazed that I went hunting with the game warden, for they told me that he was known as a pretty tough redneck character who would bust his own mother if he caught her poaching. In any case, these good old boys were amiable toward me, and I enjoyed being out traipsing around in the meditative quiet of the forest.

After I had been in Louisiana for about four weeks, the presidential election, scheduled for the fifth of November, was just a week away. The sitting president, Lyndon B. Johnson, had decided not to run for a second term due to his failing popularity as a result of U.S. military setbacks in the Vietnam War, particularly because of the unanticipated surprise attacks by the Vietcong and the North Vietnamese at the beginning of the Tet Offensive of a year ago.

The front-running candidate, Bobby Kennedy, had been assassinated nearly five months ago, and the seven remaining candidates had now been narrowed down to three: there were the Republican candidate Richard Nixon, the Democratic candidate Hubert Humphrey, and the radically conservative Southerner George Wallace. Among my squirrel-hunting buddies, one would not even think about talking in support of the Democrats, or one might end up in the stew with the squirrels.

It was bad enough talking in favor of Richard Nixon, but at least one wouldn't be tarred and feathered. This would be the first presidential election for which I was eligible to vote. During the previous election, back in November 1964, when Lyndon B. Johnson had run against Barry Goldwater, I was eighteen, and was thus under the legal voting age of twenty-one. Now I was twenty-two, and so I excitedly exercised my Constitutional right to vote by completing my absentee ballot and sending it off to California. Eighteen-year-olds, as a result of the twenty-sixth Amendment, would be eligible to vote in the next presidential election (November 1972).

The warden and all of his buddies actively supported George Wallace, and, on the day of the election, they were bragging amongst themselves as to how many votes each of them had cast in support of their favorite candidate. Perhaps it was all bravado, because it sounded to me like each of them had broken numerous federal laws, though maybe it wasn't bravado at all, for they seemed to be talking in earnest. I sat silent in the car, because we were heading out into the woods in search of squirrels, and we were all holding shotguns.

In any event Richard Nixon won the election, in large part because he chose to distance himself from the liberal wing of the Republican Party by casting aside Nelson Rockefeller and John Lindsay in favor of Spiro Agnew, a bigot, to be his vice presidential running mate. By this act, Nixon made it clear that he was openly soliciting the white backlash vote across America in response to the persistent race riots that had occurred over the last four years, beginning with the Watts riot of 1965. This was certainly a winning strategy on the part of Nixon, because he was able to bring traditional white Southern Democrats over to the Republican Party, where they loyally remained up through the millennium. These people, in large part, felt that the Johnson Administration and the Democratic Party had harshly targeted them by pushing through the Civil Rights Act of 1964.

Nixon didn't give a rat's ass whether he received a single black vote. I had fought alongside too many black Americans in Vietnam to share the same viewpoint. When my father was terminally ill (in 2004) and I was caring for him, my father brought up the time that he and I had visited his old World War II buddy after my return from the war. My father and I had never discussed that visit during all these years. Yet during our visit, this friend of my father had irritated me when he spoke disparagingly about blacks in World War II, and I had set him straight by telling him that in Vietnam, the majority of the soldiers in my platoon were black, and that we steadfastly relied on one another for our very survival. And we needed each other so desperately that I owed every soldier in my platoon, regardless of their color, my undying gratitude for my very existence. I was self-consciously aware at the time that I had pretty much ruined the evening and most likely embarrassed my father. So I was quite surprised when my father brought the subject up, and told me that he had been very proud of the way that I had gently and articulately put the man in his place. My father made it clear to me that he realized, during that visit, that the man was nothing more than a bigot, and not worthy of any special respect. I found it interesting that my father, so close to death, had made a point of bringing up this incident that had so acutely distressed me at the time. However, the key issue that boosted Nixon to victory was that he gave the impression to the American public that he had devised a plan for ending the shedding of any more American blood in Vietnam.

VI

Although I enjoyed my time in Louisiana, I did not really get close to anyone, except an elderly gray-haired woman, named Stella, who lived in the heart of the French Quarter in N'awlins, and who put me and my friends up at her place whenever we were in the city. Stella loved to collect exotic stamps from faraway places, and she frequently accompanied me and my friends around the streets of her native city.

I found the people in the South to be quite hospitable; they seemed to move at a more leisurely pace than the people out West. In the South I often saw elderly people operating their own stores, while in California everything was youth-orientated and moving faster. In California, one sometimes had the impression that the elderly were not treated with the same respect as in the South; in California, it almost seemed that the elderly were considered to be in the way.

I must confess that I was one of the very few Army officers who never did purchase a set of dress blues, which were to be worn at black-tie affairs. Perhaps I did have an attitude problem, but I felt that I had so few occasions to wear this formal dress blue uniform that cost quite a bit of money, and so I simply borrowed someone else's dress blues whenever I was required to appear at fancy affairs.

On one occasion, I, along with all of the other officers at Fort Polk, received one of those nice engraved invitations to appear at the colonel's Christmas party. I had little desire to attend these formal affairs with the boys and I did not have any dress blue uniform to wear, and I would not be able to borrow one since every junior officer was invited. In any case, the colonel's party happened to have been scheduled on the same day as Stella's birthday, which some friends and I were planning to celebrate in N'awlins, so I elected to decline the colonel's invitation.

A couple of days later, while I was out at the rifle range at Fort Polk providing instruction to the troops regarding ambush tactics, I observed the colonel's jeep approaching. The colonel's driver drove right toward me, stopped the vehicle, and the colonel hopped out and rapidly approached me. I issued up a snappy salute, which the colonel returned, and then he said to me, "Lieutenant Lawrence, I noticed that you were unable to attend my Christmas party last week."

I replied, "Yes, sir. Regretfully, I had another commitment."

He inquired, "Did you make your commitment before you received my invitation?"

I replied, "Yes, sir, just in advance of receiving your invitation."

He regarded me severely and said, "Lieutenant, next time I host a gathering, I'm going to make sure that you receive your invitation well in advance."

I replied, "Yes, sir. Thank you very much, sir." Then I snapped to attention and gave him a crisp salute, and he departed.

All of the staff sergeants, and some junior lieutenants, standing around were observing this exchange of pleasantries with suppressed yet mirthful smiles. Of course, if I had any desire to make the Army a career, this episode had marked the end of it. I'm quite certain that my next Officer Efficiency Report (OER) would note that I lacked social graces, or was deficient in social etiquette, or words to that effect. These reports were always written in such a Byzantine manner that promotion boards could only decipher them by reading between the lines for the subtle signals underscoring the officer's evaluation, which would reveal those deemed to have no further potential for promotion.

I suppose that this is precisely what is meant when people talk about a short-timer's attitude. I had less than two months left to go in the Army, and I was already out-processing in my mind. I couldn't have cared less whether I received an outstanding Efficiency Report or a deficient one; I would soon be returning to the civilian world. I had done my bit for Uncle Sam, and I had earned the right to adopt most any kind of attitude I chose. This was not an uncommon attitude of men coming back from the war, and perhaps it would be viewed as a detriment in later years—this attitude problem, which from my point of view simply meant that I could take only so much bullshit, while reserving the right to make my own choices regarding most matters that affected me.

Actually I don't believe that I had an attitude problem toward authority; I generally respected my elders; this never changed, but people in authority, in my opinion, also had an obligation to earn my respect, and if I sensed that people were abusing their authority, then I suppose they would see the reproof in my eyes, and sometimes, I realized, they saw something even more menacing that seemed to unsettle them. Besides, in my more lucid moments, I wondered whether I really had an attitude problem at all, or whether my supposed attitude problem was simply a flawed perception of the person in authority.

I asked myself whether I was the only one who had a problem with this person, because it began to seem to me that the very people who determined that I had an attitude problem were just as quick to perceive attitude problems in others as well. These people, generally in positions of authority, were relentlessly ferreting out people with attitude problems. In a Freudian sense, this might be interpreted to mean those subordinates who did not appear sufficiently obsequious in demonstrating the fawning respect that these people in authority expected.

Actually an attitude problem can only arise in an atmosphere where there is a superior/subordinate relationship, because it necessarily involves the superior's perception of the subordinate. We've probably all observed those parents who berate their children by accusatorially telling them that they have an attitude problem, which is clearly one of those malicious criticisms that is calculatedly intended to strike at, and diminish, a person's self-esteem. Behavior of this sort invariably reveals the shortcomings of the parent.

In any event, the year was drawing to a close, and I had less than two months remaining in the Army. It was hard to believe that I had first entered the Army just about three years ago, during January 1966. Three years! I was nineteen when I entered the Army as a private; now I was twenty-two and a first lieutenant. Most of my high school friends had remained in school and had already graduated from college during the summer, and they would now be moving forward in their careers and earning lucrative salaries.

My annual salary this year (1968), most of which I spent in Vietnam as a first lieutenant, totaled $5,345, which included eight months of supplemental combat pay at $65 per month.

The previous year (1967), when I was a second lieutenant, I earned a total of $3,554, though that year only included four months of combat pay. Was this adequate recompense for putting my life on the line?

Well, it's not really about the money, is it?

VII

I celebrated New Year's Eve, welcoming in 1969, in New Orleans. It had been four months since I had departed the jungles of Vietnam, and on this New Year's Eve I found myself in a seedy bar in the French Quarter with another Vietnam vet. My friend was being loud and obnoxious to the point where several redneck bouncers were telling him to "shut the fuck up!" I vaguely recall asking the tough-looking bouncers if they wanted to fight about it, and then about all I remember was three guys coming at me, and I was swinging, and they were hitting on me, and then I was pitched out onto the street, just as my friend came cruising around the corner in his car. He got out and helped me into the car, and I said, "Where the hell were you?" He said, "Bert, I didn't want to get killed."

The next morning I had to go out in front of a hundred soldiers who were sitting in the bleachers waiting for my introduction, which invariably started off with a couple of dirty jokes, something about "nip on nees" and "chu man chu" that alluded to fantasized sexual predilections of Asian women, which got some laughs, though I don't think the military tells dirty jokes as a prelude to training presentations any more, but back in those days it was expected. However, on this day, I had two black eyes, which I somewhat concealed behind a pair of aviator sunglasses, though I also had a swollen nose and a busted lip that I could not hide. Since the show must go on, I proceeded to go through my spiel in front of the troops, while looking as though I had just returned from the war that very morning. Still, I was dressed in my sharp, crisp, tailored garrison fatigues, and I was wearing my Combat Infantryman's Badge and they all respected that.

On the twentieth of January 1969, Republican Richard M. Nixon was sworn in as the thirty-seventh President of the United States:

> I, Richard Milhous Nixon, do solemnly swear that I will faithfully execute the office of President of the United States, and will, to the best of my ability, preserve, protect and defend the Constitution of the United States.

It was strikingly similar to the oath I had sworn to when I was appointed an officer in the United States Army, during which I also did "solemnly swear that I" would "defend the Constitution of the United States," although my oath was twice as long as that of the president's. Nixon finally revealed his plan for ending he war, which he called "Vietnamization."

This plan outlined the president's intention to turn more of the fighting over to the South Vietnamese who would continue to be supplied and supported by the United States. The president assured the American public that, as the South Vietnamese took over more and more of the fighting, the number of American combat troops would be decreased and ultimately withdrawn from the war. Many of the listening public only realized at that moment that Nixon's plan would not lead to a quick end to the fighting, and that Nixon had absolutely no intention of calling for an immediate cease-fire and an end to the war.

Ironically, Nixon's stated pledge to withdraw American troops, albeit ever so slowly, marked the point when the morale of the American troops in Vietnam began to plummet, as the soldiers in the field no longer wanted to risk their lives in a war from which their leaders intended to disengage. Under these contradictory and disheartening circumstances, during Nixon's first year in office, 9,585 Americans died in combat (including KIAs, died of wounds, missing in action/declared dead, or captured/declared dead), and they continued to die in significant numbers throughout Nixon's first four years in office, before the killing tapered off.[2]

These fatalities of war did not even take into account those combat soldiers, who, in adopting the new "clear and hold" concept, were brought in from the jungles to base camps where they became heroin addicts, while dejectedly waiting to be shipped home. This was the period depicted in the Francis Ford Coppola (1979) film, *Apocalypse Now*, when the "horror, the horror" of it all was beginning to set in, even though this morbid uttering was borrowed from Joseph Conrad's story, *Heart of Darkness*, published back in 1902.

Some critics attacked Nixon's plan as nothing more than political waffling that would continue to keep American troops fighting and dying until such time as the South Vietnamese were considered sufficiently capable of fighting the war on their own, and not many people had a great deal of confidence that this would happen anytime soon. In fact, during the little more than five and a half years that Nixon was in office, more than a million Americans were sent to Vietnam, and Nixon aggressively took the war into Cambodia and Laos.

VIII

During my time in Vietnam I observed a fair amount of pot smoking, but I never observed anyone shooting up heroin; besides, heroin would have only been done back in the rear base camps, not by soldiers out humping the boonies. However, years later, when I was back in the States, I ran into quite a few heroin addicts who were Vietnam vets, and, for the most part, they had picked up their habits between 1969 and 1972, following Nixon's Vietnamization (withdrawal) announcement.

One of the world's primary heroin-producing areas is the Golden Triangle, very close to Vietnam, an area that covers parts of Laos, Thailand and Burma (re-named Myanmar in 1989), and which is extremely conducive for the clandestine growing of the opium poppy. At the beginning of the nineteenth century it was discovered that by dissolving opium in acid, and then neutralizing it with ammonia, one could extract morphine from opium. Then, in 1895, a German scientist discovered that, by diluting morphine with acetyls, he could produce a drug (diacetylmorphine) that did not appear to have the same debilitating side effects as morphine; it was called heroin. Initially envisioned as a step-down cure for morphine addiction, heroin was soon revealed to be just as addictive as morphine.

Drug use, in the form of opium, had been endemic among the French Foreign Legionnaires in Indochina throughout the colonial period. With the arrival of the Americans in Vietnam, drug use became a problem both within the Army and the Marine Corps, as drug use in both services from 1969 onwards climbed above twenty percent.[3] Ultimately, the Department of Defense moved to eradicate the problem by implementing urinalysis, which was first used by the services in the spring of 1972 in order to weed out the stoners and the junkies.

Nixon's withdrawal plan unfortunately became an inexorably slow process that went on for more than four years, into the spring of 1973, during which time soldiers were still expected to continue fighting and dying. There was certainly little wonder in my mind as to why these dispirited troops took to using heavy drugs, although there was not much understanding or compassion expressed by most Americans back home for these crippled soldiers. People back home generally felt that most of us were school dropouts and losers in general, who probably had a propensity for drugs and other sordid or psychotic behavior. Of course, these were the same people who considered the bright young men from prestigious universities, who had avoided the draft, to be the stalwarts of society. The people back home seemed to look for any rationale to distance themselves from us, while shouldering as little responsibility or guilt as possible.

I traveled down to New Orleans most every weekend. I generally rented a cheap motel room when I was not crashing at Stella's, and then I hit the bars. One night I was pulled over by a couple of police cars for speeding, driving while intoxicated, and going the wrong way down a one-way street. With their red lights flashing behind me, I staggered out of my car, and the police could see that I was in a sorry state. Still, they saw the Army officer sticker on my car, and when they checked my ID, they could see that it had been recently issued and, being as how I was a first lieutenant, they assumed that I had probably just returned from 'Nam, and so one of the policemen asked me, "Where ya staying?"

I slurred, "Some motel."

He said, "What's the name of it?"

I muttered, "I don't know, but I got the key right here in my pocket," and I pulled out the key, the kind with a big plastic motel tag attached.

The police officer took the key, noted the name of the motel, then looked at me and said, "Can you drive?"

I said, "Sure."

He said, "All right, then follow me. Stay right behind me, ya hear, and I'll guide you back to yer motel."

I said, "Okay." I followed him with one eye open, trying to focus, till his rear lights went off, and there I was in front of my motel.

The policemen got out of their cars and compassionately said to me, "You okay now?"

I replied, "I'm okay now," as I staggered to my cheap motel room. The policemen wrote me no citation. Maybe I was a bit of a mess back then, but at least I was in Dixie, where the people respected the military.

I completed my active-duty military obligation during February 1969. That was it, a pat on the back, some papers in hand, changing out of my uniform and into civilian clothes, then getting into my little Triumph sports car and heading out of Louisiana, westward toward California. "Free at last," or such were my feelings at the time. Actually, the piece of paper I was issued was a DD (Department of Defense) Form 214, which only separated me from active duty, but did not discharge me from my reserve obligation, which continued in effect for nearly three more years, into January 1972, during which time I could be recalled to active duty if the government deemed it necessary, for the Army is actually comprised of three components: the active Army, the Army Reserve, and the Army National Guard.

IX

The experience of war is a defining moment in one's life. The scars of war, even those not discernable to the naked eye, run deep. Readjustment back to civilian life is not an easy transition. Most people just assume that the returning soldier will simply pick up from where he left off, be it in school or at work.

As soon as I returned to California, I hung up my Army uniform in the far recesses of my mother's closet, and disguised myself in civilian garb, for Vietnam was not a war that anyone wanted to talk about, particularly in the San Francisco Bay Area. Not many veterans displayed their medals and ribbons, except in a cardboard box in some unobtrusive corner of the garage. And we sat in lonely solitude, reflecting on the years we had served in our nation's military and been sent off to war without receiving much public support. Certainly this created conflicts in the minds of the soldiers who fought in that war, and survived.

My schoolboy friends were still enjoying their youth, but I had been exposed to deeper realities of life, which, though less innocent, nevertheless substantially expanded my understanding of life, and would no doubt lead me down different paths—far from the youth that I had recently, and abruptly, left behind. I had learned one of the most sobering lessons of life—that war is nothing more than sanctioned murder that forever affects one's soul. To kill another human being, albeit with national approbation, contravenes one's moral and religious precepts, namely that "Thou shalt not kill," which came straight out of the Old Testament (books of Deuteronomy and Exodus, chapters 5 and 20 respectively).

Efforts to prepare the soldier for reentry to society after the horrific experience of war can only achieve partial success, for a nation cannot instruct its youth to go forth and kill, then do an about-face and tell its discharged soldiers to go home, live peacefully, and forget about all the killing and the dying.

Perhaps a victory parade down Main Street with flags waving and people cheering aids in the healing process of a wounded soul, though I wouldn't know, for there were not many parades down Main Street for this war that my country soon ignominiously lost. No, this was a war best to be forgotten. I could never have fit back into my neighborhood and become involved to any great extent in the things in which the boys and girls of my age were interested. My schoolmates, with whom I had been so close before the Army, seemed immature, and their fraternity lives and fraternity pranks appeared juvenile to my eyes. They probably perceived me as too morose for their world in any case, where light-hearted youth prevailed.

When the people who stayed behind asked me about the war, and if I had killed anybody, how could I even begin to describe the ghastliness of the time I spent striving to kill people with bullets, grenades, and artillery shells, or the ear-piercing cacophony of my silent screams? And yet I had survived, with all of my limbs intact, and so I felt I had no entitlement to complain. The road back home had become interminably long; the distance had expanded exponentially and the breach was beyond repair. Perhaps it was safer, and saner, to look away and choose another path, another avenue of escape.

If I hadn't had a job waiting for me back on the ships, I don't know what I would have done. I had some anger, obviously, but it wasn't anger against society or my government; rather it was anger against myself, for what I had become — desensitized. It was as though all the levity and feelings of any kind had been sucked right out of me, like when the air is let out of a balloon. I would not have done very well in the neighborhood of my youth. I certainly could not imagine sitting around a junior college campus with a lot of high school kids and a bunch of Vietnam vets. I never wanted to hang out with veterans anyway; I didn't want to remember. I was thinking to myself that denial might be a most effective therapy.

I just closed the door on the war and headed back out to sea. Going to sea seemed to be a great escape; in fact it was one of the best, for I could leave all of my troubles behind, and all of my romantic entanglements; well, perhaps at this time in my life, I did not really have too many of those—fortunately, and so I could just sail away, into the sunset, literally. Going to sea is a purifying experience, for it is a simple routine, encompassed within a solitary lifestyle. At sea, I could spend all the time alone I desired, and then some.

15

Return to Civilian Life

I

My return to civilian life was not at all like the days following World War II, when the victorious soldiers returned to grand parades. Rather we were an embarrassment; we were losers, and nobody wants to be around a loser. People did not rush out to welcome Vietnam vets back into the workforce; in fact our places had been taken by others. In any event, I was less ambitious after the war, though I was not indolent, I wasn't afraid of work; it's just that the idea of working for the Bank of America for the next thirty years did not seem particularly appealing; money seemed unappealing. I was not attracted to these values; they appeared empty to me, and so I chose to reject them. Would I one day regret my decision? Would the world pass me by? More than ever I wanted to live life intensely, and to see and travel the world. I knew at the time that materialism was meaningless, that mortgages and car payments were meaningless. You can't take your house with you when you die. What you have in life are your experiences; these nobody can take away from you.

I returned to my old job at sea during March 1969 on cruise ships to Hawaii and the South Pacific, interspersed with a couple summer runs from San Francisco up to Alaska, though I was now twenty-two, yet in the same position I had previously held before I was called into the Army. I guess one could say that I had lost a little more than three years in my ascent up the corporate ladder while serving in the Army insofar as my future earnings potential was concerned, but I wasn't complaining, for I was one of the lucky ones.

I suppose I was falling behind my contemporaries, the guys my age who had stayed in school and therefore avoided the military. By now they had all graduated from university, and were well on their way toward riches and success.

I worked with another junior officer who was several years older than I, named Jonathan Hartfield, who had graduated from the prestigious and expensive private university of Stanford to the south of San Francisco. He seemed to drink quite a bit for a young man, while I had virtually stopped drinking after leaving the Army. He was one grade above me, but, after all, he was a Stanford graduate. On a couple evenings, when Jonathan was deep into his cups, he would lament the fact that he had gone out of his way to avoid the draft by falsely claiming some physical abnormality in front of his draft board, and thus received his 4-F Selective Service System classification (not acceptable for military service under established physical, mental or moral standards). It almost seemed as though he wanted to confess his sins to me in order to expiate his guilt.

I did not really give a shit about whether or not Jonathan had suited up for Vietnam, and yet it seemed that he had singled me out as the one to hear his confession. The only thing that surprised me was that he truly felt some degree of remorse for taking the easy way out, while most of the others I had met, who had avoided the draft and Vietnam by claiming high blood pressure or by joining the National Guard, were generally self-congratulatory about how clever they were. I just sat there and felt kind of sorry for Jonathan, but not as sorry as I felt for the poor souls whom I knew were still struggling to survive out in their jungle foxholes in Vietnam. Years later I heard that Jonathan had fulfilled his dream and opened a liquor store in Oakland. I never could understand why a young man who had graduated from prestigious Stanford University would embark on a career in the merchant marine, but even more perplexing to me, was why such a privileged man would take to drink? One might have thought that I would have been the one most likely to be afflicted by alcoholic demons as a result of my wartime experiences.

In any case I was just a workingman who had returned to his lot in life, though I was a ship's officer, which garnered some respect from the crew. My contemporaries who had stayed in school and had appeared so juvenile to my eyes would now be passing me by. They would engender respect because they were considered to be well educated with bright future prospects, while here I was, nearly five years out of high school, with only one year of college under my belt, and it did not appear that I was going to be earning a university degree any time soon.

I really didn't mind. I was back at sea — alone, with some money in my pocket; it's all I really wanted. I felt comfortable being with working men who were without intellectual pretensions. The preppy college boy thing appeared frivolous to my mind. Some vets returned from Vietnam with driving ambitions and accomplished much in politics and business, but many veterans seemed to slide downwards, toward the dark abyss — losing themselves in drugs and alcohol. Which direction would I take?

It's too easy to say that we simply make choices, as though they are set out in front of us like on a sheet of music, as though we can just follow some formal outline that will ensure us happiness and success. I found myself not caring much about making any choices for the future. I felt more than ever that I simply wanted to live in the present, where a job and some money in my pocket were sufficient.

There were no loud noises at sea, no honking horns, no trucks or cars backfiring. The ocean, except for the occasional storm, was a peaceful and contemplative environment. Since I was a Vietnam vet, my superiors just assumed that I was a weapons expert, which, in my case, happened to be true. Consequently, one of my "other duties as assigned" was to be in charge of the trap-shooting off the fantail (rear) of the ship. We used 12-gauge shotguns and I was able to take a lot of shooting practice. I became able, on average, to hit ninety-eight clay pigeons out of a hundred. This was nice duty — to be assisting the passengers on warm sunny days, while sailing over calm, blue, glassy water in the South Pacific.

I sought solitude, which I found aplenty at sea. I suppose that I was living just for myself in the most selfish sense. I wasn't seeking greater responsibility; I had my share of that in Vietnam. I no longer wanted to be responsible for others, only for myself; although I wanted to accomplish things, I had no clear vision at the moment as to what these things might be. Had the war hampered or enhanced my life? I suspected that this would be revealed to me over time as I proceeded on my own personal odyssey through life. As an army infantry officer I had been trained to lead men into combat and to engage and kill the enemy at close quarters, but this did not appear to be such a useful skill in the civilian world where the preppies reigned supreme because they were long on classroom academics, though notoriously short on experience.

Life at sea was very therapeutic. To be out on the ocean, far far away from the war, was cleansing. And yet the war continued to follow me, for there were times when I found myself afflicted with a malarial attack, a residual scourge from Vietnam (because the malaria parasites can persist in a dormant state for months, or even years, where they grow and develop, after which they work their way back into the bloodstream and attack the red blood cells, causing a relapse).

Carmen, the young, pretty, dark-haired ship's nurse, had no drugs on hand to treat malaria, so she would just hold me, until we became lovers. Carmen held the cure, for her ministrations brought me back to a far greater sense of well-being than could ever have been achieved by the ingestion of quinine.

Many of the ship's officers, whom I had known before I went away to the Army, treated me differently. I was still the youngest officer on the ship at twenty-two years of age, while virtually all of the other ship's officers were more than twice my age, but I was no longer treated as a boy; rather, I was treated as one of them, while Jonathan, though several years older than I, was still condescendingly treated as a boy by the other officers.

The world had indeed changed in my absence; California especially had changed in my absence; it wasn't just me who had changed. The fact is that everything changes, for change is the one constant in life. One dramatic change I observed was that young American women were becoming liberated, and they were much more aggressive about sex. I no longer had to make all the overtures; in fact, women now seemed to be making most of the moves.

II

It was always a thrill to sail under the Golden Gate Bridge and glimpse the city of San Francisco hugging the hills off the starboard side of the ship as we entered the beautiful bay. On one occasion, after tying up to the pier, my old Army buddy Don O'Brien unexpectedly came walking right out of the past, and up the gangway to greet me. We had been in Basic Training together when we first entered the Army. Don had recently moved to San Francisco and contacted my mother regarding my whereabouts, though I had not seen him nor heard a word from him during the past three years.

I was astonished to learn that Don never did attend Engineer Officer Candidate School. He confided to me that after a month into his advanced engineer training in Virginia, he inexplicably began to feel depressed, thinking that perhaps he might be suffering from a sense of confinement that one sometimes feels in the military. Don went through his chain of command, up to his commanding officer, to request an appointment with the base psychiatrist to discuss his bouts of depression.

As I was listening to Don, I was thinking to myself that the military is the last place in the world to seek compassion or sympathy, even from its medical officers. Shortly after his meeting with the psychiatrist, Don was informed that his nomination to OCS had been revoked. Perplexed, Don went to see his commanding officer to ask why he had been pulled out of the officer program. His CO looked at Don and said, "Soldier, you needed to see a shrink, and therefore you are no longer considered to be officer material." Don told me that he was so stunned, and further depressed by this pronouncement, that he simply walked out of the CO's office and right off the base, where he unobtrusively boarded a Greyhound bus—bound for New York City.

After being AWOL (Absent Without Official Leave) for about six months Don turned himself in to the authorities, who promptly confined him in the stockade at Fort Dix, New Jersey. Ultimately Don received a medical discharge, which was eventually converted to a general discharge, which was something less than an honorable discharge, though not as bad as a dishonorable discharge. Still, it cast a shadow that followed Don for the rest of his life.

III

During March 1969, after only two months in office, Nixon authorized the secret bombing of Cambodia and its infiltration routes into South Vietnam. Norodom Sihanouk had been the leader of Cambodia since 1953 and had maintained a delicate balancing act in keeping his country out of active military participation in the Vietnam War. He did not favor the presence of large numbers of North Vietnamese in Cambodia's eastern regions, but militarily his country was weak. The American bombing was conducted by B-52s out of Guam, each of which carried a mix of over a hundred 500-pound and 750-pound bombs. This was clearly a violation of the Geneva accords of 1954, whereby the United States was violating the neutrality of Cambodia. No doubt Nixon justified his actions as a necessary response to purported violations of Cambodian neutrality by the North Vietnamese; still, he clearly and knowingly concealed the bombing campaign from Congress as well as the American public.

At this time I had been out of the war for just a little over six months. Some soldiers with whom I had fought were still fighting, and some soldiers whom I had trained at Fort Polk had arrived in Vietnam by then, and fought and bled over the next twelve months. I could empathize with what they must be going through, whereas it seemed that the people around me could not, for there is a certain degree of detachment within a person who is reading about a war in a newspaper at home, because war is pretty much an abstract for the non-participant. You read the printed words, which can evoke sympathetic emotions and enhanced understanding, but still the reader is not subjected to the physical hardships or emotional trauma of the wartime experience, and so, for the reader, war is more of a detached intellectual exercise.

There is the world of the participant, and the other world — the passive world of spectators and observers. The spectators profess to have all sorts of opinions, and evince no hesitation in giving their pontifical advice, but do they really understand the terror of the soldier under fire? Can the spectator ever truly empathize with the soldier who is trying to submerge himself in the primordial ooze of the rice paddy to avoid being killed and is so terrified that he cannot control his bowels and thus fouls himself unabashedly, while ignominiously clinging to survival in the face of death?

The wartime experience for survival is not an experience that one is exposed to in our orderly societies, and perhaps this is not an experience for which any sane person would choose to voluntarily submit; rather, it is an experience that is thrust upon a person, like a woman giving birth, or the act of falling in love. These are experiences for which words are inadequate to describe; these experiences exist solely in the emotive experiential act of the individual, and they are so profound that they defy description by the written or the spoken word. We come to find that language, being linear in construction, has its limitations.

Six months away from the war and I could still feel it. I could still empathize with the pain and suffering that my comrades had endured, and were continuing to endure, yet there was no one around me to whom I could express my feelings. I retreated further into my books and the soothing contemplative environment that only truly existed for me far out at sea.

IV

During April 1969 the number of American troops in Vietnam reached its zenith of 543,300, yet throughout the war the enemy was able to match U.S. forces in equivalent strength, such that whenever the United States increased its troop strength in Vietnam, the communists were capable of doing the same. From this point, the number of troops in Vietnam began to decline.

On 20 July 1969, American astronaut Neil Armstrong became the first human being to set foot on the moon—"That's one small step for a man, one giant leap for mankind." It was the fruition of an American dream, born eight years earlier, when President Kennedy articulated his vision in a speech to Congress in 1961, just four months after taking office, when he said, "I believe that this nation should commit itself to achieving the goal, before this decade is out, of landing a man on the moon and returning him safely to the earth."

During the first week of September, Ho Chi Minh, our indomitable adversary, died of natural causes at the age of seventy-nine, yet his mantle of authority remained in capable hands. Also during September, President Nixon announced that, since the military had fulfilled its quota for the year with more than 280,000 draftees, draft calls would be canceled for November and December. However, in reality, the Administration was replacing the traditional draft, which had become unpopular, with the new draft lottery that was to go into effect on the 1st of December. Draft calls for October were stretched out over the final quarter of the year and were henceforth limited to nineteen-year-olds.[1]

On the sixteenth of November 1969, the *New York Times* broke the story of the My Lai Massacre. Army lieutenant William Calley was court-martialed and sentenced to life in prison at hard labor for his role in the atrocity. However, after just a couple days in the stockade at Fort Leavenworth, Kansas, President Nixon made the decision to have Calley released pending appeal of his sentence. Calley remained under house arrest in his quarters at Fort Benning, in Columbus, Georgia, for three and a half years, after which he was released on bail, and eight months afterwards he was paroled.

Americans seemed shocked that red-blooded American boys could commit such dreadful atrocities during wartime. However, I had no doubts that soldiers of every nation, in just about every war, have committed atrocities. We train people in the military to kill, which is against their religious and moral teachings, then we tell them to go forth and kill for the glory of their country, and then we are shocked to hear that some have acted in excess. War is replete with ignoble behavior. What Lieutenant Calley and his soldiers did was unconscionable, and they are condemned to live with their unpardonable sins for the rest of their lives, and my heart goes out to the victims, but I was not shocked to learn of these reprehensible acts, for I was no longer that naive. Shortly after Calley was set free on parole, he met and married a wealthy local girl, and then worked for the next thirty years in her father's jewelry store in Columbus, Georgia.

The United States, ever so slowly, began to reduce its military forces in Vietnam, with the result that, by the end of 1969, there were still 474,000 troops in Vietnam, a reduction of less than 13 percent for the year. This withdrawal process became so protracted that American soldiers continued to be killed in Vietnam in significant numbers for another four years. During 1969 alone, 8,239 soldiers were killed in action, the third highest number of KIAs during all the years of the war, exceeded only by 1968 and 1967 respectively.[2]

"As withdrawals proceeded, more and more U.S. troops in the field came to see the war as futile. No one wanted to be the last man killed or wounded. Mutinies, or 'combat refusals,' as the army called them, rose dramatically as men refused to go on search-and-destroy missions. More and more combat soldiers took heroin. A frightening jump occurred in episodes of soldiers attacking officers with guns or hurling fragmentation bombs into their tents— 'fragging,' it was called. Racial tensions shot up at bases around the world. Nurses found the self-inflicted injuries and drug overdoses of the last years of the war sadder and more bewildering than the wounds suffered from enemy fire at the height of the fighting.... An Army study identified a 'sociopathological riptide' among soldiers in the last years of the American presence in Vietnam."[3]

V

Though the Ho Chi Minh Trail through southern Laos, adjacent to South Vietnam, had been subject to B-52 bombing under the Johnson Administration, President Nixon, during February 1970, expanded this bombing to include northern Laos, around the Plain of Jars, to thwart advances by communist Pathet Lao and North Vietnamese troops. At the time I was sipping rum punches in Tahiti and reading about Vietnam and Southeast Asia in the newspapers, though I could not really escape the war, for it continued to follow me far out to sea. I wondered whether it would even follow me into marriage, somewhere in the distant future. I wondered whether the war would follow me all the way into old age.

One day at sea some passengers were checking on their baggage in storage, and I noticed that their family name was Turnbull, which was not your everyday name. I had known a young man in the Army who had been in my class at Officer Candidate School, whose name was Robert Turnbull, and so when I saw these people out on the promenade deck, I approached them and mentioned that I had known a young man in the Army, who was about my age, whose name was Robert, and I asked them if they might be related in any way.

They excitedly informed me that Robert was their son, and they seemed so very happy to talk with me about him. They even vividly recalled their son's experiences at OCS, and the humorous incident about the candy bar that required Robert to go back and repeat the last six weeks of officer training. Robert was a nice guy; he was from Andover, New Jersey, and he and I used to spend quite a bit of time together, training to become young infantry platoon leaders in our country's war against communism, though of course training was a far cry from reality, but I suppose we were in the John Wayne mode back in those days.

Robert's parents knew the story about the "unauthorized" candy bar, yet they were delighted to hear my version, and it seemed as though they breathlessly hung on my every word, and we all laughed together when I concluded my simple but elaborate tale. Then they told me that Robert had arrived in Vietnam during the fall of 1967, not long after me, and that he had been killed during the first week of February 1968, less than two years ago, at the beginning of the Tet Offensive.

They were probably taking this cruise, much like me, to get as far away as possible from the plaguing memories of war and death, and I was probably a sad reminder to these grieving parents of their young son who had forever been taken away from them. Most likely it was both a steady torment as well as a somber comfort for them to speak to me about their son, for war is such a sorrowful time, because it is a time when parents bury their children, whereas in the natural order of life, the sequence is reversed. Robert is listed on panel 38E of the Vietnam Veterans Memorial in Washington, D.C.

It was hard for me to imagine that Jim Shea, from my hometown, who was shot down in Vietnam on 20 April 1965 (one year to the day after he arrived in Vietnam), is etched on panel 1E, while Robert, who was killed about two and a half years later on the seventh of February 1968, is etched on panel 38E.

The panels become smaller as they extend out from the vertex to the wings, such that there are more than six hundred names on panel 1E, which stands more than ten feet high, but only five names on panel 70E. More than 29,000 names are etched on the Wall from panel 1E out to panel 70E (covering the period 1959 to May 1968), though it should be noted that in 1999, a death was added to the Wall that occurred in 1956.

The names of the fallen are picked up again on panel 70W (May 1968) and come back to panel 1W at the vertex. Thus the list of those who died in the Vietnam War ends (1975), just where it begins (1959). The Wall was completed seven years after the end of the war, of which its black granite panels have been immeasurably healing for all of us Vietnam vets.

VI

During March 1970, Cambodia's defense minister, Lon Nol, overthrew Norodom Sihanouk and took over control of the country. Sihanouk threw his support to the communists, blaming his ouster on CIA collusion, which resulted in an expansion of Khmer Rouge (Cambodian communists) and North Vietnamese military activity throughout Cambodia. Henry Kissinger, in a recent memoir, denies that there was any CIA involvement in the overthrow of Sihanouk.[4]

Lon Nol proceeded to look to the United States to assist him in kicking the North Vietnamese out of Cambodia. His pro-American stance provided the justification for President Nixon to authorize the invasion of Cambodia that commenced toward the end of April, which included both American and South Vietnamese Army troops. Ultimately the two-month invasion of Cambodia by U.S. and ARVN forces was only moderately effective; however, the genocide inflicted by Cambodians upon one another in their destabilized country, as a consequence of the war in Vietnam, was inordinately effective.

On the fourth of May 1970, Ohio National Guardsmen fired more than sixty rounds of live ammunition into a crowd of students at Kent State University, killing four and wounding nine, while suffering no casualties of their own. Some critics said that the protesters were all hippies who did not even go to school, but all thirteen victims were registered students at the university and attending classes.[5] They were among a group of around 2,000 students conducting a campus protest against the Vietnam War; more particularly, they were protesting Nixon's decision to invade neutral Cambodia.

Our government was now killing student protestors. We thought that this was something that could only happen in China, the Soviet Union, Hungary, Czechoslovakia, or some dictatorial South American country. Kent State was in Ohio, America's heartland, where it was believed that family values and respect for authority held sway. Kent State wasn't considered a hotbed of student radicalism, as was the perception of the University of California at Berkeley. A large segment of the population felt that the president was not disengaging from the war fast enough, for even after Kent State more than 7,000 Americans died in Vietnam.

During September 1970, after a year and a half at sea, I celebrated my twenty-fourth birthday. I was standing by the railing in the late afternoon, while our ship was heading south along the Alaskan coast on its way back to California. We were close in to land, and I was leaning over the ship's portside railing, staring in wonder as the impending sunset behind me cast shafts of light, imbued with yellow and orange pastels amongst the evergreen trees that appeared to grow so far down to the ocean's edge that they appeared to be marching into the sea. It was at this very moment that I had an epiphany of sorts, for I resolutely pledged to myself to leave this seafaring life and return to school just as soon as our ship put into port in San Francisco.

I had lost time during my three years in the Army, and, after being discharged, I just assumed that I was behind the eight ball, and that those who stayed at home had moved ahead. However, what if that was not the case at all? What if all of these disparate experiences that we have in life actually coalesce to form an even stronger alloy than could ever be achieved by spending all our youth in school? Maybe we, who had sustained the hard knocks of the Army and the experience of working for a living, were actually the very people that would eventually pull ahead. What if, many years from now, it was determined that somehow even my marginal working experiences had been the essential contributors to my future successes, because they had taught me humility and provided me with the understanding that all work is honorable.

By the end of 1970, the highest draft lottery number for draftees was 125, which meant that young American men born in the other 240 (66 percent) random numbered dates would not have to worry about being drafted. "Nixon quickly ended most student deferments, replacing them with an annual lottery whereby men were drafted on the basis of their birthdays..., the lottery system removed some of the obvious inequities of the deferment system.... After the lottery took hold, over two-thirds of men born in any year breathed more easily since only those with lower lottery numbers were likely to be drafted. This development alone substantially reduced the number of young men likely to engage in anti-war activities."[6]

PART IV: 1970–PRESENT

16

The Journey (1970–Present)

I

Looking back over the more than thirty years since I left the merchant marine to return to school, I have come to the realization that we have much more control over steering our own ship of fate than I had ever imagined when I stepped ashore at the age of twenty-four. After I left the sea during September 1970, I initially found a place to live in a small town astride the Pacific Ocean, to the north of San Francisco, during which time I returned to school at a nearby junior college for my second year of study. I received some G.I. Bill educational assistance; it wasn't very much, $175 a month at the time, but I was grateful nevertheless. I mean, it wouldn't even cover the tuition at a major university, but it covered the cost of my books at junior college, where there was no tuition.

Even with the draft lottery in place, more than 162,000 young men were drafted during 1970, and 3,659 Americans were killed in action in Vietnam during that year.[1] However, the number of U.S. troops in Vietnam began to incrementally decline, falling to 335,800 by the end of the year. During February 1971, the Nixon Administration supported a plan whereby U.S. combat forces would take up blocking positions near the northwestern portion of the DMZ, while South Vietnamese military forces would thrust into Laos and sever a main junction of the Ho Chi Minh Trail, and thus postpone any major North Vietnamese offensives into South Vietnam for a year. The 17,000 ARVN troops ran into stiff opposition from North Vietnamese soldiers, and were sent hightailing back across the border. It was becoming clear that the South Vietnamese were no match against the hardened warriors of the north, unless they were supported by overwhelming artillery and air support.

By the summer of 1971, there were no longer any American combat troops up in the central highlands; they had all been pulled out and redeployed along the coast, turning the security of the highlands over to the ARVN in concert with Nixon's Vietnamization plan, while many in Congress were applying pressure on the president to accelerate American troop withdrawals. It had been more than two and a half years since I had departed those highland jungles; however, I have come to realize that time is truly relative, and that two or three years is really no time at all, for, even after that period, I still could not get the smell of the dead bodies and the muddy paddies out of my nostrils.

That same summer, during June 1971, I completed my studies at junior college, and applied for admission to the prestigious University of California at Berkeley, directly across the bay from San Francisco. The administrators told me that so many people were trying to get into Berkeley that I would have to wait at least six months, and perhaps as long as a year, before they would be able to let me know whether or not I would be accepted. I told them I would wait, and, in the interim, I headed out for Central America in a battered old pick-up truck and soon found a job cutting bananas. Six months later, during December, a forwarded letter made its way out to me in the remote jungles of Costa Rica's Nicoya Peninsula, informing me that I had been accepted by the University of California (UC). A total of 1,206 Americans were killed in action in Vietnam this year.[2]

I commenced my studies at UC Berkeley during January 1972 where I majored in philosophy, while additionally taking several French classes. Quite a few people at the time told me that a degree in philosophy was not very practical and that I would probably end up being a shoe salesman. Nevertheless, I studied Aristotle's *Ethics*, and I read about how Kierkegaard felt we should deal with the dilemma of love, which he considered to be forever and impossible at the same time. I enjoyed my studies immensely, for I suppose that after enduring the lunacy of war I was in search of some deeper understanding of mankind, and the field of philosophy provided me the opportunity to explore the vital ethical, political, and religious issues that shape humanity.

On the last day of March 1972, North Vietnam unleashed a major offensive involving twelve of its thirteen regular combat divisions, sending three divisions across the DMZ (in clear violation of the Geneva Accords), supported by more than 200 Soviet-made tanks. Additional thrusts were made from out of Laos against Kontum and Pleiku in the central highlands, and toward Saigon from out of Cambodia. Three years of troop withdrawals had reduced U.S. troop strength to around 69,000, most of whom were support personnel, compelling the South Vietnamese to take over the ground fighting, while the U.S. provided air support with massive B-52 and carrier air strikes against targets in both South and North Vietnam (including Hanoi and Haiphong), as well as the mining of North Vietnamese ports in order to halt the flow of Soviet war materials to the communists. By September South Vietnamese forces had gone over to the offensive and were driving back the North Vietnamese, which thus significantly strengthened America's hand at the Paris Peace Talks and its negotiations pertaining to the release of our POWs.[3] By autumn all U.S. combat troops had departed Vietnam, leaving behind just 43,500 airmen and support personnel. Still, 327 Americans were killed in action in Vietnam during 1972.[4]

On New Year's Eve, 1973, I was with a group of fellow students who had not made any plans for the evening, and so, at the last minute, we all decided to drive across the Bay Bridge into San Francisco. The girls were looking cute as they made coat hanger hats for their heads, and we found ourselves on the corner of Columbus and Broadway, where Chinatown and the Italian neighborhood of North Beach intersect, just as the clock was approaching midnight.

During February, North Vietnam began its release of the 591 American MIAs who had ultimately been classified as prisoners of war (POWs). That still left 2,585 American MIAs unaccounted for, which enflamed the ire of family members and veteran's groups who doubted the veracity of the North Vietnamese assertions that these 591 Americans, representing less than 20 percent of all those Americans listed as missing in action, were all that remained alive. However, the Nixon Administration wanted to rapidly extricate itself from this debacle and seemed willing to accept the claims of the North Vietnamese that all of the other 2,585 MIAs were dead. But if so, then where were the bodies? Or such were my thoughts at the time.

During March 1973, at the age of twenty-six, I received my Bachelor of Arts degree from Berkeley. The war for the United States was winding down, although 23,000 American troops were still in Vietnam, impatiently awaiting their return home, while twenty more Americans were killed in action during the first three months of 1973.[5] The war continued for another two years amongst the Vietnamese — all the way into the spring of 1975, while some Marines remained behind to guard the U.S. Embassy, before they themselves were forced to evacuate Saigon under the unstoppable onslaught of the Vietcong and the NVA. Even during these days, when the war was winding down, the United States was still not the most comfortable place for a Vietnam vet.

I wanted to get away, and felt that I could justify my existence by continuing with my formal education abroad. At least I had an objective upon which to focus my energies, and that always seemed to help, so I purchased a one-way plane ticket to Europe and headed out into my future. I arrived in Europe toward the end of March 1973. This was it. I suppose that if I found myself being lonely, insecure, unhappy, or unloved, there would be nothing I could do about it. I had no idea as to how I was going to get back to the States, but somehow I would have to earn my way, and who knew how long that would take?

I felt such an incredible sense of liberation, pretty much because I had no plans for the future. In fact I had no future; for the first time in my life, since infancy (and also perhaps when I was in the war), I was living in the moment, for better or for worse. I was living my own renaissance; I would make friends and acquaintances strictly on my own merits, with very little money in my pocket. I would certainly not have to contend with the insecurity of the affluent who seemed to continually be worrying about whether people liked them for who they were, or for what they possessed. It was ironic that I would be traveling to the Old World to fashion my new world — it was exhilarating.

I ended up spending nearly three years in France, during which time I attended the University of Paris–Sorbonne in the heart of the Latin Quarter for two years, while working in restaurants as a dishwasher, waiter, and bartender. Toward the end of my time in France, some successful American businessmen came into the restaurant in Pigalle where I was bartending and suggested that I consider applying to the American Graduate School of International Management (Thunderbird) in Arizona. They told me that in less than two years I could earn a master's degree in international management, which was like a MBA (Master's degree in Business Administration), but with the additional requirement of a demonstrated proficiency in a foreign language, and they pointed out that since I was already conversant in French, I should easily be able to satisfy the stringent language requirements, and I would therefore only need to focus on the business requirements. Then, once I received my master's degree, I should be able to easily obtain an overseas assignment and return to Europe.

I was aware that Thunderbird was consistently ranked as the #1 international business school in the United States, and admitted only a small number of students without undergraduate degrees in business; nevertheless, I proceeded to gather up all of my university transcripts and submitted an application. If accepted, I would constitute the tiny segment of the student population that had little or no prior exposure to business studies.

The following month I received a letter from the Thunderbird Business School. I opened the letter with some trepidation, but was happily surprised to read that I had been accepted. Was I just dreaming, or was it possible for a twenty-eight-year-old bartender and Vietnam vet to make something more of his life? Or, was it already too late for me? Weren't most of my contemporaries back in the States already well on their way in their chosen career fields, buying their houses and raising their children? Here I was, heading toward thirty, and yet I had none of these things. I came to find that the business school curriculum was nothing more than pure practicality, simple common sense really, as well as learning the buzz words so that one could speak the language of business.

I got married along the way. I actually married a woman with whom I went to high school; we were in the same class and her parents had been regular customers at the restaurant in which I had worked after school. My wife had graduated from San Francisco State College in 1968, which was at the hub of student protests against the Vietnam War when I was overseas fighting. We met in Paris, simply by chance, in a café, after not seeing one another for more than ten years— since our high school days. My wife had been adamantly against the war, so we never discussed the subject between us during our first seven years together.

Within a year of our meeting, I became the proud father of a lovely baby girl when I was twenty-nine, and I graduated from Thunderbird at the age of thirty. After a short stint working in San Francisco's Financial District, I decided to enter government service and was soon thereafter offered a civilian job with the Navy in Europe, primarily because they were looking for a French speaker. Who would have thought that hanging out in France for nearly three years would be the deciding factor, to my benefit, in securing a position with the federal government in Europe?

II

I ended up working as a civilian for the government for nearly twenty-seven years, fifteen of which were overseas. I spent thirteen years living and working out of Italy, and two years in Japan. I never really escaped the grasp of the Vietnam War; it was as though it had firmly entrenched itself within me, and I still could not clearly discern whether this state of being had been for better or worse. I was frequently approached at my work to handle hazardous contingency assignments pertaining to the evacuation of American citizens from areas of civil unrest (referred to as Noncombatant Evacuation Operations [NEOs]) that took place in West Africa for the most part. I had been selected for these assignments primarily because I was a Vietnam vet, which prompted my superiors to believe that I would hold up under pressure, and this was nearly thirty years after my return from the war.

A Navy captain with whom I had worked in West Africa during 1996, and who considered me to be the Navy's subject matter expert on these types of evacuations, had encouraged me to apply for entry into the Naval War College's prestigious College of Naval Command and Staff, believing that I had some critical knowledge and experience to impart to the Navy officer community.

The United States Naval War College is the oldest war college in the United States, and the oldest continuing War College for professional military officers in the world. By professional, I mean that it is an academic institution for military officers who have already received their commissions and who have been serving in the military for twelve to fifteen years. Therefore, it was somewhat unusual for an older guy like me to be enrolled. However, shortly after the millennium, I graduated right along with the rest of my classmates.

The College of Naval Command and Staff is designed to educate midgrade officers who have compiled outstanding performance records during their careers. The curriculum is rigorous and the courses focus on areas intended to enhance the leadership performance of the attending officers, as well as groom them for positions on the staffs of any of our nation's nine Unified Combatant Commands, such as CINCPAC (Commander in Chief, U.S. Pacific Command) to which MACV had been a subordinate command, or CINCCENT (Commander in Chief, U.S. Central Command) whose area of responsibility covers much of the Middle East. It should be noted that during 2002, the Secretary of Defense changed all of the Commander in Chief (CINC) designates to Commander

(COM), reserving the Commander in Chief designate solely for the president of the United States.

All officers who attend this college have their bachelor's degrees, over half possess their masters' degrees, and some even have their PhDs. A board of senior officers is convened annually to consider which officers will be selected for attendance. Consequently, those selected are considered to be the cream of the crop. Attendance by civilians, like me, is by endorsement of their federal agencies, which in turn nominate their respective candidates using similar selection criteria as for Navy officers. My nine other classmates, who were in their mid-thirties and virtually all graduates of the Naval Academy, provided me the opportunity to reflect upon my Vietnam experiences, because in the eyes of my fellow classmates, Vietnam was still considered the last really big war.

I told them that I felt, from my perspective, that there had been four wars going on in Vietnam. There was the war down in the lowlands and the Delta region around Saigon that was primarily an urban war fought primarily against South Vietnamese communists (VC) where it was difficult to discern the good guys from the bad guys, so that a perceptible degree of cynicism developed amongst the soldiers who fought there. Then there was the war fought primarily by the Marines up along the DMZ against North Vietnamese Army (NVA) regulars and big gun artillery that seemed to me to be a very tough form of trench warfare for the most part. Thirdly, there was the war in the central highlands, fought in thick jungles, also against the NVA, where there was almost a pristine purity to the fight, and little confusion as to who were the bad guys. Most of the fighting up through 1968, including all three phases of the Tet Offensive, had resulted in bloody tactical defeats for the communists, notwithstanding the immense strategic victory the communists had gained during phase one with its attack against the U.S. Embassy in Saigon when many Americans back home lost the will to continue the fight. Fourthly, there was the war that was fought from 1969 to 1973, for a little more than four years, under the Nixon presidency and the application of his Vietnamization plan, during which the United States was striving to extricate itself from the war, such that morale suffered, as soldiers did not want to be the last person to die in a lost cause.

The communist victory was narrower than many people realize, as the mobility and superior firepower of the Americans had consistently been winning the tactical battles with devastating effect. I suppose, in retrospect, that I considered myself fortunate to have departed the war during September 1968, four months before President Nixon took office, and I do not say this because I agreed or disagreed with Nixon's plan, but rather because, all the way up through 1968, the bloodiest year of the entire war, we soldiers out in the bush on our search-and-destroy missions still believed. We sincerely believed we were fighting the good fight and beating back the communist onslaught, and that our comrades had not died in vain.

During my time in Vietnam I had peered behind the velvet curtain and seen the elephant, and thus was forced to see a harsher reality than that to which most people are exposed. I suppose I had acquired an enhanced understanding of life, at the expense of losing my youthful innocence. Still, I have always retained a positive attitude, especially after surviving the ordeal of war, for I was just so happy to be alive. I rarely sweat the small stuff.

I did not shed a single tear in Vietnam, not even after seeing so many young men die. I wasn't the only one. We didn't cry. Perhaps because we were soldiers, men, and Americans, though I am not particularly ashamed about this fact, for this was how we were raised as young boys. During my childhood years, if a boy was to cry after the age of eight he would be pitilessly taunted by his child peers as being a baby; it was part of our cultural toughening-up process, to prepare us for the harsh world of reality that most all of us would confront in the imminent future — at the end of adolescence.

I developed a deeper appreciation for camaraderie and friendship as a result of the war, though some women have said I was selfish and like a stone. I listened, although I was aware that men are more closed off emotionally than women, yet I have attempted to loosen up and reach out more to people. I concede that I have been selfish — to the extent that I wanted to educate myself and accomplish things in life, and thus I felt compelled to focus on my goals without permitting others to sidetrack or deter me.

Except for the time after the war when I went squirrel hunting around Fort Polk with the game warden, and, shortly afterwards, when I was in charge of the trapshooting off the fantail of the cruise ship up through the age of twenty-three, I have not picked up a rifle or a shotgun. I can't really explain why. I simply felt no inclination to do so. I cry more easily now. I cry when I see young children suffer, elderly people lonely, or when my mind, which oftentimes seems to have a will of its own, takes me on habitual journeys back to Vietnam, where I am prompted to remember, as though it was yesterday, the brave young men who died there. I feel that I am becoming better; I am no longer a stone.

Appendix A

Comparison of Vietnam War Casualties to Other American Wars

More than two-thirds (68 percent) of all the 58,220 American deaths in Vietnam occurred within just three years (1967, 1968, and 1969), though these 39,361 deaths include both hostile and non-hostile deaths.[1] However, if one were to consider just those Americans killed in action (KIA), then these same three years (1967, 1968, and 1969) comprised slightly more than 72 percent (29,698) of all the 40,934 Americans killed in action during the war, with 1968 being by far the bloodiest year, during which 32 percent (13,005) of all U.S. KIAs occurred, followed by 1967 (8,454) and 1969 (8,239) at about 20 percent each.[2]

Statistics indicate that 3.7 soldiers were wounded for each man killed in action (153,303 ÷ 40,934) in Vietnam, which was a better survival ratio than during World War II, for in Vietnam, with helicopter medevacs, the wounded were evacuated from the battlefield more rapidly than in previous wars, resulting in more survivors from serious wounds. As a consequence, the Vietnam War produced 5,283 amputees, one amputee for every 11 deaths (a ratio which includes both hostile and non-hostile deaths), a better ratio of amputees to deaths than in previous wars; during World War II, for example, there were 54 deaths for every amputee.[3] If the Vietnam War had been conducted without the helicopter, then the number of soldiers killed would have been far greater.

If one were to consider just combat (hostile) deaths and wounded together, while excluding "other deaths" such as deaths from accidents and disease, one could make the following comparisons[4]:

- First would be **World War II** (1941 to 1945) with the greatest number of casualties at **964,403** (292,557 combat deaths and 671,846 wounded);
- Second would be the **Civil War** (1861 to 1865) at **633,819** (214,938 total combat deaths [74,524 Confederates killed and 140,414 Union soldiers killed], plus 418,881 total wounded [137,000 Confederates wounded and 281,881 Union soldiers wounded]);
- Third would be **World War I** (1917 to 1918) at **257,404** (53,402 combat deaths and 204,002 wounded), though the war had started for the French and Germans in 1914;
- Fourth would be the **Vietnam War** at **200,737** (47,434 combat [hostile] deaths [includes 40,934 killed in action] and 153,303 wounded). I have included the figure

of 153,303 for the number of wounded, which includes only those wounded that required hospitalization.
- Fifth would be the **Korean War** (1950 to 1953) at **137,025** (33,741 combat deaths and 103,284 wounded);
- Sixth would be the **Second Iraqi War** (19 March 2003 through 3 August 2009 and continuing) at **34,918** (3,464 combat [hostile] deaths and 31,454 wounded [of which 13,853 were considered more serious than the others]).[5] It should be noted that President Barack Obama provided an exit strategy on 27 February 2009 when he stated that by the end of August 2010 "our combat mission in Iraq will end." Though even after that time, 35,000 to 50,000 U.S. military personnel will remain in Iraq to assist in training the Iraqis, after which they too will be pulled out of Iraq by the end of 2011.
- Seventh would be the **War of Independence** (1775 to 1783) at **10,623** (4,435 combat deaths and 6,188 wounded);
- Eighth would be the **War of 1812** (1812 to 1815) at **6,765** (2,260 combat deaths and 4,505 wounded);
- Ninth would be the **Mexican War** (1846 to 1848) at **5,885** (1,733 combat deaths and 4,152 wounded);
- Tenth would be the **War in Afghanistan** (7 October 2001 through 3 August 2009 and continuing) at **3,886** (514 combat [hostile] deaths and 3,372 wounded [of which 2,139 were considered more serious than the others]).[6]

It is astonishing that the American phase of the Vietnam War persisted for twenty years (1955 to 1975). Perhaps some might say that American ground troops in force were there for only eight years (mid–1965 to early 1973), which still approximates America's other longest war — our War of Independence, which lasted for more than eight and a half years.

World War II, for the United States, lasted four years, as did our Civil War, while the War of 1812 and the Korean War each lasted three years. I would say that the United States hung in there in Vietnam, though certainly not as long as our adversaries, but, after all, Vietnam was their country. Aside from all American restrictions and cautions in conducting the war in such a way so as not to provoke China or the Soviet Union into entering the war, the United States was certainly committed to fighting communism in Southeast Asia and stuck it out for a very long time.

The Vietnam War may very well have been an unwinnable war to begin with, though our political leaders had made much political capital from the domino theory, which had effectively engendered a rabid fear of communism in the minds of the American people. This was not the first time, nor would it be the last time, that our political leaders used simple analogies or slogans to instill fear in the people in order to galvanize support to take the fight overseas before the threat could reach our shores, and the people seemed to react to these slogans of fear with emotions that were as intense as religious belief, such that anyone who was in disagreement was denounced as being unpatriotic, and the bugles would start to blow, and the flags would wave, and young men would go marching off to war. It was as though reason had gone to sleep, and whoever could profess their beliefs persistently enough would carry the day. I'm not saying that our political leaders were consciously trying to mislead the people, but, as politicians, they were accomplished persuaders, as well as being our duly elected leaders, and so we believed them, yet they were people like ourselves, and quite capable of making errors in judgment.

Appendix B
Army Medals

During my military service I received the following awards: Expert Rifle Badge; Good Conduct Medal; National Defense Service Medal; Vietnam Service Medal; Republic of Vietnam Campaign Medal w/60 Device; Combat Infantryman's Badge; Bronze Star and Purple Heart.

We wore our **rifle qualification badge** on our uniforms—Expert, Sharpshooter, or Marksman. It was a very demanding qualification, such that less than 10 percent qualified as Expert, as one had to achieve a score of at least 225 points out of 250, and we were required to fire from the standing, kneeling, and prone positions. Everyone in the Army qualifies at the end of Basic Combat Training (as do the Marines at the end of Boot Camp) and then they receive the qualification badge that they will wear throughout their entire military careers, for all the world to see, except in the case of enlisted men like me who went on to OCS, where we were given a second opportunity to qualify, this time as officers. It seemed that at OCS we were provided a lot more practice at the rifle range so a much higher percentage of us qualified as experts. Everyone was impressed when they saw the Expert Rifleman Badge, as everyone knew how difficult it was to acquire.

The **Army Good Conduct Medal (AGCM)** is only awarded to enlisted men, and not to officers. However, I had been an enlisted soldier for a little more than a year before becoming an officer. Normally the medal requires three years of qualifying enlisted service, but an exception is made if the individual enters an officer school, then the individual must have a minimum of one year of enlisted service.

The recipient must meet the following five criteria:

(1) The immediate commander must evaluate the soldier's character as above reproach.
(2) The soldier has willingly complied with the demands of the military environment.
(3) The soldier has been loyal and obedient to his superiors.
(4) The soldier has faithfully supported the goals of his unit and the Army.
(5) The soldier has conducted himself in such an exemplary manner as to distinguish himself.[1]

Ironically, the wearing of the Good Conduct Medal by officers stigmatized them as the plebeians of the officer corps in the eyes of their fellow officers, advertising to all that we had attended OCS instead of West Point or some glitzy ROTC program, making it definitively known to all that our advance up the ranks would be slower than for the others. Soldiers who were in the enlisted ranks before becoming officers were referred to as Mustangs. And of course the West Point officers could distinguish themselves from the ROTC officers by the wearing of their Academy rings. In fact, the very first American academic institution to introduce the class ring was the U.S. Military Academy at West Point back in 1837, though it wasn't until around 1935 that West Point graduates began wearing heavy gold signet rings that displayed their year of graduation and their school insignia. The elite officers out of West Point could easily recognize other Academy alumni by their signet rings, and these guys, who dominated the military hierarchy, were well aware of the fact that they were on the fast track for promotions and success, hence the term "ring knockers," for these officers would subtly, yet unmistakably, publicize to everyone in the room that they were the top dogs.

The **National Defense Service Medal (NDSM)**, at the time, was awarded for honorable active military service during either the Korean War or the Vietnam War.

The **Vietnam Service Medal (VSM)** was awarded to members of the Armed Forces who served in the war anytime during the nearly eight years between July 1965 and March 1973, during which time ground units were deployed in Vietnam, when most of the combat deaths occurred.

The **Campaign Medal for the Republic of Vietnam (RVNCM)** is a foreign medal, awarded by the Government of the Republic of Vietnam (RVN) to U.S. Armed Forces personnel who served at least six months in the RVN between March 1961 and March 1973. It was also awarded if the soldier was wounded, captured, or killed in action inside of the six-month requirement. The medal came with a "60" device bar (1960-), with the last date to be decided after the war was over. The ending period remains blank because the Government of the Republic of (South) Vietnam had ceased to exist by the time the war was over.

The **Combat Infantryman's Badge (CIB)** was established back in World War II by the War Department, because it was recognized that the infantryman, unlike all other soldiers, continuously operated under the worst conditions, and performed a mission that was not assigned to any other soldier. It was observed that the infantry, though representing only a small portion of the total Armed Forces, suffered the most casualties while receiving the least public recognition.

These factors led to the establishment of the CIB, an award that provided special recognition of the unique role of the Army *infantryman, **the only soldier whose daily mission is to close with, and destroy, the enemy***, as well as seize and hold terrain. Soldiers must meet the following three criteria before they can be awarded the Combat Infantryman's Badge:

1. The soldier must have been an infantryman satisfactorily performing infantry duties,
2. The soldier must have been assigned to an infantry unit during such time as the unit was engaged in active ground combat, and
3. *The soldier must have actively participated in such ground combat.*[2]

There are four medals that the Army can bestow upon its infantry soldiers, on the ground, for distinguished military action against enemy forces.

The **Medal of Honor** is the highest honor, awarded "For Conspicuous Gallantry and Intrepidity at the Risk of Life, Above and Beyond the Call of Duty, in Action Involving Actual Conflict with an Opposing Armed Force." My battalion had one Medal of Honor recipient in Vietnam, awarded posthumously to Platoon Sergeant Elmelindo Smith for his actions on the sixteenth of February 1967, six months before I arrived in country. Sergeant Smith's platoon had been engaged by mortars, rocket, and machine-gun fire from three sides, yet Platoon Sergeant Smith continued to position and inspire his men even after being severely wounded three times, and he continued to fight on and lead his men until his dying breath.

Next comes the **Distinguished Service Cross**, awarded for "Extraordinary Heroism in Connection with Military Operations Against an Opposing Armed Force." Then comes the **Silver Star**, awarded "For Gallantry in Action Against an Opposing Armed Force," followed by the **Bronze Star**, which is awarded (by direction of the president) "For Heroic or Meritorious Achievement of Service in connection with Operations Against an Opposing Armed Force." The Navy/Marine Corps awards the Navy Cross, in lieu of the Distinguished Service Cross, for "Extraordinary Heroism."[3]

The **Purple Heart** is the oldest American military decoration, established by General George Washington during America's War of Independence. The Purple Heart is awarded to those individuals who sustain a wound "which necessitates treatment by a medical officer and which is received in action with an enemy."

Appendix C
U.S. Hostile (Combat) and Non-Hostile Deaths

Hostile Deaths: There were a total of 47,434 hostile deaths during the Vietnam War as set forth below:

	KILLED IN ACTION	DIED OF WOUNDS	DECLARED DEAD	Total
1959-1960	4			4
1961	10	1	1	12
1962	30	1		31
1963	71	7	5	83
1964	146	4	14	164
1965	1,313	110	63	1,486
1966	4,432	596	212	5,240
1967	8,454	996	212	9,662
1968	13,005	1,630	272	14,907
1969	8,239	1,180	130	9,549
1970	3,659	568	74	4,301
1971	1,206	163	65	1,434
1972	327	27	135	489
1973	20	10	15	45
1974				0
1975	18		3	21
After 1975		6		6
Total	40,934	5,299*	1,201**	47,434

*Six (6) individuals died of their wounds after 1975.
**Includes missing in action/declared dead (1,085); and captured/declared dead (116).

Appendix C

Non-Hostile Deaths: There were a total of 10,786 non-hostile deaths during the Vietnam War as set forth below:

	PRESUMED DEAD	ACCIDENT	HOMICIDE	ILLNESS	SELF-INFLICTED	Total
1956			1			1
1957		1				1
1959		1				1
1960		1		1		2
1961		2		1	1	4
1962	1	18	1	2		22
1963		22		10	7	39
1964	1	38	1	9	3	52
1965	7	369	6	54	6	442
1966	9	952	29	98	22	1,110
1967	17	1,499	17	133	35	1,701
1968	23	1,684	28	174	83	1,992
1969	36	1,882	37	182	94	2,231
1970	21	1,562	72	144	73	1,872
1971	8	787	38	97	50	980
1972		228	6	28	8	270
1973		19		4		23
1974		1				1
1975		41				41
After 1975				1		1
Total	123	9,107	236	938*	382	10,786

*One (1) individual died of illness after 1975.

Total Deaths (Hostile and Non-Hostile): There were a total of 58,220 American deaths during the Vietnam War.

*Seven (7) individuals died of their wounds or from illness after 1975.

The author was provided these statistics by the Director of the Department of Defense Statistical Information Analysis Division (SIAD)/Defense Manpower Data Center (DMDC) during December 2007.

Copyright © 2009 by Albert T. Lawrence. All rights reserved.

	Total
1956	1
1957	1
1959	2
1960	5
1961	16
1962	53
1963	122
1964	216
1965	1,928
1966	6,350
1967	11,363
1968	16,899
1969	11,780
1970	6,173
1971	2,414
1972	759
1973	68
1974	1
1975	62
After 1975	7
Total	58,220*

Chapter Notes

Chapter 1

1. Annual Report to the Congress of the United States from the Director of Selective Service, various issues; and David Card and Thomas Lemieux, "Going to College to Avoid the Draft: The Unintended Legacy of the Vietnam War," paper presented at the Meeting of the American Economics Association, January 2001.
2. Speech by the Hon. James H. Webb, Jr., Asst. Secretary of Defense for Reserve Affairs, given at the Commonwealth Club of California, San Francisco, August 28, 1986; and Arthur T. Coumbe, "Why ROTC? The Debate over Collegiate Military Training 1969–1973," *Air & Space Power Journal* (September 1999), http://www.airpower.maxwell.af.mil/airchronicles/cc/coumbe.html.
3. Office of the Under Secretary of Defense, *Personnel and Readiness: Population Representation in the Military Services, Active Component Officers* (Washington, D.C.: Department of the Army, 2004).
4. Arthur T. Coumbe, "Why ROTC? The Debate over Collegiate Military Training 1969–1973," *Air & Space Power Journal* (September 1999), http://www.airpower.maxwell.af.mil/airchronicles/cc/coumbe.html; and Howard Zinn, *A People's History of the United States: 1492–Present* (New York: HarperCollins, 2003), 491.
5. "Commissions OK'd In Combat by MC," *New York Times*, November 1, 1967; and Mark A. Smith, "A Brief History of Battlefield Commissions in the Armed Forces" (Washington, D.C.: National Order of Battlefield Commissions, 1986).
6. Milton J. Bates, Lawrence Lichty, Paul L. Miles, Ronald H. Spector, and Marilyn Young (eds.), *Reporting Vietnam: American Journalism: 1959–1975* (New York: Library of America, 2000), 779, 782.

Chapter 2

1. Bernard B. Fall, *Street without Joy* (Mechanicsburg, PA: Stackpole Books, 1994), 385; and Micheal Clodfelter, *Vietnam in Military Statistics: A History of the Indochina Wars, 1772–1991* (Jefferson, NC: McFarland & Company, 1995), 33.
2. Larry H. Addington, *America's War in Vietnam: A Short Narrative History* (Bloomington: Indiana University Press, 2000), 6.
3. Douglas Porch, *The French Foreign Legion* (New York: HarperCollins, 1991), 203.
4. George C. Herring, *America's Longest War: The United States and Vietnam: 1950–1975*, 4th ed. (New York: McGraw-Hill, 2002), 10–11, 24.
5. Bernard B. Fall, *Hell in a Very Small Place: The Siege of Dien Bien Phu* (Cambridge, MA: Da Capo Press, 2002), 483.
6. Addington, *America's War in Vietnam*, 44.
7. John Ernst, *Forging a Fateful Alliance: Michigan State University And the Vietnam War* (East Lansing, Michigan State University Press, 1998), 21.
8. Herring, *America's Longest War*, 48–49.
9. Ibid., 11–13.
10. Addington, *America's War in Vietnam*, 52–53.
11. Stanley Karnow, *Vietnam: A History* (New York: Penguin Books, 1983), 242–243.
12. Lisle A. Rose, *Power at Sea: A Violent Peace, 1946–2006* (Columbia, MO: University of Missouri Press, 2007), 52; and David

L. Anderson, *Trapped by Success: The Eisenhower Administration and Vietnam, 1953–61* (New York: Columbia University Press, 1991), 21, 23.

13. Robert D. Schulzinger, *A Time for War: The United States and Vietnam: 1941–1975* (Oxford: Oxford University Press, 1997), 71–72, 77.

14. "President Eisenhower's News Conference, April 7, 1954," in *The Pentagon Papers, Gravel Edition*, vol. 1 (Boston: Beacon Press, 1971), 597–598.

15. The Vietnam Veterans Memorial.

16. Ward Just, introduction, in *Reporting Vietnam: American Journalism: 1959–1975*, ed. Milton J. Bates, Lawrence Lichty, Paul L. Miles, Ronald H. Spector, and Marilyn Young (New York: Library of America, 2000), xv; and Congressional Research Service Report for Congress, *American War and Military Operations Casualties: Lists and Statistics, Updated June 29, 2007*, CRS-11, http://www.fas.org/sgp/crs/natsec/RL32492.pdf.

17. Addington, *America's War in Vietnam*, 53–55.

18. Ibid., 55.

19. Karnow, *Vietnam: A History*, 265; and Rose, *Power at Sea*, 156.

20. Schulzinger, *A Time for War*, pp. 112–116.

21. Archive of Nuclear Data from National Resources Defense Council's Nuclear Program; Rose, *Power at Sea*, 155, 157–168; and Tim Weiner, *Legacy of Ashes: The History of the CIA* (New York, Doubleday, 2007), 200, 205–206.

22. Stanley Karnow, "Ho Chi Minh: He Married Nationalism to Communism and Perfected the Deadly Art of Guerrilla Warfare," *Time*, April 13, 1998. Uncle Ho was the affectionate name given to Ho Chi Minh by his countrymen, giving rise to the image of a humble and benign man, although he was a seasoned revolutionary.

23. Henry Kissinger, *Ending the Vietnam War: A History of America's Involvement in and Extrication from the Vietnam War* (New York: Simon & Schuster, 2003), 35.

24. Addington, *America's War in Vietnam*, 66–67.

25. Kissinger, *Ending the Vietnam War*, 35–36; and Karnow, *Vietnam: A History*, pp. 294, 326.

26. Kissinger, *Ending the Vietnam War*, 34.

27. Schulzinger, *A Time for War*, 127.

28. Addington, *America's War in Vietnam*, 74–77; and Weiner, *Legacy of Ashes*, 239–243.

29. Fall, *Street without Joy*, 244.

30. Robert A. Pape, *Bombing to Win: Air Power and Coercion in War* (New York: Cornell University Press, 1996), 190 (for Hanoi and Haiphong); and Thomas C. Thayer, ed., *A Systems Analysis View of the Vietnam War 1965–1972, vol. 9: Population Security* (Washington, D.C.: OASD(SA) RP, Southeast Asia Intelligence Division, 1977), 89 (for Saigon); and "A Matter of Time?" *Time*, March 12, 1965 (for Da Nang).

31. Department of Defense Statistical Information Analysis Division (SIAD), Defense Manpower Data Center, casualty figures provided to author on 31 December 2007.

32. Karnow, *Vietnam: A History*, 513.

33. Schulzinger, *A Time for War*, 210, and Rose, *Power at Sea*, 152.

34. Chris Bellamy, *Absolute War: Soviet Russia in the Second World War* (New York: Alfred A. Knopf, 2007), 8.

35. Karnow, *Vietnam: A History*, 344–345.

36. Department of Defense Statistical Information Analysis Division (SIAD), Defense Manpower Data Center, casualty figures provided to author on December 31, 2007.

Chapter 3

1. Shelby L. Stanton, *Vietnam Order of Battle: A Complete Illustrated Reference to U.S. Army Combat and Support Forces in Vietnam 1961–1973* (Mechanicsburg, PA: Stackpole Books, 2003), 347; and the United States Military Academy at West Point, Public Affairs Office, casualty figures provided to author on September 23 2008.

2. Department of Defense Statistical Information Analysis Division (SIAD), Defense Manpower Data Center, casualty figures provided to author on 31 December 2007.

3. William Shakespeare, *Hamlet*, Act I, Scene 3, lines 79–81.

Chapter 4

1. Joseph Balkoski, *Utah Beach: The Amphibious Landing and Airborne Operations on D-Day* (Mechanicsburg, PA: Stackpole Books, 2005), 180, 195–198, 220, 232.
2. K. Fedra, V. R. Pantulu, and L. Winkelbauer, "Expert Systems for Environmental Screening: An Application in the Lower Mekong Basin." IIASA Research Report RR-91-019 (Laxenburg, Austria: International Institute for Applied Systems Analysis, 1991), 1–180.
3. Theophilus Frances Rodenbough and William L. Haskin, *The Army of the United States: Historical Sketches of Staff and Line with Portraits of Generals-in-Chief* (New York: Maynard, Merrill, & Co., 1896), 511–525.
4. Shelby L. Stanton, *Vietnam Order of Battle: A Complete Illustrated Reference to U.S. Army Combat and Support Forces in Vietnam, 1961–1973* (Mechanicsburg, PA: Stackpole Books, 2003), 369.
5. Department of the Army, Technical Manual No.9-3071-1, Chapter 1, 11, 6 January 1958.
6. Ibid.
7. Tim Page and John Pimlott (eds.), *Nam: the Vietnam Experience: 1965–67* (New York: Mallard Press, 1988), 310.
8. Vietnam Veterans Association of Australia, Victorian Branch (Incorporated), Article, "NVA/VC Weaponry." Melbourne, Australia.
9. Department of the Army, Office of the Adjutant General, *Operation Sam Houston Conducted by the 4th Infantry Division*, Declassified Confidential Report, June 28, 1967.
10. *Personnel-General Military Awards: Army Regulation 600-8-22* (Washington, D.C.: Department of the Army, 2006), 81.
11. Karnow, *Vietnam: A History*, 551.
12. John H. Hay, Jr., "Vietnam Studies: Tactical And Material Innovations" (Washington, D.C.: U.S. Government Printing Office, 1989), 11, 12.
13. First Cavalry Division (Airmobile), First Battalion, Seventh Cavalry After Action Report (December 9, 1965), 2.
14. Stephen C. Bankes, Carl H. Builder, and Richard Nordin. *Command Concepts: A Theory Derived from the Practice of Command and Control*. Santa Monica, CA: Rand Corporation, 1999.
15. Harold G. Moore and Joseph L. Galloway, *We Were Soldiers Once ... and Young: Ia Drang: The Battle That Changed the War in Vietnam* (New York: HarperPerennial, 1993), 233.
16. Ibid., 261.
17. Harold G. Moore and Joseph L. Galloway, *We Are Soldiers Still: A Journey Back to the Battlefields of Vietnam* (New York: HarperCollins, 2008), 123–124.

Chapter 5

1. United States Department of Veterans Affairs, Office of Academic Affiliations, Vietnam Health Issues Readings.
2. Dave E. Lounsbury, *Military Preventive Medicine: Mobilization and Deployment*, vol. 1 (Falls Church, VA: Office of the Surgeon General, Department of the Army, 2003), 118–121.
3. Shelby L. Stanton, *Vietnam Order of Battle: A Complete Illustrated Reference to U.S. Army Combat and Support Forces in Vietnam 1961–1973* (Mechanicsburg, PA: Stackpole Books, 2003), 347; and *Vietnam Conflict-Casualty Summary*, June 2004, assembled by the Department of Defense Statistical Information Analysis Division (SIAD).
4. Stanton, *Vietnam Order of Battle*, 347.
5. Jonathan Wright, who is involved with the London Zoo and has a BSC degree in Zoology, says that "tigers rarely attack people. They are usually good-tempered and prefer to avoid people and generally give a wide berth to people. Even when provoked, tigers normally give a warning growl and allow the intruder to back off. Tigers may object if a person comes too close to cubs or a kill. If a growl is not effective, the tiger may make a short rush, accompanied by terrifying roars. The tiger will only attack if an intruder ignores these warnings."

Chapter 6

1. *Hydrology of Lower Mekong Basin*, the Mekong River Commission, Vientiane, Laos, 2005; and University of Utah, Department of Meteorology (for Seattle).

2. Richard K. Kolb, "Korea and Vietnam: Comparing Participants and Casualties," *VFW Magazine*, June-July 2003; and Melvin R. Laird, "Iraq: Learning the Lessons of Vietnam," *Foreign Affairs* 84:6 (November/December 2005), http://www.foreignaffairs.org.

3. Terry H. Anderson, *The Movement and the Sixties* (New York: Oxford University Press, 1995), 374.

4. Department of Defense Statistical Information Analysis Division (SIAD), Defense Manpower Data Center, casualty figures provided to author on December 31, 2007.

Chapter 7

1. John Macdonald, *Great Battlefields of the World* (New York: Macmillan Publishing Company, 1984), 109.

2. Fourth Infantry Division After Action Report, No. AD390643, Operation MacArthur, "Battle For Dak To"— Search and destroy, 25 October–1 December 1967, Adjutant General's Office [Army], Washington, D.C. (April 29, 1980); 13, 16, 20, 39, 92, 110, 365.

3. *Ibid.*, 30.

4. *Ibid.*, 57.

5. *Ibid.*, 5, 13, 16, 30, 56, 57, 141.

6. Larry Gormley and Kimberly Cloutier. "U.S. Army Divisions in World War II," http://www.historyshots.com/usarmy/; and Fourth Infantry Division History.

7. Fourth Infantry Division After Action Report, "Battle For Dak To," 4–7, 38, 56, 57.

8. Harry G. Summers, Jr., "Duty, Duplicity, and Design, the Army's Reaction to Tet," paper presented at the Colloquium on Contemporary History, seminar 11, Naval Historical Center, Washington, D.C., September 29, 1998.

9. Robert S. McNamara, with Brian Van De Mark, *In Retrospect: The Tragedy and Lessons of Vietnam* (NY: Times Books, Random House, 1995), 306, 307, 311.

10. Karnow, *Vietnam: A History*, 285.

11. *Statement of Vietnam Veterans of America* (cites the 15 percent figure), submitted to the Subcommittee on Post Traumatic Stress Disorder (PTSD) and the Institute of Medicine on 6 July 2006; and Melvin R. Laird, "Iraq: Learning the Lessons of Vietnam," *Foreign Affairs* 84:6 (November/December 2005), http://www.foreignaffairs.org (cites 10% infantry figure).

Chapter 8

1. Lewis Sorley, *Vietnam Chronicles: The Abrams Tapes, 1968–1972* (Lubbock: Texas Tech University Press, 2004), 17.

2. Charles K. Armstrong, "America's Korea, Korea's Vietnam." *Critical Asian Studies* 33:4 (December 2001): 527–540; and James Sterngold, "South Korea's Vietnam Veterans Begin to Be Heard," *New York Times*, May 10, 1992.

3. Andrew Schlesinger, *VERITAS: Harvard College and the American Experience* (Chicago: Ivan R. Dee, 2005), 228, 268.

4. Department of Defense Statistical Information Analysis Division (SIAD), Defense Manpower Data Center, casualty figures provided to author on December 31, 2007.

5. Stanley Karnow, *Vietnam: A History* (New York: Penguin Books, 1983), 23.

6. New Jersey State Council, Vietnam Veterans of America, Inc., Bayonne, NJ; and "Vietnam Warriors: A Statistical Profile," *VFW Magazine* (January 2003).

7. Joseph Balkoski, *Utah Beach: The Amphibious Landing and Airborne Operations on D-Day* (Mechanicsburg, PA: Stackpole Books, 2005), 31.

8. Marshall Hanson, with Scott Beaton, "Historical Reflections: The Vietnam War Revisited," http://www.navy-reserve.org/ (2000).

9. *History of the Army National Guard*, Information Courtesy of the Army National Guard, as re-printed by Rod Powers during 2003.

10. Brian C. Harris, "Relevance of Army National Guard Infantry Units in the Force Structure and Their Role in Combat," Strategy Research Project. U.S. Army War College (2004), 5.

11. *VFW Magazine* (April 1997); and Army National Guard White Paper, "Participation in the Global War on Terrorism," 2005, 7.

12. John Donne, "Meditation XVII," *De-*

votions upon Emergent Occasions and Death's Duel (New York: Random House, 1999), 107.

13. John Ferling, *Almost a Miracle: The American Victory in the War of Independence* (Oxford: Oxford University Press, 2007), 196; and Geoffrey C. Ward, *The Civil War: An Illustrated History* (New York: Alfred A. Knopf, 1990), 129, 242–245.

Chapter 9

1. The Peoples of the World Foundation and Joshua Project (A Ministry of the U.S. Center for World Mission, Colorado Springs, CO).
2. Thomas C. Thayer, ed., *A Systems Analysis View of the Vietnam War 1965–1972, vol. 9: Population Security* (Washington, D.C.: OASD(SA) RP, Southeast Asia Intelligence Division, 1977), 12.

Chapter 10

1. Henry Kissinger, *Ending the Vietnam War: A History of America's Involvement in and Extrication from the Vietnam War* (New York: Simon & Schuster, 2003), 41; and Department of State, Office of the Historian, Bureau of Public Affairs, *Foreign Relations of the United States (FRUS), Vol. III, 1964–1968, Vietnam, June-December 1965* (Pittsburgh: U.S. Government Printing Office, 1996).
2. Ngo Vinh Long, "The Tet Offensive and Its Aftermath," in *The Tet Offensive*, ed. Marc Jason Gilbert and William Head (Westport, CT: Praeger, 1996), 89.
3. Thomas Mathew Rienzi, "Vietnam Studies: Communications-Electronics 1962–1970" (Washington, D.C.: U.S. Government Printing Office, 1972), 103; and Shelby L. Stanton, *Vietnam Order of Battle: A Complete Illustrated Reference to U.S. Army Combat and Support Forces in Vietnam 1961–1973* (Mechanicsburg, PA: Stackpole Books, 2003), 7.
4. Telegram from the Commander of the Military Assistance Command, Vietnam (Westmoreland) to the Commander in Chief, Pacific Forces (Sharp) and the Chairman of the Joint Chiefs of Staff (Wheeler) /1/Saigon, January 30, 1968, 1255Z.
5. George C. Herring, *America's Longest War: The United States and Vietnam: 1950–1975*, 4th ed. (New York: McGraw-Hill, 2002), 231, 232.
6. Evan Thomas, *John Paul Jones, Sailor, Hero, Father of the American Navy* (New York: Simon & Schuster, 2003), 132.
7. Robert D. Schulzinger, *A Time for War: The United States and Vietnam: 1941–1975* (Oxford: Oxford University Press, 1997), 263–264; and Lisle A. Rose, *Power at Sea: A Violent Peace, 1946–2006* (Columbia, MO: University of Missouri Press, 2007), 151.
8. Schulzinger, *A Time For War*, 247, 266; Robert Dallek, *Nixon and Kissinger: Partners in Power* (New York: Harper-Collins, 2007), 62; and Stanley Karnow, *Vietnam: A History* (New York: Penguin Books, 1983), 258.
9. Robert L. Bartley, "Iraq: Another Vietnam? The Truth about the Tet Offensive Is That We Won." *Wall Street Journal*, November 3, 2003.
10. Robert A. Doughty, "Leavenworth Papers: The Evolution of US Army Tactical Doctrine, 1946–79" (Fort Leavenworth, KS: Combat Studies Institute, U.S. Army Command and General Staff College, August 1979), 31, 32.
11. Robert S. McNamara, with Brian Van De Mark, *In Retrospect: The Tragedy and Lessons of Vietnam* (New York: Times Books, Random House, 1995), 277.
12. Schulzinger, *A Time For War*, 247, 266; Dallek. *Nixon and Kissinger*, 62, and Karnow, *Vietnam: A History*, 572–579.
13. Schulzinger, *A Time For War*, 240.

Chapter 11

1. Ronald H. Spector, *After Tet: The Bloodiest Year in Vietnam* (New York: The Free Press, 1993), 146; and Shelby L. Stanton, *Vietnam Order of Battle: A Complete Illustrated Reference to U.S. Army Combat and Support Forces in Vietnam 1961–1973* (Mechanicsburg, PA: Stackpole Books, 2003), 139, 372.
2. Dennis M. Simon, *The War in Vietnam: 1965–1968* (Dallas, TX: Southern Methodist University, 2002); and the Vietnam Veterans Memorial, Washington, D.C.

3. Bernard B. Fall, *Street without Joy* (Mechanicsburg, PA: Stackpole Books, 1994), 240; and Bernard B. Fall, *Hell in a Very Small Place: The Siege of Dien Bien Phu* (Cambridge, MA: Da Capo Press, 2002), 425–430.

4. Committee to Review the Health Effects in Vietnam Veterans of Exposure to Herbicides, Institute of Medicine, *Veterans and Agent Orange: Health Effects of Herbicides Used in Vietnam* (Washington, D.C.: The National Academies Press, 1994), 74.

5. 173rd Airborne Brigade.

6. Kevin M. Generous, *Vietnam: The Secret War* (London: Bison Books, 1985), 180–181.

7. Department of Defense Statistical Information Analysis Division (SIAD), Defense Manpower Data Center, casualty figures provided to author on 31 December 2007; and, *Vietnam Conflict-Casualty Summary*, June 2004, assembled by the Department of Defense Statistical Information Analysis Division (SIAD); and Congressional Research Service Report for Congress, *American War and Military Operations Casualties: Lists and Statistics, Updated June 29, 2007*, CRS-11, http://www.fas.org/sgp/crs/natsec/RL32492.pdf.

8. John T. Correll, "Casualties: Until Recently, Large Numbers of Killed and Wounded Were an Inevitable Part of Warfare," *Air Force Magazine, Journal of the Air Force Association* 86:6 (June 2003): 48–53.

9. John Prados, "Khe Sanh: The Other Side of the Hill," *Vietnam Veterans of America* (July/August 2007), http://www.vva.org/veteran/0807/khesanh.html.

10. Larry Gormley and Kimberly Cloutier. "U.S. Army Divisions in World War II," http://www.historyshots.com/usarmy/; and Fourth Infantry Division History; and Stanton, *Vietnam Order of Battle*, 93–94.

11. Harold G. Moore and Joseph L. Galloway, *We Are Soldiers Still: A Journey Back to the Battlefields of Vietnam* (New York: HarperCollins, 2008), 28.

12. Department of Defense SIAD, Defense Manpower Data Center, 31 December 2007.

13. *Vietnam Conflict-Casualty Summary*, June 2004.

14. Richard K. Kolb, "Korea and Vietnam: Comparing Participants and Casualties." *VFW Magazine*, June–July 2003.

15. Congressional Research Service Report for Congress, *American War and Military Operations Casualties: Lists and Statistics, Updated June 29, 2007*, CRS-3, CRS-4, http://www.fas.org/sgp/crs/natsec/RL32492.pdf.

16. George C. Herring, *America's Longest War: The United States and Vietnam: 1950–1975*, 4th ed. (New York: McGraw-Hill, 2002), 267 (for wounded figure); and Department of Defense SIAD, Defense Manpower Data Center.

Chapter 12

1. Robert Service, "The Absinthe Drinkers," *Collected Poems of Robert Service* (New York: G. P. Putnam's Sons, 1940), 456.

2. Dennis M. Simon, *The War in Vietnam: 1965–1968* (Dallas, TX: Southern Methodist University, 2002).

3. Stephen E. Ambrose, *D-Day: The Climactic Battle of World War II* (New York: Simon & Schuster, 1994), 48–49.

4. Arthur Marwick, *The Sixties: Cultural Revolution in Britain, France, Italy, and the United States, c.1958–c.1974* (Oxford: Oxford University Press, 1998), 585–675.

Chapter 13

1. Donald Johanson and Blake Edgar, *From Lucy to Language* (New York: Simon & Schuster Editions, 1996), 38, 43, and 239.

2. William Shakespeare, *Julius Caesar*, Act II, Scene 2, lines 32–37.

Chapter 14

1. Arline Kaplan, "Hidden Combat Wounds: Extensive, Deadly, Costly." *Psychiatric Times* 25:1 (January 1, 2006): 1–3; and "The Invisible Casualties." *The Week* (July 4–11, 2008): 15.

2. Department of Defense Statistical Information Analysis Division (SIAD), Defense Manpower Data Center, casualty figures provided to author on 31 December 2007.

3. Gabriel, Richard A., "Professionalism Versus Managerialism in Vietnam," *Air University Review* 32:2 (January/February 1981): 77–84.

Chapter 15

1. Henry Kissinger, *Ending the Vietnam War: A History of America's Involvement in and Extrication from the Vietnam War* (New York: Simon & Schuster, 2003), 102.
2. Department of Defense Statistical Information Analysis Division (SIAD), Defense Manpower Data Center, casualty figures provided to author on 31 December 2007.
3. Robert A. Schulzinger, *A Time for War: The United States and Vietnam: 1941–1975* (Oxford: Oxford University Press, 1997), 279.
4. Kissinger, *Ending the Vietnam War*, 133.
5. Kent State University, Libraries and Media Services, Chronology, May 1–4, 1970.
6. Selective Service System; and Schulzinger, *A Time For War*, 281.

Chapter 16

1. Annual Report to the Congress of the United States from the Director of Selective Service, various issues; David Card and Thomas Lemieux, "Going to College to Avoid the Draft: The Unintended Legacy of the Vietnam War," paper presented at the Meeting of the American Economics Association, January 2001 (for draft statistics); and Department of Defense Statistical Information Analysis Division (SIAD), Defense Manpower Data Center, casualty figures provided to author on 31 December 2007 (for KIA figures).
2. Department of Defense SIAD, Defense Manpower Data Center, 31 December 2007.
3. Henry Kissinger, *Ending the Vietnam War: A History of America's Involvement in and Extrication from the Vietnam War* (New York: Simon & Schuster, 2003), 233, 245, 252, 262, 319.
4. Department of Defense SIAD, Defense Manpower Data Center, 31 December 2007.
5. *Ibid.*

Appendix A

1. National Archives, Southeast Asia Combat Area Casualties File (CACCF).
2. Department of Defense Statistical Information Analysis Division (SIAD), Defense Manpower Data Center, casualty figures provided to author on 31 December 2007.
3. Congressional Research Service Report for Congress, *American War and Military Operations Casualties: Lists and Statistics*, Washington, D.C., June 29, 2007, CRS-9, http://www.fas.org/sgp/crs/natsec/RL32492.pdf (considers only those American wars that ended prior to 2008).
4. Congressional Research Service (CRS) Report for Congress, *American War and Military Operations Casualties: Lists and Statistics, Updated June 29, 2007* (for all American wars except the Second Iraqi War and the War in Afghanistan), pp. CRS-2, CRS-3, CRS-10, CRS-11.
5. U.S. Department of Defense, http://www.defenselink.mil/news/casualty.pdf.
6. *Ibid.*

Appendix B

1. *Personnel-General Military Awards: Army Regulation 600–8-22* (Washington, D.C.: Department of the Army, 2006), 57.
2. *Ibid.*, 98.
3. Department of the Navy, SECNAVINST 1650.1H, August 22, 2006 (Washington, D.C.: Pentagon, 2006): 2–13.

Bibliography

Addington, Larry H. *America's War in Vietnam: A Short Narrative History.* Bloomington: Indiana University Press, 2000.

Ambrose, Stephen E. *Crazy Horse and Custer: The Parallel Lives of Two American Warriors.* New York: Anchor Books, 1996.

_____. *D-Day: The Climactic Battle of World War II.* New York: Simon & Schuster, 1994.

Anderson, David L. *Trapped by Success: The Eisenhower Administration and Vietnam, 1953–1961.* New York: Columbia University Press, 1991.

Anderson, Terry H. *The Movement and the Sixties.* New York: Oxford University Press, 1995.

Aristotle. *Nicomachean Ethics.* New York: The Bobbs-Merrill Company, Inc., 1962.

Armstrong, Charles K. "America's Korea, Korea's Vietnam." *Critical Asian Studies* 33:4 (December 2001): 527–540.

Balkoski, Joseph. *Utah Beach: The Amphibious Landing and Airborne Operations on D-Day.* Mechanicsburg, PA: Stackpole Books, 2005.

Bankes, Steven C., Carl H. Builder, and Richard Nordin. *Command Concepts: A Theory Derived from the Practice of Command and Control.* Santa Monica, Calif: Rand Corporation, 1999.

Bartley, Robert L. "Iraq: Another Vietnam? The Truth about the Tet Offensive Is That We Won." *Wall Street Journal,* November 3, 2003.

Bates, Milton J., Lawrence Lichty, Paul L. Miles, Ronald H. Spector, and Marilyn Young (eds.). *Reporting Vietnam: American Journalism: 1959–1975.* New York: Library of America, 2000.

Beevor, Antony. *Stalingrad: The Fateful Siege: 1942–1943.* New York: Penguin Books, 1998.

Bellamy, Chris. *Absolute War: Soviet Russia in the Second World War.* New York: Alfred A. Knopf, 2007.

Card, David, and Thomas Lemieux. "Going to College to Avoid the Draft: The Unintended Legacy of the Vietnam War." Paper presented at the Meeting of the American Economics Association, January 2001.

Clausewitz, Carl von. *On War.* Trans. Michael Howard and Peter Paret. New Jersey: Princeton University Press, 1976.

Clodfelter, Micheal. *Vietnam in Military Statistics: A History of the Indochina Wars, 1772–1991.* Jefferson, NC: McFarland & Company, 1995.

Coddington, Edwin B. *The Gettysburg Campaign: A Study in Command.* New York: Charles Scribner's Sons, 1964.

Committee to Review the Health Effects in Vietnam Veterans of Exposure to Herbicides, Institute of Medicine, *Veterans and Agent Orange: Health Effects of Herbicides Used in Vietnam.* Washington, D.C.: The National Academies Press, 1994.

Cook, Michael. *A Brief History of the Human Race.* New York: W. W. Norton, 2003.

Correll, John T. "Casualties: Until Recently, Large Numbers of Killed and Wounded Were an Inevitable Part of Warfare." *Air Force Magazine* 86:6 (June 2003): 48–53.

Coumbe, Arthur T. "Why ROTC? The Debate over Collegiate Military Training, 1969–1973." *Air & Space Power Journal* (September 1999), http://www.airpower.maxwell.af.mil/airchronicles/cc/coumbe.html.

Dallek, Robert. *Nixon and Kissinger: Partners in Power*. New York: HarperCollins, 2007.

Davis, Paul K. *100 Decisive Battles from Ancient Times to the Present: The World's Major Battles and How They Shaped History*. Oxford: Oxford University Press, 1999.

Donne, John. *Devotions upon Emergent Occasions and Death's Duel*. New York: Random House, 1999.

Doughty, Robert A. "Leavenworth Papers: The Evolution of US Army Tactical Doctrine, 1946–79." Fort Leavenworth, KS: Combat Studies Institute, U.S. Army Command and General Staff College, August 1979.

Dyhouse, Tim. "Dak To: 33 Days of Violent, Sustained Combat." *VFW Magazine* (March 2006): 33.

Edgar, Blake, and Donald Johanson. *From Lucy to Language*. New York: Simon & Schuster Editions, 1996.

Ernst, John. *Forging a Fateful Alliance: Michigan State University and the Vietnam War*. East Lansing: Michigan State University Press, 1998.

Fall, Bernard B. *Hell in a Very Small Place: The Siege of Dien Bien Phu*. Cambridge, MA: Da Capo Press, 2002.

_____. *Street without Joy*. Mechanicsburg, PA: Stackpole Books, 1994.

Farrow, Edward Samuel. *A Dictionary of Military Terms*. New York: Thomas Y. Crowell, 1918.

Fedra, K., V. R. Pantulu, and L. Winkelbauer. "Expert Systems for Environmental Screening: An Application in the Lower Mekong Basin." IIASA Research Report RR-91-019. Laxenburg, Austria: International Institute for Applied Systems Analysis, 1991.

Ferling, John. *Almost a Miracle: The American Victory in the War of Independence*. Oxford: Oxford University Press, 2007.

First Cavalry Division (Airmobile). First Battalion, Seventh Cavalry After Action Report, December 9, 1965.

Fourth Infantry Division. After Action Report, No. AD390643, Operation MacArthur, "Battle for Dak To"—Search and destroy, 25 October–1 December 1967, Adjutant General's Office [Army], Washington, D.C., April 29, 1980.

Gabriel, Richard A. "Professionalism Versus Managerialism in Vietnam." *Air University Review* 32:2 (January/February 1981): 77–84.

Generous, Kevin M. *Vietnam: The Secret War*. London: Bison Books, 1985.

Gibbons, Ann. *The First Human*. New York: Doubleday, 2006.

Gillam, James T. *War in the Central Highlands of Vietnam 1968–1970: An Historian's Experience*. Lewiston, NY: Edwin Mellen Press, 2006.

Gormley, Larry, and Kimberly Cloutier. "U.S. Army Divisions in World War II." http://www.historyshots.com/usarmy/.

Halberstam, David. *The Coldest Winter: America and the Korean War*. New York: Hyperion, 2007.

_____. *The Fifties*. New York: Villard Books, 1993.

_____. *War in a Time of Peace: Bush, Clinton, and the Generals*. New York: Scribner, 2001.

Hanson, Marshall, with Scott Beaton. "Historical Reflections: The Vietnam War Revisited," http://www.navy-reserve.org/ (2000).

Harris, Brian C. "Relevance of Army National Guard Infantry Units in the Force Structure and Their Role in Combat." Strategy Research Project. U.S. Army War College, 2004.

Hay, John H., Jr. "Vietnam Studies: Tactical and Material Innovations." Department of the Army. Washington, D.C.: U.S. Government Printing Office, 1989.

Herring, George C. *America's Longest War: The United States and Vietnam: 1950–1975*, 4th ed. New York: McGraw-Hill, 2002.

Holliday, J. S. *Rush for Riches: Gold Fever

and the Making of California. Berkeley: University of California Press, 1999.

"The Invisible Casualties." *The Week* (July 4–11, 2008): 15.

Josephy, Alvin M., Jr., ed. *The American Heritage History of World War I.* New York: Bonanza Books, 1982.

Just, Ward. Introduction. In *Reporting Vietnam: American Journalism: 1959–1975*, edited by Milton J. Bates, Lawrence Lichty, Paul L. Miles, Ronald H. Spector, and Marilyn Young. New York: Library of America, 2000.

Kaplan, Arline. "Hidden Combat Wounds: Extensive, Deadly, Costly." *Psychiatric Times* 25:1 (January 1, 2006): 1–3.

Karnow, Stanley. "Ho Chi Minh: He Married Nationalism to Communism and Perfected the Deadly Art of Guerrilla Warfare." *Time*, April 13, 1998.

_____. *Vietnam: A History*. New York: Penguin Books, 1983.

Keegan, John. *The First World War.* New York: Vintage Books, 1998.

Kierkegaard, Søren. *Fear and Trembling and the Sickness unto Death.* Princeton: Princeton University Press, 1954.

Kissinger, Henry. *Ending the Vietnam War: A History of America's Involvement in and Extrication from the Vietnam War.* New York: Simon & Schuster, 2003.

Kolb, Richard K. "Korea and Vietnam: Comparing Participants and Casualties." *VFW Magazine*, June–July 2003.

Kurlansky, Mark. *1968: The Year That Rocked the World.* New York: Random House Trade Paperbacks, 2005.

Laird, Melvin R. "Iraq: Learning the Lessons of Vietnam." *Foreign Affairs* 84:6 (November/December 2005), http://www.foreignaffairs.org.

Langguth, A. J. *Our Vietnam: The War 1954–1975.* New York: Touchstone, 2000.

Larrabee, Eric. *Commander in Chief, Franklin Delano Roosevelt: His Lieutenants, and Their War.* New York: Touchstone, 1987.

Leakey, Richard. *Origins Reconsidered: In Search of What Makes Us Human.* New York: Anchor Books, 1992.

Lengel, Edward G. *To Conquer Hell: The Meuse-Argonne, 1918.* New York: Henry Holt and Company, 2008.

Long, Ngo Vinh. "The Tet Offensive and Its Aftermath." In *The Tet Offensive*, edited by Marc Jason Gilbert and William Head, 89–124. Westport, CT: Praeger, 1996.

Lounsbury, Dave E. *Military Preventive Medicine: Mobilization and Deployment*, vol. 1. Falls Church, VA: Office of the Surgeon General, Department of the Army, 2003.

Macdonald, John. *Great Battlefields of the World.* New York: Macmillan Publishing Company, 1984.

Marwick, Arthur. *The Sixties: Cultural Revolution in Britain, France, Italy, and the United States, c.1958–c.1974.* Oxford: Oxford University Press, 1998.

Maslowski, Peter, and Don Winslow. *Looking for a Hero: Staff Sergeant Joe Ronnie Hooper and the Vietnam War.* Lincoln: University of Nebraska Press, 2004.

Mason, Robert G. *Life in Space.* Alexandria, VA: Time-Life Books, 1983.

"A Matter of Time?" *Time*, March 12, 1965.

McNamara, Robert S., with Brian Van De Mark. *In Retrospect: The Tragedy and Lessons of Vietnam.* New York: Times Books, Random House, 1995.

Mondadori, Arnoldo, ed. *The History of Art.* Leicester, England: Blitz Editions, 1989.

Moore, Harold G., and Joseph L. Galloway. *We Are Soldiers Still: A Journey Back to the Battlefields of Vietnam.* New York: HarperCollins, 2008.

_____ and _____. *We Were Soldiers Once ... and Young: Ia Drang: The Battle That Changed the War in Vietnam.* New York: HarperPerennial, 1993.

Page, Tim, and John Pimlott (eds.). *Nam: the Vietnam Experience: 1965–67.* New York: Mallard Press, 1988.

Oren, Michael B. *Six Days of War: June 1967 and the Making of the Modern Middle East.* New York: Ballantine Books, 2002.

Pape, Robert A. *Bombing to Win: Air Power and Coercion in War.* New York: Cornell University Press, 1996.

Porch, Douglas. *The French Foreign Legion*. New York: HarperCollins, 1991.

Prados, John. "Khe Sanh: The Other Side of the Hill." *Vietnam Veterans of America* (July/Aug. 2007), http://www.vva.org/veteran/0807/khesanh.html.

"President Eisenhower's News Conference, April 7, 1954." In *The Pentagon Papers, Gravel Edition*, vol. 1. Boston: Beacon Press, 1971.

Prochnau, William. *Once upon a Distant War*. New York: Vintage, 1995.

Rienzi, Thomas Mathew. "Vietnam Studies: Communications-Electronics 1962–1970." Washington, D.C.: U.S. Government Printing Office, 1972.

Rodenbough, Theophilus Frances, and William L. Haskin. *The Army of the United States: Historical Sketches of Staff and Line with Portraits of Generals-in-Chief*. New York: Maynard, Merrill, & Co., 1896.

Rose, Lisle A. *Power at Sea: A Violent Peace, 1946–2006*. Columbia: University of Missouri Press, 2007.

Schlesinger, Andrew. *VERITAS: Harvard College and the American Experience*. Chicago: Ivan R. Dee, 2005.

Schulzinger, Robert D. *A Time for War: The United States and Vietnam: 1941–1975*. Oxford: Oxford University Press, 1997.

Service, Robert. *Collected Poems of Robert Service*. New York: G. P. Putnam's Sons, 1940.

Shakespeare, William. *The Works of Shakespeare*. New York: Oxford University Press, 1938.

Simon, Dennis M. *The War in Vietnam: 1965–1968*. Dallas, TX: Southern Methodist University, 2002.

Smith, Mark A. "A Brief History of Battlefield Commissions in the Armed Forces." Washington, D.C.: National Order of Battlefield Commissions, 1986.

Sorley, Lewis. *Vietnam Chronicles: The Abrams Tapes, 1968–1972*. Lubbock: Texas Tech University Press, 2004.

Spector, Ronald H. *After Tet: The Bloodiest Year in Vietnam*. New York: The Free Press, 1993.

Stanton, Shelby L. *Vietnam Order of Battle: A Complete Illustrated Reference to U.S. Army Combat and Support Forces in Vietnam, 1961–1973*. Mechanicsburg, PA: Stackpole Books, 2003.

Sterngold, James. "South Korea's Vietnam Veterans Begin to Be Heard." *New York Times*, May 10, 1992.

Summers, Harry G., Jr. "Duty, Duplicity, and Design, 'The Army's Reaction to Tet.'" Paper presented at the Colloquium on Contemporary History, seminar 11, Naval Historical Center, Washington, D.C., September 29, 1998.

Thayer, Thomas C., ed. *A Systems Analysis View of the Vietnam War 1965–1972, vol. 9: Population Security*, Washington, D.C.: OASD(SA) RP, Southeast Asia Intelligence Division, 1977.

Thomas, Evan. *John Paul Jones: Sailor, Hero, Father of the American Navy*. New York: Simon & Schuster, 2003.

Timberg, Robert. *The Nightingale's Song*. New York: Touchstone, 1995.

Tolkien, J. R. R. *The Lord of the Rings Trilogy*. New York: Ballantine Books, 1965.

Toll, Ian W. *Six Frigates: The Epic History of the Founding of the U.S. Navy*. New York: W. W. Norton & Company, 2006.

Trumbo, Dalton. *Johnny Got His Gun*. New York: Bantam Books, 1982.

United States. Congressional Research Service. Report for Congress. *American War and Military Operations Casualties: Lists and Statistics, Updated June 29, 2007*. Washington, D.C., http://www.fas.org/sgp/crs/natsec/RL32492.pdf.

———. Department of Defense. Office of the Under Secretary. *Personnel and Readiness: Population Representation in the Military Services, Active Component Officers*. Washington, D.C.: Department of the Army, 2004.

———. ———. Statistical Information Analysis Division (SIAD), Defense Manpower Data Center. Vietnam casualty figures, 31 December 2007.

———. Department of State. Office of the Historian, Bureau of Public Affairs. *Foreign Relations of the United States (FRUS), Vol. III, 1964–1968, Vietnam, June–December 1965*. Pittsburgh: U.S. Government Printing Office, 1996.

_____. Department of the Army. Office of the Adjutant General. *Operation Sam Houston Conducted by the 4th Infantry Division*, Declassified Confidential Report, June 28, 1967.

_____. _____. *Personnel-General Military Award: Army Regulation 600-8-22*. Washington, D.C.: Department of the Army, 2006.

Urwin, Gregory J. W. *Custer Victorious: The Civil War Battles of General George Armstrong Custer*. Edison, NJ: Blue & Grey Press, 1983.

Ward, Geoffrey C. *The Civil War: An Illustrated History*. New York: Alfred A. Knopf, 1990.

Webb, James H., Jr. Speech at the Commonwealth Club of California, San Francisco, CA, August 28, 1986.

Weinberg, Gerhard L. *A World at Arms: A Global History of World War II*. Cambridge: Cambridge University Press, 1994.

Weiner, Tim. *Legacy of Ashes: The History of the CIA*. New York: Doubleday, 2007.

Wert, Jeffry D. *Custer: The Controversial Life of George Armstrong Custer*. New York: Simon & Schuster, 1996.

Zinn, Howard. *A People's History of the United States: 1492–Present*. New York: HarperCollins, 2003.

Index

1st Cavalry Division (Airmobile) 27, 42, 44–45, 61–63, 97–99, 127–28, 160; 1st Battalion, 7th Cavalry 61–62; 2nd Battalion, 5th Cavalry (Regiment) 62; 2nd Battalion, 7th Cavalry 62–63, 97; 2nd Battalion, 8th Cavalry 98–99; 2nd Battalion, 12th Cavalry 98–99
1st Infantry Division 127–28
2nd Infantry Division (Korean War) 18
3rd Infantry Division (World War II) 100
3rd U.S. Infantry Regiment (The Old Guard) 8
4th Infantry Division 41–42, 45–48, 54, 77, 108, 111, 124, 127–29, 138, 140, 149, 161, 164, 171; battle of Dak To 98–101; 2nd Brigade 42, 46, 47, 98–99, 128, 138, 140, 171
4th Infantry Division, 1st Brigade 46, 98, 128, 140; 1st Battalion, 8th Infantry (Regiment) 41–42, 45, 98–99, 100; 3rd Battalion, 8th Infantry 41–42, 45, 98–99; 3rd Battalion, 12th Infantry 41–42, 98–100
4th Infantry Division, 2nd Brigade 42, 46, 47, 98–99, 128, 138, 140, 171; 1st Battalion, 12th Infantry 41–42, 60, 99; 1st Battalion, 22nd Infantry 41–42, 60; 2nd Battalion, 8th Infantry 41–42, 45, 47, 55, 60, 96–98, 138, 140, 149, 163–64, 171
4th Infantry Division, 3rd Brigade (from 25th Division on 1 August 1967) 46, 140, 161; 1st Battalion, 14th Infantry 46, 161; 1st Battalion, 35th Infantry 46, 161; 2nd Battalion, 35th Infantry 46, 161
8th Division (World War I) 45
9th Infantry Division 100, 127–28
11th Light Infantry Brigade 127–28, 136–37; C Company, 1st Battalion, 20th Infantry 136–37
17th Cavalry 127
23rd Infantry Division (Americal) 127–28, 136–37
25th Infantry Division 46, 127–28, 161; 3rd Brigade (from 4th Infantry Division on 1 August 1967) 41–42, 46, 161; 3rd Brigade, 2nd Battalion, 12th Infantry 41–42, 46, 161; 3rd Brigade, 2nd Battalion, 22nd Infantry 41–42, 46, 161; 3rd Brigade, 3rd Battalion, 22nd Infantry 41–42, 46, 161

34th Armor, squadron of 127–28
42nd Division "Rainbow" (World War I) 108
69th Armor, squadron of 127–29
75th Infantry Regiment 146
82nd Airborne Division, 3rd Brigade 128
101st Airborne Division 15, 44, 127–28, 140, 172
173rd Airborne Brigade 44–45, 95–96, 98–99, 127–28, 146, 172; 1st Battalion of the 503rd Infantry 98–99; 2nd Battalion of the 503rd Infantry 96, 98–99; 4th Battalion of the 503rd Infantry 98–99
196th Light Infantry Brigade 127–28
198th Light Infantry Brigade 127–28
199th Light Infantry Brigade 127–28

Abrams, Gen. Creighton W. 133
Absinthe 162–63
Acid 125–26
Advanced Infantry Training (AIT) 9, 30–31, 181
Advisers (U.S. military) 20, 22, 23
Afghanistan, War 218
Agent Orange 106, 145–46
Agnew, Spiro 190
Air Force, U.S. see U.S. Air Force
AIT 30–31, 181
AK-47, Soviet 28, 53–54, 89, 90, 184
Alaska 199, 207
Albuquerque, New Mexico 177
Alexandria, Egypt 11
Algeria 16, 22
Ambush duty 69–71, 81
Amendment (26th) 115, 190
American Express 173
American Graduate School of International Management (Thunderbird) 212
Amputees 217
Amsterdam 39, 50, 56
Andover, New Jersey 206
Annam, Vietnam 16
Antiwar movement 29, 169, 181, 207–08, 212
AOR (area of operations) 98–99, 171–72
Apache Wars 45
Apocalypse Now (movie) 194
Aristotle 85, 210

239

240 Index

Arkansas 186
Armed Forces Radio Network 125
Armor 9, 12, 46, 74, 102, 127–29, 154–55, 159
Armored personnel carrier (APC) 149–52
Armstrong, Neil (astronaut): Moon landing 204
Army, U.S. *see* U.S. Army; *individual units*
Army of South Vietnam (ARVN) 21–23, 27, 96, 98–100, 127–30, 141–43, 151, 207, 209–11; 3rd Army Reserve 196
Artillery 9, 12, 34, 45–46, 48, 58, 62, 69, 72, 73, 74, 83, 91, 93, 98, 102, 114–15, 119, 159, 163–64, 169–70, 209, 214; Tet attack on Pleiku 128–31
ARVN *see* Army of South Vietnam
ARVN Cavalry Squadron 129; 22nd ARVN Ranger Battalion 129
Augusta, Georgia 12, 37–38
Australians 128, 146
Automatic Teller Machines (ATMs) 173
AWOL (Absent Without Official Leave) 180, 202

B-52 strategic bomber 62, 153, 203, 205, 210
Baby Boomers 21
Bachelor of Arts (B.A.) degree 211
Bahnar *see* Montagnards
Bamboo (green tree) vipers 67, 69, 71
Ban Me Thuot, South Vietnam 128, 171
Bangkok, Thailand 162–63
BankAmericard 173
Basic Combat Training (BCT) 7–14
Battlefield commissions 13
Bay of Pigs, Cuba 21
Beatles (singing group) 125, 186
Beer, Vietnamese 134
Ben Hai River 15
Ben Het, South Vietnam 96
Berkeley, California 27, 105, 113, 169, 207, 210–11
Berlin 36, 169
Bible 30, 197
Bien Hoa, South Vietnam 41
Bigot 190–91
Bivouac 96, 152
"Black Is Black" (song) 123
Black Panthers (U.S.) 137
Blacks 6, 31–32, 123, 136–37, 140, 188–89, 190; percentage in the Army 52
Blonde on Blonde (music album) 126
Body count 100, 105–106, 130
Bombing (of North Vietnam and Cambodia) 26, 125, 137, 140, 202–03
Boots, jungle 79, 148
Branches of the Army (i.e. Infantry, Armor, etc.) 102, 159
Brennan's Restaurant, New Orleans 187
Brezhnev, Leonid 23–24
Bronson, Charles (actor) 167
Bronze 152

Bronze Star 171, 178, 220, 222
Buddhists 19; self-immolation 22
Buis, Major Dale 20
Bulgaria 53
Burma 16, 96, 195
Bush, George H.W. (41st U.S. President) 110–11
Bush, George W. (43rd U.S. President) 110

C-4 (Explosive, plastic) 57, 70–71, 152
C-130 (military aircraft) 44, 171
C-rations 57, 80–81, 83, 156
Calley, Lt. William L., Jr. 136–37; sentencing and parole 204
Cam Ranh and Cam Ranh Bay 15, 127, 172
Cambodia 16, 26–27, 42–44, 49, 55, 62, 96, 101, 119, 195, 206–07; secret bombing of 202–03
Cambodian communists 206–07
Camp Enari 45, 131
Campaign Medal for the Republic of Vietnam (RVNCM) 220–21
Carbine 54, 97, 119
Casualties *see* Amputees; Hostile and non-hostile (related) death statistics; Killed in action (KIA); Missing in action (MIA); Wounded
Casualties, enemy, NVA and VC killed during the war 107
Casualties, U.S. Army: 4th Infantry Division battlefield casualties in Vietnam vice World War II 100; deaths (hostile) borne by infantry, artillery, etc. 160; officers killed 34–35
Catholics 14, 19, 21
Cell phones 173
Central Highlands 26, 41, 42, 44, 46–47, 49, 55, 61–63, 64, 95, 101, 118–19, 128, 140, 171–72, 210, 214; rainfall 87
Central Intelligence Agency (CIA) 21, 206–07, 209; Phoenix Operation 151–52
Cheney, Richard Bruce "Dick" (Vice President under George W. Bush) 110
USS *Chesapeake* 10
Chicago, Democratic Convention 169
Chicom Type-56 automatic rifle 53, 84
China 16, 18, 19, 22, 23, 25–29, 43–44, 96, 109, 119, 134, 162, 207, 218
Chinook helicopter 58
Cholon (district of Saigon) 128
CIA 21, 151–52, 206–07, 209
CIB 117, 160, 164, 170, 178, 220–22
CIDG 61, 95, 98–100
Cigarettes 30, 33, 47, 70, 79–80, 116, 152, 156, 158, 164, 168, 175
Civil Rights Act (Public Law 88–352) 31, 189, 190
Civil War 10, 31, 41, 46, 52, 66, 90, 133, 151, 167, 185–86, 188–89, 217–18; conscription 112

Civilian Irregular Defense Group (CIDG) forces 61, 95, 98–100
Claymore mine 57, 70–71, 80, 182
Clear and hold (strategy) 133, 194
Clinton, William Jefferson "Bill" (42nd U.S. President) 110–11
Coast Guard (U.S.) 112
Cobra gunships 45, 158
Cochin China, South Vietnam 16
Code of Conduct 8, 85
Colt (Colt's Inc., Firearms Division) 53
Columbia University 169
Columbus, Georgia 31, 204
Combat fatigue 184–85
Combat Infantryman's Badge (CIB) 117, 160, 164, 170, 178, 220–22
Combat sweep 133
Commander in Chief, US Central Command (CINCCENT) 213
Commander in Chief, US Pacific Command (CINCPAC) 213
Compact discs (CDs) 123
Con Thien, South Vietnam 145
Congress, U.S. 24, 31, 109, 115, 133, 203, 209
Conrad, Joseph (author) 194
Conscription 5–7, 11, 24, 29, 75, 107–08, 110, 112, 115, 119, 200, 204, 208–09
Constitution see United States Constitution
Constitutional Amendment (26th) 115, 190
Copper 152
Coppola, Francis Ford (movie director) 194
Corps (military regions I, II, III, and IV) 42–43, 128, 137, 146
Corps-level command (I Field Force) 44
Costa Rica 210
Credit cards 173
Creole 187
Cuba 11
Cuban missile crisis 22, 23
Custer, George Armstrong 47, 54, 61–63, 67, 113; Little Big Horn, battle of 97–98
Czechoslovakia 53, 169, 207

Da Nang, South Vietnam 15, 29, 41, 127–28, 137; population (1965) 27
Dak To, Battle of 26, 56, 95–101, 123, 128, 171, 173
Dalat, South Vietnam 127
Darvon 67
DD Form 214, 196
Death statistics see Hostile and non-hostile (related) death statistics
Deer Hunter (movie) 166
Demilitarized Zone (DMZ) 15, 26–27, 42, 44, 128, 129, 133, 145, 155, 210, 214
Desegregation of the U.S. armed forces 31
Diem, Ngo Dinh 18–23
Dien Bien Phu, North Vietnam 17–19, 142, 151
Diners Club 173

Distinguished Flying Cross 92–93
Distinguished Service Cross 55, 224
Dixie 186, 196
DMZ 15, 26–27, 42, 44, 128, 129, 133, 145, 155, 210, 214
DNA identification of remains 82–83
Dog tags 82–83
Dollar Steamship Lines 11
Domino theory: cited by Eisenhower 19–20, 218–19
Donne, John (poet) 111–12
Donut Dollies 47, 138
Dover Air Force Base, Delaware 39
Dow Chemical Company 106
Draft (Selective Service) 5–7, 11, 24, 29, 75, 107–08, 110, 112, 115, 119, 200, 204, 208–09
H.M.S. Drake (British frigate) 131
Drill Instructor (Marine Corps) 7
Drill Sergeant (Army) 7–8
Drug (urinalysis) testing 195
Drug use 126, 194–95, 205
Dubček Alexander 169
Dulles, John Foster 19
Dust-off see Helicopters (including medevacs)
Dylan, Bob 125–26

Eggs Benedict 187
Eisenhower, Dwight D. (35th U.S. President) 17–21, 31, 106, 148, 169
Élan 55
Embassy, U.S. 37, 131, 211, 214; during Tet 128
Enari, Mark 1st LT 45
Entrenching tool 49, 60, 68, 124, 146, 153

F-4 Phantom 107
F-111 tactical strike fighter jet 37–38
Federal Communications Commission (FCC) 173
Firebase 58
Fitzgibbon, Richard B., Tech Sgt. USAF 20
Flare, parachute 78–79
Floyd, Eddie (singer) 123
Fort Belvoir, Virginia 12
Fort Benning, Georgia 12, 31, 37, 52, 72, 204
Fort Dix, New Jersey 202
Fort Gordon, Georgia 12, 37–38, 52
Fort Knox, Kentucky 12
Fort Leavenworth, Kansas 204
Fort Lewis, Washington 172
Fort Mason, San Francisco, California 11
Fort Ord, California 6–7, 14, 52, 125
Fort Polk, Louisiana 177, 178, 181–82, 185, 188, 191–93, 203, 215
Fort Sill, Oklahoma 12
Fragging 94, 205
France 16–22, 23, 39, 100, 108, 125, 142, 162, 169, 211–13
France, Vichy 16
French Battalion (in Korean War) 18

242 Index

French Indochina 16–17, 19–20, 96, 195
French Union forces 16
Friendly fire 58, 72, 73, 136, 154

Galloway, Joseph L. 27, 45, 130
"Gary Owen" (Irish song) 61–62
USNS *Gen. LeRoy Eltinge* (T-AP-154) 15
Geneva Conference of 1954 and Accords 18–19, 21, 25, 100–01, 142, 203, 210
Georgetown University 110
G.I. (Government Issue) 33, 178
G.I. Bill 209
Giap, Gen. Vo Nguyen 17
Golden Triangle 195
Goldwater, Barry 190
Good Conduct Medal (AGCM) 220–21
Gore, Al (Vice President under Clinton) 110
Grand Ole Opry 125
Great Depression 174
Green Berets 14, 21, 48, 50, 61, 96, 98, 127, 129, 146
Grenades and grenade launchers 9, 33–34, 48–49, 65, 71, 80, 94, 117, 148, 159, 182
Grunts 49
Guam 62, 203
Gulf of Mexico 186
Gulf of Tonkin see Tonkin Gulf
Gurevich, Mikhail 107

Haiphong, North Vietnam 44, 210; population (1965) 27
Halazone 157
USS *Hancock* 26
Hanoi, North Vietnam 16, 18, 22, 43, 107, 125, 210; population (1965) 27
Harriman, Averell 137
Harvard University 105, 106, 110
Hawaii 162, 199
Heart of Darkness (novel) 194
Helicopters (including medevacs) 21, 45, 46, 49, 56, 58, 61, 65, 73, 86, 92–93, 102–03, 146, 148–49, 153–54, 158–59, 160, 163–65, 169, 171, 217
Helmet, M-1 49–50
Hensel AAF (Army Air Field) 124
Herbicides 106, 145–46
Heroin 186, 194–95, 205
"Hey Jude" (song) 186
Hill 875 (Dak To) 98–99
Hippies 126, 207
Hmong see Montagnards
Ho Chi Minh 19, 20, 21–22; death of 204
Ho Chi Minh sandals 72
Ho Chi Minh Trail 26–27, 42, 95, 205, 209
Hoi An, South Vietnam 128
Homo sapiens sapiens 175
Hong Kong 11, 162
Honolulu 11
Hope, Bob 125
Hostile and non-hostile (related) death statistics: death ratio of officers to enlisted 65; deaths (hostile) sustained by the Air Force, Army, Navy and Marine Corps 160; deaths (hostile and non-hostile) 154; deaths (non-hostile) compared to other wars 154; deaths of draftees (hostile and non-hostile) 107
Howitzer 46, 58, 114–15, 12
Hué, South Vietnam 16, 127, 129
Huey (UH-1 utility helicopter) 158–59, 165, 169
Humphrey, Hubert H. 189
Hungary 207

"I Wish It Would Rain" (song) 123
Ia Drang, Battle of the 27, 45, 56, 61–63, 64, 97, 101
Immersion foot 148
India 16, 17, 29; 1962 border war with China 22
Indochina 16–17, 19–20, 96, 195
International Red Cross 47, 138
Iraqi War, 2nd 218
Iron Age 152
Israel: Six-Day War of 1967 (3rd Israeli-Arab war) 51
Italy 213

Jack Daniel's (whiskey) 35, 84
Jacket, field 125, 126–27
Jacket, flak 145, 158
Japan and Japanese 16, 20, 47, 101, 105, 213; attack on Pearl Harbor 11
Jarai see Montagnards
Jealousy 157
Jody 156
Johnson, Lyndon Baines (36th U.S. President) 28, 24–25, 29, 31, 102, 109, 125, 137, 189, 205
Jones, John Paul 131
Jungle rot 51
Junkies 195

Kalashnikov, Mikhail 53
Kennedy, John F. (35th U.S. President) 20–23, 102, 105, 204
Kennedy, Robert 137, 155, 169, 189
Kent State University 207
Kerry, John (U.S. Senator) 110
Kesey, Ken (author) 126
Khe Sanh, South Vietnam 42, 129, 145
Khmer Rouge 206–07
Khrushchev, Nikita 17, 23; Cuban Missile Crisis 22
Kierkegaard, Søren (philosopher) 210
Kill ratios 105–06
Killed in action (KIA): (1955–1964) 27; (1965) 29; (1966) 35; (1967) 217; (1968) 160, 217; (1969) 205, 217; (1970) 209; (1971) 210; (1972) 210; (1973) 211

Index 243

King, Martin Luther, Jr. 155; assassination 137
Kissinger, Henry A. 206–07
"Knock on Wood" (song) 123
Koho see Montagnards
Kontum, South Vietnam 95, 97, 98–99, 101, 128, 210
Korean Army (Republic of [South] Korea [ROK]) 106, 128
Korean War 17, 18, 19, 28, 83, 108, 109, 147, 154, 177, 218, 221
Kosygin, Alexey Nikolayevich 23
Kuala Lumpur, Malaysia 162
Kubrick, Stanley (movie director) 137

Laos 16–17, 20–21, 24, 26–27, 42, 43, 95–96, 101, 119, 159, 195, 205, 209, 210
Lawrence, Captain James, U.S. Navy 10
Lenin, Vladimir llyich 17
Liaison Officer (LNO) 73, 91, 115, 129
Liberia, West Africa 37
Lindsay, John (mayor of New York City) 190
Line company 74, 93
Line officers 9, 46
Listening post 71–72, 182
Little Big Horn 97–98
Lon Nol see Nol, Lon
Long, Huey 186
Long Binh Army Base, South Vietnam 41
Long Range Patrol (LRP) 146
Long range reconnaissance patrol (LRRP) 146, 158
Los Bravos (Spanish singing group) 123
Louisiana 177, 178, 184, 185–87, 188, 189, 191, 193, 196
Louisiana Northwestern State University 185
LSD (lysergic acid diethylamide) 125–26
"Lucy in the Sky with Diamonds" (song) 125

M14 see Rifle, automatic
M16 see Rifle, automatic
M40 recoilless rifle 78
M72 LAW (Light antitank weapon) 78
M79 grenade launcher 48, 53
M203 grenade launcher 48
MAAG (Military Assistance and Advisory Group) 20, 22–23
MacArthur, Gen. Douglas 147, 170
Machine guns 30, 53, 67, 72, 80, 82, 93, 150–51, 154, 158–59, 169
MACV (Military Assistance Command, Vietnam) 22–23, 29, 44, 105, 124, 141, 213
Main Street (USA) 197
Malaria 52, 69, 79, 86, 120, 131–32, 149, 201; cases and preventative treatment 64–65
Malaysia 16, 119, 162
Mang Yang Pass, South Vietnam 151
Manila, Philippines 162
Maps, scale of 58
Marine Corps, U.S. see U.S. Marine Corps

Marseilles, France 11
MASH (Mobile Army Surgical Hospital) 47, 148
Mason-Dixon Line 52, 178
Matson Navigation Company 11
Mattel 53
McCarthy, Senator Eugene 137
McCarthy, Senator Joseph R. 17
McCartney, Paul (singer-songwriter) 186
MCIs (Meal, Combat, Individual) 81
McNamara, Robert S. 102, 105
McQueen, Steve (actor) 167
Medal of Honor 47, 55, 170, 222
Medals: Bronze Star 171, 178, 220, 222; Campaign Medal for the Republic of Vietnam (RVNCM) 220–21; Distinguished Flying Cross 92–93; Distinguished Service Cross 55, 224; Good Conduct Medal (AGCM) 220–21; Medal of Honor 47, 55, 170, 222; National Defense Service Medal (NDSM) 220–21; Navy Cross 222 ; Rifle qualification badge 220; Silver Star 45, 55, 85, 224; Vietnam Service Medal (VSM) 220–21
Medevac see Helicopters (including medevacs)
Mekong River 43
Mekong River Delta 42–43, 46, 87
Memphis, Tennessee 137
Merry Pranksters 126
Mexican War 45, 218
Mexico 6, 11, 24, 146, 169
MIA (missing in action) 27, 154, 160, 194, 211
Midway 11
MiG-19 107
MiG-21 107
Mikoyan, Anastas 23
Mikoyan, Artem 107
Military Assistance and Advisory Group (MAAG) 20, 22–23
Military Assistance Command, Vietnam (MACV) 22–23, 29, 44, 105, 124, 141, 213
Military-industrial complex 106
Military Police 46, 102, 172
Militia 108
Mine, land 82, 104, 150–51, 152
Mini-Tet 141
Missile gap 22
Missing in action (MIA) 27, 154, 160, 194, 211
Mission District, San Francisco 6, 14, 39
Mississippi River 43, 186
USS *Missouri* 16
Missouri River 186
"Mr. Tambourine Man" (song) 125
Mnong see Montagnards
Montagnards 61, 75, 95, 116, 117–22, 124
Moon landing 204
Moore, Harold G. (Lt. Gen. Ret.) 27, 45, 61–63, 130
Morphine 195

Mortars (NVA) 78, 128, 145
Mortars (U.S.) 30, 34, 45, 47–48, 54, 72, 78, 80, 82, 114, 124, 126–30, 134–36
MOS (military occupational specialty) 12
Motown music 123, 125
Mustangs 221
My Lai massacre 136–37, 204

Napalm 106
Naples, Italy 11
National Defense Service Medal (NDSM) 220–21
National Guard (U.S. Army) 11, 13, 108–13, 181, 196, 200; at Kent State 207
National Liberation Front (NLF) 20, 125
Naval War College (U.S.) 213–214
Navy see U.S. Navy
Navy Cross 222
NCO see Officers and non-commissioned officers
New York 11, 12, 29, 169, 202
New York Times 204
New Zealanders 128
Ngo Dinh Diem see Diem, Ngo Dinh
Nha Trang, South Vietnam 128
Ninety Day Wonders (World War II) 32
Nixon, Richard (37th U.S. President) 169, 189–90, 194–95, 202–03, 205, 206–07, 209, 211, 214
Nol, Lon 206–07
Noncombatant Evacuation Operation (NEO) 213
North Carolina 32, 151
North Vietnam see Vietnam (North), Democratic Republic of
North Vietnamese Army (NVA) 26–29, 34, 44–45, 47, 61–63, 71–72, 75–76, 78, 95–101, 106, 114, 128–31, 137, 140–43, 145, 150–52, 155, 160, 163–64, 210–11, 214
North Vietnamese Army 1st Division 98, 140; 24th Infantry Regiment 95, 98–99; 32nd Infantry Regiment 62–63, 98–101; 40th Artillery Regiment 98; 66th Infantry Regiment 62–63, 98–99; 174th Infantry Regiment 98–99; 304th VC battalion (attached) 98–99
North Vietnamese Army 325th Division 140
North Vietnamese Army 33rd Infantry Regiment 61, 63
Nuclear powers, threats, and submarines 19, 20, 22, 23, 28, 133
NVA see North Vietnamese Army (NVA)

Oakland, California 6, 39, 200
Oath, Presidential 194
Oath, U.S. Army 36
Obama, Barack Hussein (44th U.S. President) 218
Oceanic Steamship Company 5, 11
OER (Officer Efficiency Report) 192

Officer Candidate School (OCS) 10–14, 31, 32–37, 48, 65, 181, 202, 205–06, 220–21
Officers and non-commissioned officers (NCOs) 9, 11–13, 34–36, 46, 65, 84, 102–03, 136, 138–39, 160–61, 184–85, 192–93
Ohio River 186
Oklahoma City 177
The Old Guard (3rd U.S. Infantry Regiment) 8
Operation Pegasus 42
Operation Sam Houston 55
Opium 162, 195
Oxford University 110
Oxymoron 73, 154

P-38 (can opener) 83
Pasadena, California 31, 174
Paris Peace Talks 127, 147, 210
Pathet Lao 20–21, 24, 96, 205
Patton, Gen. George S. 31, 155
Pearl Harbor 11
Peers, Lt. Gen. William 77, 100–101
Penang, Malaysia 162
Philadelphia 29
Philippine Insurrection 45
Philippines 16, 128, 146
Phnom Penh, Cambodia 43
Phoenix Program 151–52
Picasso, Pablo (painter) 167
Pistol, 45-caliber semi-automatic 53, 134
Platoon (movie) 161
Plei Me, South Vietnam 61, 63
Pleiku, South Vietnam 44, 49, 61, 62, 97–98, 124–25, 127, 134, 140, 151, 171, 210; Tet attacks 128–31
Point, of patrol 56–58, 59–60, 66, 113
Point, rally (ambush) 182
Poncho 68–69, 125
Post-traumatic stress disorder (PTSD) 184–85
Pot (marijuana) 126, 134
POWs (Prisoners of War) 141–43; release of American POWs 211
Prague see Czechoslovakia
PRC-25 portable radio 69, 114
Presidential Oath 194
Presidential Unit Citation 55
Presley, Elvis 37
Prisoners of war 141–43, 211
PTSD 184–85
Public Law 88–352 (Civil Rights Act) 31, 189, 190
Public Law 99–145: pertaining to Purple Heart 154
Puff the Magic Dragon (Douglas AC-47) 114
Pungi stake 79, 88, 148–49
Purple Heart 154, 160, 178–79, 220, 222
PX 44, 165, 175

Index

Quayle, Dan 110
Qui Nhon, South Vietnam 151

R&R 162–63
Rabies 126
Racial issues 31–32, 123, 136–37, 140, 188–89, 190, 205
Radiotelegraph operator (RTO) 34–35, 52, 57, 65, 75–76, 83, 90–91, 138
USS *Ranger* 131
Rawls, Lou (singer) 168
RDX (cyclotrimethylene-trinitramine) 57
Reach-echelon motherfuckers (REMFs) 103
Reconnaissance in force 61, 133
Red Cross 47, 138
Red River 43–44
Reserve Officer Training Corps (ROTC) 10, 12–13, 50, 113, 181, 220–21
Rest & Recuperation (R&R) 162–63
Reveille 33
Rhade see Montagnards
Richmond, California 6
Rifle, automatic (AK-47 & Chicom) 28, 53–54, 84, 89, 90, 184
Rifle, automatic (M14 & M16) 7–8, 30, 48, 53–54, 75, 82, 89, 169, 182
Rifle, recoilless 78
Rifle, Winchester repeating 54, 97
Rifle qualification badge 220
Ring knockers 13, 221
Revolutionary War see War of Independence
Robinson, Jackie 31
Rockefeller, Nelson 190
Rockets, 122-millimeter 128, 130, 145
Rockwell, Norman 174
Rome, Italy 169
Roosevelt, Brigadier General Theodore, Jr. 42
Roosevelt, Theodore (26th U.S. President) 42
ROTC 10, 12–13, 50, 113, 181, 220–21
Route 66 (highway) 177
RPG, grenade launcher 78, 128, 131, 150
RTO 34–35, 52, 57, 65, 75–76, 83, 90–91, 138
Rules of Engagement 151
Russian Revolution 28–29

S-1, S-2, S-3, S-4, and S-5 (Army staff elements) 73, 88, 92, 163, 168–69, 179
Saigon 16, 20, 22, 27, 41, 42–44, 46, 54, 87, 105, 125, 131, 139, 145, 210–11, 214; Tet 128
SAMs, (surface to air missiles) 107
San Jose State University 126
San Francisco, California 5–6, 11, 14, 21, 25, 29, 31, 39, 60, 105, 126, 173, 175, 181, 197, 199, 202, 207, 209–11, 212
Search and destroy (strategy) 27, 56, 57, 67, 72–73, 74, 95, 98, 133, 145, 149, 205, 214
Segregation 31–32, 123, 189

Selective Service System see Draft
Self-immolation by Buddhists 22
Seminole Wars 45
Service, Robert (poet) 163
Shake-and-bake sergeants 84
Shakespeare, William 8, 40, 167, 174–75
Shanghai, China 11
H.M.S. *Shannon* (British frigate) 10
Shea, Lt. James 25–26, 206
Shell-shock 184–85
Shelter half (groundsheet) 50, 68–69, 83, 126, 153–54
Short timer 165, 192
Siam 43
Sihanouk, Norodom 202, 206–07
Silver Star 45, 55, 85, 224
Singapore 11, 16, 162; Sling (cocktail) 35
Sisyphus (King of Corinth) 81–82
Six-Day (Israeli-Arab) War 51
Slicks see Helicopters
Smith, Sgt. Elmelindo, U.S. Army 222
SNCC (Student Nonviolent Coordinating Committee) 137
Song Dynasty, death by a thousand cuts (Ling Chi) 103
Sorbonne, Paris, France 212
SOS (shit on a shingle) 7
South Africa 49
South China Sea 15, 43, 46, 137, 172
South Vietnam see Vietnam (South), Republic of
Southeast Asian Treaty Organization (SEATO) 19
Soviet Union 17–19, 21–29, 53, 107, 109, 169, 207, 218
Spanish-American War 10
Special Forces 14, 21, 48, 50, 61, 96, 98, 127, 129, 146
Spinal meningitis 177
Spit-shine 32, 178
Spoiling attack 133
Stalin, Joseph 17
Stanford University 199
Stars & Stripes (newspaper) 125
Statistics of death see Hostile and non-hostile (related) death statistics
Stieng see Montagnards
Stone, Oliver 161
Stone Age 152
Stoners 126, 195
Student Nonviolent Coordinating Committee (SNCC) 137
Studies and Observations Group (SOG) 95
Suez 11
Sydney, Australia 5, 162

TAC (Teach, Assess and Counsel) officers 32–34
Tahiti 146, 205
Taipei, Nationalist China 162

Tan Canh, South Vietnam 128
Tarawa 50
Temptations (singing group) 123
Tennessee 186
Tet Offensive 56, 97, 101, 109, 123, 125, 132–33, 137, 140–41, 147, 151, 155, 164, 189, 206, 214; three phases of Tet Offensive 127–28
Texas 185–86
Thailand 16, 43, 96, 128, 162–63, 195
"They Don't Give Medals to Yesterday's Heroes" (song) 168
Tigers 70
Title 38 of the United States Code 185
Tokyo 16, 162, 169
Tolkien, J.R.R. (author) 77
Tomb of the Unknown Soldier 8, 82–83
Tonkin, Vietnam 16
Tonkin Gulf incident 24–25, 44
Tonkin Gulf Resolution 24–25, 109
Travis Air Force Base, California 39, 172
Trench foot 148
Troop levels in Vietnam (U.S.) 13, 23, 29, 102, 160, 204, 209–11
Truman, Harry S. (34th U.S. President) 16–17, 18–19, 20, 31
Trump, Donald (business magnate) 110–11
Turnbull, Robert, Lt. 36, 205–06
2001: A Space Odyssey (movie) 137

Unified Combatant Commands, U.S. 213
Union of Soviet Socialist Republics (USSR) see Soviet Union
United Kingdom (Great Britain and Northern Ireland) 17, 23
U.S. Air Force 21, 26, 37–38, 39, 62, 73, 112, 153, 172, 203, 205, 210
U.S. Army: officers and non-commissioned officers (NCOs) 9, 11–13, 34–36, 46, 65, 84, 102–03, 136, 138–39, 160–61, 184–85, 192–93; see also Army Reserve; Casualties, Army; United States Army War College
U.S. Army units see individual units
United States Army War College 109
U.S. Coast Guard 112
United States Constitution 25, 31, 36, 108, 115, 190, 194
U.S. Embassy (Saigon): Tet attack 128, 131, 211, 214
U.S. Marine Corps 7, 9, 13, 15, 27, 29, 37, 41, 42, 44, 46, 48, 49–50, 73, 108, 112, 127–29, 139, 145, 155, 160, 177, 195, 211, 214, 222; 1st Division 27, 127, (battle for Hué) 129; 3rd Division 27, 127, (9th Marine Expeditionary Brigade) 27
U.S. military (total) that served in Vietnam 109, 160
U.S. Navy 9–11, 25, 41, 73, 108, 112, 131, 148, 210, 222
United States Supreme Court 31

University of California at Berkeley 27, 105, 113, 169, 207, 210–11
University of California at Los Angeles (UCLA) 12, 31
University of Michigan 29
University of Paris, Sorbonne 212
University of Pennsylvania 110
University of Wyoming 110
USO (United Service Organizations Inc.) 125, 139

Vance, Cyrus 137
VC 20, 34, 43, 44, 62, 98–99, 127–30, 151, 164, 214
Vichy France see France, Vichy
Veterans 54, 55, 65, 101, 115, 117, 146, 157, 178, 179–81, 184–85, 188, 193, 195, 197–98, 199, 200–01, 207–08, 211, 212, 213
Veterans Hospitals 177, 185
Vietcong (VC) 20, 34, 43, 44, 62, 98–99, 127–30, 151, 164, 214
Vietminh 17, 18, 19, 20, 142
Vietnam (North), Democratic Republic of 18, 22, 24–29, 42–44, 51, 96, 106–07, 125, 127, 130, 134, 137, 140, 143; release of American POWs 211; see also North Vietnamese Army (NVA)
Vietnam (South), Republic of 15, 18, 19, 21–23, 27, 42–44, 95–96, 102, 118, 125, 127–28, 134, 140, 143, 151, 181, 221; see also Army of South Vietnam (ARVN)
Vietnam Conflict 20; see also Vietnam War
Vietnam Service Medal (VSM) 220–21
Vietnam Veterans Memorial ("The Wall") 26, 149, 206
Vietnam War 6, 13, 20, 22, 25, 29, 30, 34–35, 43, 52, 82–83, 97, 100, 105, 106–13, 133, 141–43, 154, 159–61, 169, 184–85, 189, 202–03, 212, 214–15, 217–18, 221
Vietnamization 194–95, 209, 214
Viper, bamboo (green tree) 67, 69, 71
Visa 173
Vung Tau, South Vietnam 127

"The Wall" (Vietnam Veterans Memorial) 26, 149, 206
Wallace, George Corley, Jr. (Governor of Alabama) 189–90
War of annihilation 133
War of 1812 10, 218
War of Independence 10, 131, 133, 218, 222; conscription 112
Warrant officers 65
Warsaw and Warsaw Pact 53, 169
Washington, George (1st U.S. President) 222
Watts, South Los Angeles, California 140, 190
Wayne, John (actor) 10, 167, 183, 206
We Were Soldiers Once ... and Young (book & movie) 27, 45, 64, 130
Welch, Raquel (actress) 125

West Point (military academy) 12, 13, 50, 124, 147, 221; killed in action in Vietnam 35
Western Union 173
Westmoreland, Gen. William C. 23, 132–33, 146
White phosphorus 48
Willy Pete 48
World War I 45–46, 77, 83, 108, 114, 133, 147, 159, 170, 185, 217–18
World War II 6, 10, 13, 16, 20, 21, 30, 32, 41–42, 51, 53, 55, 77, 78, 83, 100, 105–06, 108, 110, 114, 133, 136, 150, 154, 159, 168, 174, 177, 179, 185, 190, 199, 217–18, 220–22
Wounded: requiring hospitalization 160, 217–18; treated at field aid stations 160

Yale University 110
Yangtze River 43
Yellow River 43
Yosemite, California 96

Z-Card (U.S. merchant marine) 10–11
Ziegfeld Follies 12
Zippo lighter 79–80

www.ingramcontent.com/pod-product-compliance
Ingram Content Group UK Ltd.
Pitfield, Milton Keynes, MK11 3LW, UK
UKHW041937140426
5217IPUK00014B/530